H

A ROMANOV
FANTASY

A ROMANOV FANTASY

life at the court of

ANNA ANDERSON

FRANCES WELCH

W. W. Norton & Company
New York London

For Craig

All rights reserved
Printed in the United States of America

For information about permission to reproduce selections from this book,
write to Permissions, W. W. Norton & Company, Inc., 500 Fifth Avenue,
New York, NY 10110

For information about special discounts for bulk purchases, please contact
W. W. Norton Special Sales at specialsales@wwnorton.com or 800-233-4830

Manufacturing by Courier Westford
Production manager: Anna Oler

Library of Congress Cataloging-in-Publication Data

Welch, Frances, 1957–
A Romanov fantasy : life at the court of Anna Anderson / Frances Welch.
— 1st American ed.
p. cm.
Includes bibliographical references.
ISBN 978-0-393-06577-0 (hardcover)
1. Anderson, Anna. 2. Anastasiia Nikolaevna, Grand Duchess, daughter of
Nicholas II, Emperor of Russia, 1901–1918. 3. Impostors and
imposture—Biography. I. Title.
CT9981.A53W45 2007
947.08'3092—dc22
[B]   2007023232

W. W. Norton & Company, Inc.
500 Fifth Avenue, New York, N.Y. 10110
www.wwnorton.com

W. W. Norton & Company Ltd.
Castle House, 75/76 Wells Street, London W1T 3QT

1 2 3 4 5 6 7 8 9 0

CONTENTS

The world wants to be deceived.
Sebastian Brant, *Ship of Fools* (1494)

To know your ruling passion, examine
your castles in the air.
Archbishop Whately, *Apophthegms* (1864)

DRAMATIS PERSONAE

* **Alexander II** (1818-1881): Tsar of Russia
* **Alexander III** (1845-1894): Tsar of Russia
* **Alexandra Feodorovna** (1872-1918): Tsarina of Russia
* **Alexis Nikolaievich** (1904-1918): Tsarevich of Russia
* **Anastasia Nikolaievna** (1901-1918): Grand Duchess of Russia
* **Andrew Vladimirovich** (1879-1956): Grand Duke of Russia; supported Anna's claim
* **Botkin, Eugene** (1865-1918): physician for the Imperial Family; father of Gleb
* **Botkin, Gleb Evgenievich** (1900-1969): writer and artist; one of Anna's most devoted supporters
* **Botkin, Peter**: brother of Dr Eugene Botkin
* **Botkin, Serge Dmitrievich**: cousin of Eugene; muted supporter of Anna
* **Botkin, Serge** (1832-1889): physician at the Courts of Tsar Alexander II and III; father of Eugene
* **Botkin, Tatiana** (1898-1965): Gleb's sister; staunch supporter of Anna
* **Buxhoeveden, Baroness Sophie** (1884-1956): Tsarina's lady-in-waiting, failed to recognise Anna as Anastasia
* **Dehn, Lili**: former friend of the Tsarina; believed she recognised Anna as Anastasia
* **Ernest Louis** (1868-1937): Grand Duke of Hesse and by Rhine; one of Anna's arch-enemies
* **Frederick Ernest** (1905-1985): Prince of Saxe-Altenburg; one of Anna's most loyal supporters
* **Gibbes, Charles Sydney** (1876-1963): English tutor to the Imperial children; failed to recognise Anna
* **Gilliard, Pierre** (1879-1962): French tutor to the Imperial Family; first friend, then avowed enemy, of Anna
* **Grunberg, Inspector Franz**: played host to Anna in Berlin in the mid-1920s
* **Heydebrandt, Adele von**: Anna's friend and carer in Unterlengenhardt

* **Irene, Princess of Prussia** (1866-1953): the Tsarina's sister; failed to recognise Anna as Anastasia in Berlin in 1922
* **Jennings, Annie Burr:** Anna's supporter and host during her first trip to the US in the late 20s
* **Kleist, Baron Arthur von:** Anna's first host in Berlin
* **Kschessinska, Mathilde** (1872-1971): wife of Grand Duke Andrew; supported Anna after meeting her in 1928
* **Leeds, William:** husband of Princess Xenia of Russia and Anna's host in the late 1920s
* **Leuchtenberg, Duke George Romanovsky de Beauharnais** (1872-1929): Anna's host at Castle Seeon during 1927-28
* **Leverkuehn, Paul:** Anna's lawyer from 1940 for 20 years
* **Lilburn, Ian:** Historian and genealogist; staunch Anna supporter
* **Manahan, Dr Jack** (1919-1990): university lecturer and genealogist; married Anna in Charlottesville in 1968
* **Maria Feodorovna** (1847-1928): Dowager Empress of Russia; mother of Tsar Nicholas; survived the revolution; never met Anna
* **Maria (Marie) Nikolaievna** (1899-1918): Grand Duchess of Russia
* **Miltitz, Baroness Monica von:** supporter of Anna
* **Miliukov, Alexis:** accompanied Anna from Unterlengenhardt to Charlottesville
* **Nicholas II** (1868-1918): Tsar of Russia.
* **Olga Alexandrovna** (1882-1960): Grand Duchess of Russia; Anastasia's aunt, the Tsar's sister; appeared to recognise Anna, then seemed undecided
* **Olga Nikolaievna,** (1895–1918): Grand Duchess of Russia
* **Peuthert, Clara:** Anna's earliest supporter; met her at the Dalldorf Asylum
* **Rasputin, Gregorii** (1864 or 1865–1916): mystic faith–healer, spiritual adviser to the Romanovs
* **Rasputin, Maria:** Gregorii's daughter. Believed Anna was Anastasia for several weeks then changed her mind
* **Rachmaninov, Sergei** (1873–1943): composer and pianist; supporter and benefactor of Anna Anderson

PROLOGUE

Reunion: Charlottesville, 1968

In the summer of 1968, a tiny old woman held court in Charlottesville, Virginia. She had an unforgiving pudding-bowl haircut which made her look strangely childish. Her diminutive form was matched by a small face wrinkled in suspicion and disapproval. For nearly half a century, she had claimed to have survived the shootings of the rest of her family at Ekaterinburg in July 1918. She was, she insisted, the Grand Duchess Anastasia, youngest daughter of the last Tsar of Russia.

Fifty years after the murders of the Romanovs, 'Anastasia' – or Anna Anderson, as she now called herself – was settling into opulent new surroundings on Charlottesville's University Circle, a short walk away from the city's sumptuous University of Virginia campus. In an elegant drawing room Anna sat, unmoved and unmoving, while two admirers vied for her attention.

The younger of her two courtiers was also her host, John E 'Jack' Manahan, a millionaire and former university lecturer. A keen genealogist, Jack had paid Anna's fare from Germany; he was thrilled to be entertaining this Grand Duchess with her links to the crowned heads of Europe.

Her second courtier was an elderly Russian émigré called Gleb Botkin. His father, Dr Eugene Botkin, had been murdered with the Imperial Family. Forty years earlier, Gleb had pronounced himself convinced that Anna was none other than his childhood friend, the Grand Duchess Anastasia. It was Gleb who had orchestrated Anna's visit to Charlottesville.

It is hard to imagine which of the three friends – Gleb, Jack or Anna – an onlooker would have found most striking. Gleb, now aged 68, had anointed himself 'Most Reverend Archbishop of the Church of Aphrodite', a church he himself founded in 1938. He frequently wore robes and his appearance had given rise to comment in Charlottesville: children referred to him as Father Christmas, while one journalist compared him to a wizard. His asceticism was supplemented by a passion for Pall Mall cigarettes. An elegant cigarette holder did nothing to protect his moustaches, now stained a dark yellow.

Jack, a more youthful 49, wore his excess pounds as he wore his brightly coloured clothes, with bluff pride. He had a round, youthful face divided almost in half by a pronounced widow's peak.

Anna, now well into her 70s, shared with Jack a preference

for bright colours and had a particular passion for red which, she maintained, was the colour of the Romanovs. Though she was reputed to have an Imperial ability to sit up 'ramrod straight', she preferred to slump in her chair, resembling nothing so much as a small pile of ill-assorted clothes.

Happily neither of Anna's suitors was put off by her fading personal attractions. Nor were they ruffled by her disengaged, occasionally aggressive mode of conversation. Each accepted with equanimity her reproof as she hesitated to share the mysteries surrounding her past. 'I was living this dirt!' she snapped. 'Not sit comfortable reading a book!' Both men were dutifully silent at her bidding: 'Not interrupten!'

Tapes still exist of the trio's disjointed exchanges. Gleb speaks with a beguiling Russian accent, his voice thickened and enriched with age. Jack speaks with a reassuring sing-song southern drawl, like the good guy in a 1940s film. Jack can be heard making repeated efforts to lighten the atmosphere with offers of varieties of food. 'Cheese on bread, celery, watermelon, ice-cream, then the raisins are to be passed along like bonbons with the mints,' he instructs.

Both men, in their different ways, succeed in presenting themselves as gentlemen. Gleb struggles to divert Anna with carefully worded anecdotes, while Jack devotes himself to her physical well-being. 'She hasn't eaten enough to keep a bear alive,' he observes ruefully at one point.

Anna's responses are unpredictable: Gleb's stories do not seem to interest her any more than Jack's snacks. When she speaks, it is usually to issue put-downs in a rich, guttural

0158704З9

German accent. One of her recurring themes is that Gleb, who lays claim to being her oldest friend, has kept her in the dark. She tries to elicit sympathy from her host. 'Zis I hear for ze furst time Mr Manahan!' she snaps.

The intricacy of the relationships within obscure European Royal Families proves a popular topic. But it is Jack who is the obsessive; he has traced his own links with 50 American families including the Zangles, the Frizzells, the Stoops and the Oggs.

At one point Jack and Anna can be heard enjoying a lively exchange about the Swedish Royal Family. Their parrying with disparate pieces of information is only brought to a halt when Anna is distracted by the sound of a kitten.

Jack: 'I think her name is Queen Louise.'

Anna: 'No – her name is Ingrid of Sweden. She is the daughter of the present King of Sweden. The only daughter from the first wife.'

Jack: 'No, but Ingrid is the daughter of old King Gustaf – King Gustaf Adolf.'

Anna: 'The only daughter of this present King of Sweden is the Queen Ingrid of Denmark.'

Jack: 'I see. She has two girls – Benedicta and Louise.'

Anna: 'She has three girls.'

Jack: 'I took a picture of one of the girls.'

Anna: 'The youngest is the Queen of Greece and the wife of Constantine...' (There is the noise of mewing cats.) '... Oooh Kätzchen. Is there not yelling Kätzchen somewhere?'

Anna is always interrupting to draw attention to Jack's pets:

the animation in her voice reveals where her sympathies lie. What her two admirers made of this competition cannot be known. Both knew she had left 40 cats behind in Germany and that she had been furious when health officials insisted they be put down. They had presumably seen the photograph of her locked in a loving embrace with a mammoth of a dog called 'Baby'.

During pauses in the conversation, the sounds of birdsong and crickets mingle with incongruous noises of domesticity: lawn-mowing and washing-up. Breaking one prolonged silence, the sound of the phone causes great alarm. 'The telephone is ringing!' shouts Anna.

But Anna's dismay over the phone is as nothing compared to her consternation over awkward questions. There is the sound of tea-cups crashing on saucers as Anna refuses to answer questions about her last night at Ekaterinburg. The questions in this case are put by a more brazen fourth party, a man called Alexis Miliukov, who has accompanied Anna to Charlottesville from her home at Unterlengenhardt in Germany. While he was never to be an integral part of Anna's life, he derives importance from his role as creator of the tapes.

Miliukov: 'You should remember.'

(Bang) Anna: 'Nothing do I remember!' (Bang). 'Nothing! You are thousand times mistaken about thousand things!...'

Miliukov: 'How did it happen in night-time?'

(Bang) Anna: 'Don't ask these terrible things! I don't remember nothing for many reasons...'

Miliukov: 'The doors were taken off the bedrooms.'

Anna: 'Don't speak these things! Please not! Otherwise I get ill!'

As she fends off the questions, Anna's voice acquires a disconcerting tremor. The tireless efforts of Jack and Gleb to create a pleasant atmosphere come to nothing as a distinct chill descends upon the Charlottesville drawing room.

Anna's distress would not have posed any puzzle for those, like Gleb and Jack, who believed she was the Grand Duchess Anastasia. For them, it would have seemed quite understandable that the elderly Anastasia would be haunted by visions of her family being murdered around her.

For those who did not believe, however, this blurring of reality with fantasy was baffling and irksome. Upon what was Anna's very real upset based? Had she succumbed to others' belief that she really was Anastasia? Had she fallen prey to a subterfuge of her own making? Had Anna, in some sense, *become* Anastasia? It was in such highly charged moments that Anna Anderson's claim flourished for so many years.

CHAPTER ONE

The Murders: Ekaterinburg, 1918

During the course of her long and bizarre life, the claimant, Anna Anderson, was repeatedly asked to describe the events of the dreadful night of 17 July 1918, when the Tsar, Tsarina and their five children were shot in the cellar of the Bolsheviks' House Of Special Purpose in Ekaterinburg. Her reluctance to offer details proved, of course, controversial: while her detractors seized upon it as proof that she was simply not there, her supporters were equally quick to claim it as evidence of trauma.

She was unable to describe even the earlier, uneventful part of that night without injecting it with horror. Anna claimed to have felt terrified before the shootings and that her mother, the Tsarina, had been beside herself: 'half-fainting with fear and being almost unconscious, she perhaps took in least of the appalling things that were happening to us all then.'

In fact, the Romanovs had mercifully little intimation of their fate. Members of the execution squad who saw the Imperial Family as they passed by on their way to the cellar recalled them looking remarkably relaxed. According to one, Victor Nitrebin, the three younger daughters 'smiled naturally at us in their usual cheerful manner'; another, Michael Kudrin, said: 'The Romanovs were completely calm, no suspicion.' Even the Bolshevik leader, Yakov Yurovsky, said: 'There were no tears, no sobs, no questions.' The Tsarina herself was so relaxed that, upon entering the room, she demanded chairs: 'Is it forbidden to sit down?'

Yurovsky supplied two chairs, then told the family and the four retainers to line up against a back wall for a photograph: the authorities needed proof that the family had not escaped. He then returned with ten gunmen, each of whom had been allotted one victim; he himself was to shoot the Tsar. But when the order was given to fire, the men, fuelled with Dutch courage, all disobeyed Yurovsky's instruction, turning instead on the Tsar. As the Tsar fell, the drunkest of the men, Peter Ermakov, turned on the Tsarina and shot her at point-blank range as she tried to cross herself.

Within minutes the room was full of gunsmoke and clouds of plaster dust; the dim light from one electric bulb was obscured. The gunmen were reduced to firing randomly at moving shadows, mostly legs, just discernible beneath the layers of cloud. They were hit by their own bullets ricocheting off jewels embedded in their victims' clothes. The Grand Duchesses, it was later established, had sewn eight kilograms of jewels into their underclothes; large amounts in wadding were held in brassières. 'It was complete chaos,' recalled Nitrebin.

When Yurovsky finally screamed at the gunmen to stop shooting, only four people had actually been killed: the Imperial couple and two retainers, the cook Ivan Kharitonov and the footman Alexei Trupp, both of whom had been standing behind the Tsar. Yurovsky ordered the men out into the corridor to wait for the smoke to clear; they stumbled out of the room, eyes smarting and lungs full of toxic fumes. Several of them, overcome by the effects of the fumes and carnage, leant against the walls vomiting.

Yurovsky then selected just four men to accompany him back into the room. Doctor Botkin, who had been standing closest to the Tsar, had been hit by two bullets in the abdomen. He had turned toward the body of the Tsar, only to be hit by a third bullet in the legs, shattering his knee caps. He had then fallen to the floor. Yurovsky now saw him, covered in blood, leaning on his right arm and trying to raise himself. He shot the doctor in the head.

He then turned his attention to the fourteen-year-old Tsarevich. He shot at the boy five times, emptying his cartridge; though Alexis fell to the floor, he was still moaning. Yurovsky screamed at Ermakov to help him. Ermakov bayoneted Alexis repeatedly but also failed to kill him. The two men became desperate. Yurovsky wrote: 'Nothing seemed to work. Though injured he continued to live.' Neither of them knew that, like the Grand Duchesses, the boy had a layer of jewels sewn into his clothes. Finally, in a frenzy, Yurovsky grabbed a second gun and shot him twice in the ear.

The two men then fired at Olga and Tatiana but failed to hit them. As they moved in closer, the two elder Grand Duchesses crouched down, their arms over their heads. Yurovsky shot Tatiana in the head; Ermakov shot Olga. The third Grand Duchess, Marie, began screaming and Ermakov rounded on her, stabbing her repeatedly. But, as Yurovsky recalled: 'The bayonet would not pierce her bodice.' In the end, Ermakov claimed he shot her in the head. He then went after the seventeen-year-old Anastasia, who had backed into a corner. He made another frenzied attempt to use his bayonet; once again, he found he was unable to break through the bodice. With characteristic courage, Anastasia carried on 'screaming and fighting' until Ermakov shot her, too, in the head – or so he claimed.

The maid Anna Demidova was the last to be killed; she had risen to her feet shouting: 'God has saved me.' Ermakov immediately rounded on her with his bayonet. After a brief struggle, Demidova fell to her death; she had no jewels to protect her.

The room was at last quiet, though Ermakov carried on stabbing bodies, at one point even pinning the Tsar to the floor. The less bloodthirsty Yurovsky meanwhile ordered Kudrin to help him go round checking the bodies and feel pulses. When Yurovsky was satisfied that all eleven victims were dead, he ordered the gunmen to start moving the corpses. He himself returned upstairs to his office and lay down with a cold compress over his head.

But as the bodies were moved, it became clear that some of the victims were still breathing. One of the guards, Alexander Strekotin, recalled that as one of the Grand Duchesses was picked up 'she cried out and covered her face with her hands. Another daughter was still alive'. A second guard standing in the corridor saw one of the Grand Duchesses 'spit blood from her mouth; strange, guttural noises came from her'. Ermakov began trying to bayonet the bodies again; when this failed, he lashed out with his rifle butt until all was quiet. Shooting was no longer permitted as it was creating too much noise. The daughters who had survived the early volley of bullets were Marie and Anastasia.

According to Gleb Botkin, two men – the former guard, Anatoly Yakimov, and Feodor Gorshkov – later claimed Anastasia had survived. In fact, neither had witnessed the executions first-hand. Nonetheless their testimonies mysteriously disappeared after Anna Anderson emerged as a serious claimant in the 1920s. They were apparently misplaced while in the hands of the motor car magnate Henry Ford, who had acquired the papers from the White investigator Nikolai Sokolov in 1923, hoping to use them as evidence of a worldwide Jewish conspiracy.

As the bodies lay in the corridors, the guards began looting and Yurovsky had to be summoned from his bed. He ordered all the guards to his office where they were given 30 seconds to hand over every diamond stick-pin, brooch, necklace and gold ring. They would be searched afterwards; anyone found to have kept stolen goods would be shot. Strekotin later confessed that he had stolen Botkin's pocket-watch; he presumably failed to give it in.

While the guards were brought to order, the eleven corpses were abandoned where they lay: some had made it to the back of a truck, others simply lay in the cellar room and even in the corridors.

The cellar in Ekaterinberg

Later, when the truck was finally loaded, three guards were assigned the task of sitting in the back with the corpses. Anna Anderson's supporters subsequently made the most of their discovery that one of these guards, Andras Verhas, had refused, an hour earlier, to fire at any of the women and children. The supporters argue that the lily-livered Verhas would have been more likely to help any survivors, at this stage, than to finish them off.

Ermakov was to have taken sole responsibility for the disposal of the bodies, but, as Yurovsky said: 'It had become clear to me that he would not be able to carry this out in an orderly fashion.' So Yurovsky reluctantly joined his comrade in the front of the truck. As they made their way out of Ekaterinburg, Yurovsky asked Ermakov whether he had brought the necessary equipment to dig a grave. Ermakov mumbled that perhaps someone else could bring something; he himself had a shovel.

In the forest, the overloaded truck inched along at five miles an hour before being brought to a halt by a 25-strong band of Ermakov's factory worker friends, all of whom had been looking forward to murdering the Romanovs. To their disappointment, they now found themselves assigned the less glamorous task of unloading the corpses on to the grass as the truck became stuck in the mud.

Shortly afterwards the truck stuck for good; it had slid off the track and become wedged between two trees. At this point Yurovsky decided that Ermakov's comrades must transfer the corpses to open carts. But as they transferred the bodies, the men came upon the jewels sewn into the clothes. There was a frenzy of excitement and Yurovsky threatened to shoot anyone who stole from the victims. Meanwhile the whereabouts of the proposed grave site was becoming more and more obscure. Hectored with questions from the exasperated Yurovsky, Ermakov admitted he couldn't be sure of the spot – perhaps it was one mile west?

In an effort to get Ermakov's men away from the bodies, Yurovsky sent them to look for alternative places for the burial; he and Ermakov also set off on horseback. It was Ermakov's men who found the Four Brothers mineshaft, where the bodies were initially buried. For the next 50 years, the mine shaft was believed to be the bodies' final resting place.

Alongside the mine shaft, the corpses were unloaded, then stripped and all the clothes burnt. Yurovsky collected the jewels, to be handed over, he claimed, to the authorities in Moscow.

But as the bodies were dumped in the shaft, it became clear that it was too shallow. Although the men threw in grenades, the shaft remained just ten feet deep. At a loss, Yurovsky decided to return to Ekaterinburg to seek advice; dirt and brushwood were strewn over the shaft to hide the protruding limbs.

The chairman of the Ekaterinburg Soviet suggested an alternative mine shaft and, in the early evening, Yurovsky rode into the forest with a friend to check its suitability. Unfortunately, their horses fell and both men suffered broken legs. By the time Yurovsky had limped back to the Four Brothers at 4.00am, there was just time to lift the bodies out of the shaft, pull them to the edge of the clearing and cover them again with brushwood.

Yurovsky's final visit to the Four Brothers was at midnight on the third night after the murders; he had not slept for 70 hours. Under his direction, the bodies were loaded on to open carts, then on to a truck. Unfortunately, as this second truck entered a clearing known as Pig's Meadow, it also slid and became stuck. The corpses were unloaded, but to no avail; the truck would not shift. At the end of his tether, Yurovsky decided simply to carry out the burial there, in the middle of the clearing. The men dug a hole and threw in nine of the corpses; they pulled railway sleepers over the grave and the truck, finally free of mud, was then driven back and forth over the sleepers.

Previous attempts had been made to speed up the process by burning two of the corpses: the pair Yurovsky had intended to burn were those of the Tsarevich and the Tsarina. Two years later Yurovsky said he believed they burnt the maid, Demidova, by mistake.

It was only in the late 1980s that the messy details of the disposal of the bodies finally came out. Until then, the Imperial Family and the four retainers were believed to have been buried or destroyed at the Four Brothers. The discovery, months after the murders, of the children's dog Jimmy, still intact in the shaft, was deemed poignant proof. Jimmy, incidentally, though sometimes referred to as Anastasia's dog, was actually Tatiana's. Alexis' dog Joy, a male, was more fortunate; he survived the shootings and was rescued from the House of Special Purpose by a seventeen-year-old Bolshevik guard called Michael Leteman. Unfortunately for Letemen, Joy was later spotted by a White army officer sitting in the family's backyard. Despite having nothing to do with the murders, Leteman was executed. Joy, meanwhile, though blinded apparently by the trauma of what he had witnessed, was dispatched to England to pass his twilight years with a distinguished Russian family in Windsor.

The location of the real burial site came out with the emergence, in 1978, of a lengthy report written by Yurovsky at the time. In the years following the murders, almost every aspect of the executions had become confused in a mire of disagreement and rumour. Yurovsky and Ermakov both claimed, for instance, to have fired the bullet that killed the Tsar. Both of them donated what they claimed were the relevant revolvers to separate museums. Ermakov was unable to resist taking a photograph of himself at the burial site; the photograph proved an invaluable clue in searches which continued, over the years, for more remains.

First burial site at the Four Brothers

Either out of cussedness or because he simply did not remember, Ermakov claimed at one point that the killers had disposed of all the bodies by burning them in a large funeral pyre. In a so-called 'deathbed interview', granted in 1935, he added a personal detail: 'I then pitched the ashes into the air and the wind caught them like dust and carried them out across the woods and fields.' Insisting, at the time of the interview, that he was dying of throat cancer, Ermakov lived on happily for a further seventeen years.

In 1993, the identity of the bones of the Tsar, Tsarina and three of their five children was finally established with DNA tests. The identity of Dr Botkin was also established, but with less certainty. The missing Tsarevich, meanwhile, may have been successfully burnt, but the fate of Anastasia remains a mystery.

Ermakov later claimed to have shot both of the younger daughters in the head but, according to scientists re-assembling the bones, Marie suffered only one bullet wound, and that was to the thigh. If he did manage to hit Anastasia, the wound was not fatal, as, according to two guards, she was still alive several minutes later. In 1998 a Russian scientist claimed to have found the remains of Alexis and Marie: the Russians have always maintained it was Marie, rather than Anastasia, who was missing. However these findings have yet to be scientifically proven.

Ever since those terrible July days, there have been conflicting accounts of what really happened to the Russian Imperial Family in Ekaterinburg. The possibility that one of the five children may have been wrested from the chaos has been seized upon as a kind of solace. Stories centring upon the survival of the attractive, youngest daughter, Anastasia, have proved particularly appealing.

All the more understandable, then, that Anna Anderson rarely lacked people to tend to her financial, physical and emotional needs. It goes without saying that subsequent DNA testing which seemed to destroy her claim never dented the faith of her remaining supporters, the 'Anastasians', as they called themselves. Ninety years on, as they point out, meticulous searches around Ekaterinburg have failed to unearth any trace of the seventeen-year-old Anastasia.

While the Anastasians' initial motives were not always noble – some dreamt of money and power – they usually found themselves reduced, in the end, to acts of altruism. For her most fervent supporter, Gleb Botkin, Anna Anderson was the only surviving link in a chain binding three generations of the Botkin family to the last three Tsars of Russia.

CHAPTER TWO

The Botkins and the Romanovs

Alexander III, Emperor and Autocrat of All The Russias, was known as a bear of a man who walked through locked doors and crushed pewter tankards with his bare hands. Following a railway accident, he was said to have lifted the whole of the collapsed dining car to allow his family to escape. The menacing spectacle he presented as he bent pokers and silver plates was lent further colour by his preference for ragged peasant clothes.

While other heads of state attended the opera, Alexander III liked to gather a group together to accompany him on the tuba. Queen Victoria made no attempt to conceal her distaste for the over-sized Tsar, denouncing him as a sovereign whom she did 'not look upon as a gentleman'.

Once, during dinner, an Austrian ambassador hinted at

trouble in the Balkans, adding that his country might be mobilising two or three Army Corps. Alexander III picked up a silver fork, twisted it into a knot and threw it on to the ambassador's plate. 'That is what I am going to do to your two or three Army Corps.' On the domestic front, Alexander was no less alarming, addressing his eldest son Nicky, the future Tsar Nicholas II, as 'girlie' while pelting him with bread balls.

Gleb Botkin's grandfather, Dr Serge Botkin, was the man charged with maintaining the physical well-being of this leviathan. He had previously distinguished himself as personal physician to Alexander III's father, Alexander II. Serge Botkin relished his role as the first Russian doctor to tend a Tsar; all his predecessors were German. The Botkin family was of Scottish origin and had initially established themselves in St Petersburg as traders in tea. The young Serge broke with family tradition to study medicine. Such was his subsequent prowess that he earned himself a grand sobriquet: the 'Father of Russian Medicine'.

The Botkins later boasted of Serge's insistence upon maintaining his independence from his Imperial charges, pointing out that he always refused to live at Court. Unfortunately the doctor failed to extend this instinct for self-preservation to his physical needs. His grandson, Gleb, insisted that Serge's premature death, at 52, was caused by heart failure due to overwork.

It cannot be known which area of his professional life Serge found most exacting. There is no denying that Alexander III's father, the less intimidating Alexander II, was capable of seeing the broader picture: he took the momentous step of liberating the peasants in 1861. But he never lost his eye for detail. He complained roundly to Serge when he spotted the doctor's sons failing to cross themselves with sufficient vigour during church services.

Alexander III's dominant character would not have lent itself well to the role of patient. But Serge managed to win the respect of both Tsars; indeed, his burgeoning reputation was such that he was soon branching out from The Court, tending to the wider Russian public with 'Botkin's Powders'.

After Serge's death, the grief-stricken Alexander III refused to see any other doctors, dismissing them all as 'sawbones'. He may have been overly cavalier; Alexander III died suddenly in 1894, aged just 49, of nephritis, an inflammation of the kidneys.

Two of Serge's sons, Eugene and Serge, became doctors and in 1908, Eugene, aged 43, would follow his father to the Russian Imperial Court. It was a decision that would have been inconceivable 20 years earlier: as a young man Eugene had been a well-known agitator. According to his son Gleb, he was even forbidden from going out at night for fear he might be 'rubbed out' by government officials. Eugene had been among a group expelled from the Academy of Medicine in St Petersburg for writing a petition to the Tsar in support of student protesters. Far from being ashamed of their expulsion, the group met annually to commemorate the day they left the Academy. As each member died, a photograph would be installed in his place.

When the commemorative day came round in 1917,

Eugene was in exile in Siberia with the Imperial Family and so unable to attend. His former colleagues set up his portrait beside the table. Some weeks later, as he examined a photograph of the meeting that had been sent to him, Eugene felt a chill of foreboding; his son Gleb heard him muttering to himself: 'How strange. Am I already dead?' Months later he would be shot with the Imperial Family.

Dr Botkin, with Tatiana and Gleb in exile atTobolsk, 1918

It is indicative of the esteem in which the Botkin family was held that, despite these early revolutionary activities, Tsar Alexander III was keen to persuade Eugene to follow his father to the court. Tsar Alexander's first offer was for Eugene to act as physician to the Tsarevich Nicholas's sickly younger brother George, who died, aged just 27, of tuberculosis. Perhaps unsurprisingly, Eugene rejected the offer at this point, preferring to take courses in medicine at Berlin and Heidelberg. The decision was to stand him in good stead when, years later, he was able to act as a translator for the German-speaking Tsarina when she received Russian delegations.

According to his brother Peter, Eugene had an innate goodness, apparent even when he was a child. He wrote lyrically of Eugene: 'He was never like other children. Always sensitive, of a delicate inner sweetness of extraordinary soul, he had a horror of any struggle or fight. We other boys would fight with fury. He would not take part in our combats but when our pugilism took on a dangerous character he would stop the combatants at the risk of injuring himself. He was very studious and conscientious in his studies. For a profession he chose medicine: to help, succour, soothe and heal, without end.'

Peter would have been gratified to know that, 80 years after his brother's death, plans were going ahead for a chapel to be built in Dr Eugene Botkin's honour; the chapel would be built on the site of the House of Special Purpose. In 1992 the Orthodox Church in Russia even established a commission – the Holy Synod Commission on the Canonisation of Saints in Regard to the Martyrdom of the Imperial Family – which considered Dr Botkin and the three other murdered retainers for canonisation.

Eventually the commission, while making a special mention of Dr Botkin, decided against granting canonisations: 'The Commission does not have any evidence of broad prayerful veneration of these laymen as well as of miracles connected with them. Furthermore, there is at present a lack of any substantial evidence about the religious life and personal piety of all these laymen with the exception of some fragmentary witness about the spiritual life of E.S. Botkin.' The report continued with a rather peremptory nod to their sacrifice; the retainers, it said, were merely 'servants doing their moral duty by remaining with the Imperial Family; in fulfilling this duty, they did not commit themselves to the role of martyrs.'

By the age of 40, Eugene Botkin had abandoned his left-wing leanings and established himself as a staunch monarchist, even volunteering his services as an army doctor in the Russo-Japanese war in 1905. He served aboard the St Georgievsky Hospital Red Cross train and subsequently became Commissioner-in-Chief of the Russian Red Cross at the front.

Three years later, he made the momentous decision to take up a second offer of an Imperial appointment. This new offer had been proposed by Tsar Alexander III's son, Tsar Nicholas II. The job would entail moving his own family to the Imperial residence at Tsarskoye Selo. Before moving, Dr Botkin wrote a heavy-hearted letter to Peter: 'My responsibility is great but this is not only *vis-à-vis* the family. I find myself with a great burden, a responsibility toward not only the family but the whole country.'

***

Remembering his childhood years, Gleb depicted Tsarskoye Selo, rather disparagingly, as a place sealed off from reality. 'Tsarskoye Selo was a world apart, an enchanted fairyland to which only a small number of people had the right to entry... To the loyal monarchists, it was... the abode of the earthly gods. To the revolutionaries it was a sinister place where blood thirsty tyrants were hatching their terrible plots against the innocent population.'

From their ivory tower the Tsar and Tsarina were unable to understand their people's lives. According to Gleb, they based their views of the Russian peasant entirely on what he called the 'sugary stories' in Turgenev's *Notes of a Hunter*. When the Revolution came, the Tsarina remained convinced that the peasants were behind her. Receiving implausibly supportive telegrams from the furthest ends of the Empire, she refused to believe that these were sent by government agents and not by her beloved 'plain people'.

It is doubtful whether Dr Botkin ever found time to develop an overview of life at Tsarskoye Selo. He spent most of his waking hours managing the health crises – real and imagined – of the Tsar, Tsarina and their five children. First and foremost among his tasks was to monitor the Tsarina's famously weak heart, which had to be checked twice a day. The Tsarina's heart reduced her to prolonged periods in wheelchairs and on *chaises longues*. Her worries about her health vied with her obsessive interest in her husband's affairs. At one point she decided to have a wooden staircase erected that led to a balcony above his formal audience chamber. On the balcony, screened off by curtains, she installed a large couch where she could listen while resting.

The Tsarina is sometimes depicted as being some kind of *malade imaginaire*. But Dr Botkin certainly took her symptoms seriously; he wrote of his concern to his brother Peter. 'I am very pained about the malady of the Empress, it is a nervousness of the heart related to the cardiac muscles. This is confirmed by physicians here who I have consulted. I spoke without restrictions because I believe it to be in the best interests of the Empress. I like to let my imagination free to search for different names for the Empress's condition.'

The Tsar and Tsarina

He did not enjoy the same privilege of openness with regard to her haemophiliac son, the Tsarevich Alexis. The boy's illness was kept from the public and Dr Botkin either swore his own children to secrecy or never told them. In 1921, when his daughter Tatiana wrote her memoir, she never at any point specified the nature of Alexis's illness.

In the end perhaps it was Dr Botkin's discretion as much as his medical skills that endeared him to the Tsar. As the Tsar once said to Peter: 'Your brother is a true friend to me, we take everything to heart, and we feel comfortable describing our maladies to him.'

But if Dr Botkin was a reassuring listener and inspector of the Grand Duchesses' throats and rashes, he never fought shy of more exacting duties placed upon him by the Tsarevich. The boy was a prey to 'daredevil reaction', the medical term for haemophiliacs irresistibly drawn to risk-taking activities. He would suffer terrible haemorrhages after falling off high pieces of furniture and tobogganing down staircases. At one point he knocked his face and nearly died from a nosebleed.

Alexis

Botkin's plight as the Tsarevich's doctor was that there was little he could do to help. Morphine, which would have subdued the pain, was deemed unsuitable for a child. Years later, in exile in Siberia, the doctor was at his wits' end regarding treatment for the sick boy. He appealed to the

Imperial Family's Bolshevik captors to allow Alexis to see his tutors: 'Both teachers are completely irreplaceable for Alexis Nikolaievich and I as a doctor must admit that they sometimes bring more relief to the patient than medical teams.' The Ural Regional Soviet replied with a stiff refusal: 'Even one servant would be one too many.'

Dr Botkin may never even have told his wife the extent of Alexis's illness. Certainly Mrs Botkin did not form a favourable view of the young Tsarevich when she met him for the first time. The boy, then aged four, received her bow and friendly greeting with a fierce frown. When Mrs Botkin complained to her husband, he replied that she had obviously upset the Tsarevich with a breach of etiquette. 'Of course the Heir was angry with you. You should have bowed to him in silence, for you have no right to say anything before he himself has started to talk with you.'

Alexis, the Tsarina and Dr Botkin

The more relaxed Mrs Botkin evidently felt herself increasingly marginalised and constrained by her husband's busy professional life. Dr Botkin would be at Court throughout the day; when he finally returned home, he would be occupied with commitments to hospitals and medical academies, sometimes until 5.00am. Eventually Mrs Botkin declared with a sigh, 'Isn't this a dull provincial town?' before embarking upon a scandalous affair with a German tutor. Dr Botkin reluctantly agreed to a divorce and the 'poor young woman' he had married reverted to obscurity.

Meanwhile, Dr Botkin had long forgotten his youthful revolutionary tendencies. He irritated his eleven-year-old son Gleb by insisting the boy bow and cross himself more in church. Mindful of the reprimand his own father received from Alexander II regarding his inertia, he added: 'Your failure to do so might affect my position at court. Some member of the Emperor's suite might and undoubtedly will observe you, and then will inform Their Majesties that their personal physician is apparently neglecting the religious education of his children.' Gleb said that from then on he avoided going to the Imperial Family's church; he disliked the gestures, he explained to his father, because they involved 'a lot of unnecessary movement'.

The young Gleb had already developed a distaste for Court etiquette. He was outraged by the idea that the reception of a lady visitor at court would depend on the position of a feather or *aigrette* (a spray of gems) on her hat. As he recalled: 'When a woman was kissing the Empress's hand an aigrette was likely to get into the Empress's nose and make Her Majesty sneeze. Whenever something of the sort happened the whole Court was in uproar, and the Empress herself suspected the lady who had caused her such embarrassment of deliberate mischief and possibly of revolutionary ideas.'

Gleb embellished his recollections with a litany of courtly constraints: one should never turn one's back on the Imperial Family; one must back out of the room; one must never contradict a member of the Imperial Family or indeed say anything without being asked first. Lastly, if out walking with a member of the Imperial Family, one should neither greet nor even accept the greetings of other passers-by.

While much of Gleb's railing was light-hearted, he maintained that these extremes of formality were damaging to a sense of perspective. He was firmly convinced that the Tsar's heart had actually atrophied. But the example he offered, of the Tsar carrying on playing tennis after hearing of the destruction of the Russian naval fleet at Tsushima, was not true. In fact, the Tsar received the news from the minister of war on an Imperial train; nonetheless Gleb's point was perhaps borne out by the minister's comment upon his subsequent conversation with the Tsar: 'His composure is admirable'.

Gleb's colourful descriptions of courtiers certainly call into question the Imperial couple's ability to judge people. The Tsarina's closest friend, Anna Vyrubova, had an exhibitionist complex and would apparently strip off when she went to the doctor with a throat complaint. Sentries complained that she often appeared naked at windows. She was rumoured to have had an affair with Rasputin; after the Revolution she insisted upon having herself ceremoniously examined by a surgeon and officially declared *virgo intacta*. Gleb described her rather brutally as having had 'round naive eyes, the childish expression of which contrasted strangely with her corpulence'.

But the most controversial of the courtiers must have been the so-called holy man, Gregorii Rasputin. Dr Botkin, in a rare moment of independent judgement, refused to speak to him, turning his back whenever he saw him. Gleb does not record what his father said when the Tsarina pleaded Rasputin's case to him: 'Saints are always calumniated,' she had cried. 'He is hated because we love him.' But at one point Rasputin visited Dr Botkin, hoping to inveigle his way into the doctor's good graces by presenting some interesting ailments. He was out of luck, the doctor declared him 'healthy as a bull'.

Rasputin

Rasputin was known for expressing his freedom of spirit by masterminding orgies and exposing himself in St Petersburg nightclubs. His official counterpart, Father Vassilliev, the father confessor to the Imperial Family, might have espoused the more conventional aspects of religion, but he too prided himself on an unconventional and extremely liberal attitude: 'The devil neither smokes nor drinks nor engages in revelry and yet he is the devil.' When not teaching the Imperial children religious studies, he would conduct mass confessions during which the congregation confessed their sins in shouts and tears.

Of less importance but equal colour were some of the retainers. There was an *aide-de-camp* called Prince Friederieksz, a descendant of Finnish bankers, who was so old that he routinely fell asleep during briefs. He once installed a visiting prince in one room to wait for the Tsar who was in an adjoining room. The two were kept apart for some time, each increasingly enraged by the other's tardiness. Friederieksz's son-in-law, meanwhile, caused a scandal selling what he called radio-active water from his estate; with radioactivity not yet burdened with a bad press, he succeeded in making two million dollars in one year, selling to railway station restaurants. Lastly, there was a Prince Orlov who declared that he would not shave while foreigners were on Russian soil. Foreigners would not have deemed him much of a threat: he was too large to mount a horse and was obliged to join parades on foot.

Dr Botkin's ease with the idiosyncrasies of the pre-

Revolutionary court was undoubtedly connected with his devotion to all seven members of the Imperial Family. Over hurried evening meals, the enraptured doctor would regale his own four children with anecdotes such as the one in which the Tsar found a match in his shoe: 'How strange!' he apparently exclaimed. 'So far as I can remember, I have never lighted matches with my foot.' Another story concerned Dr Botkin's saying to Anastasia: 'You are made of gold.' She replied: 'No I'm made of ordinary leather.' On one occasion the eldest Grand Duchess, Olga, was reading a book given to her by Dr Botkin. When the Tsarina wanted to see it, Olga replied: 'You must wait until I find out whether this book is a proper one for you to read.'

Gleb never commented either upon the low-key nature of these anecdotes, or his father's overjoyed reaction. Perhaps he preferred to be true to his early perceptions: at the time, these would very likely have echoed his father's.

It would have come as no surprise to Mrs Botkin when her husband confessed that he loved the Imperial children as much as his own. At one point each of the daughters had presented him with a flower; Dr Botkin immediately put the four flowers together and took them to a jeweller who made a facsimile of them in coloured enamel. 'What better symbol of the Grand Duchesses could there be than those flowers?' he sighed. 'For they are in truth like beautiful flowers.'

The Imperial children lived an extremely narrow existence that bestowed a particular importance on outsiders. They used to play a game with Dr Botkin in which they tracked him from room to room, following the scent of his rich perfume. They were evidently fond of the doctor, with Alexis once declaring: 'I love you with my whole little heart.' The Grand Duchess Olga pronounced Dr Botkin 'a deep well of profound ideas' and addressed him in all her letters as 'Dear Well'. Gleb, incidentally, concurred, feeling the children's tutors failed to match his father in any kind of intellectual depth. He deemed the Swiss tutor, Pierre Gilliard, 'a very ordinary type of French teacher' and the children's nanny, Alexandra Tegleva, Gilliard's future wife, 'a complete nonentity'. The language teacher, Yekaterina Schneider, was so prudish that she refused to let the Grand Duchesses stage a play containing the word 'stockings'.

The Romanov Children

As to companionship, the Tsarina believed that the four Grand Duchesses should be self-sufficient. The Baroness Buxhoeveden, the Tsarina's lady-in-waiting, recalled that 'no young girls were ever asked to the Palace'. Gleb's sister, Tatiana, later claimed that Olga 'longed pathetically' for real friends. In 1912 an American magazine *Royal Mothers and Their Children* referred to the children as 'inmates of the Imperial nursery' watched over by a 'nerve-racked mother' who suffered from 'abnormal fears' for their futures.

The constraints placed upon the children adversely affected their development. As Alexander Mossolov, the head of the Imperial Chancellery, later recalled: 'Even when the two eldest had grown into real young women, one might hear them talking like little girls of ten or twelve.'

The young Olga made what would turn out to be a particularly poignant comment apropos the fate of the Welsh prince Llywelyn The Last – killed by the English in 1282 – during a history lesson. 'I really think people are much better now than they used to be, I'm very glad I live now when people are so kind.' In a further irony, it was Olga who told her nanny that all her sympathies were with 'poor Goliath' who could not have expected David to throw the stone.

Gleb later judged Olga the most thoughtful of the four girls. As a teenager she grew less convinced of people's kindness and, according to Gleb, was the only one in the Imperial Family who seemed even faintly aware of the gathering darkness. 'I had the impression that she had little illusion in regard to what the future held in store for them, and in consequence was often sad and worried.' The Tsarina also noted Olga's recurrent bad moods, complaining to the Tsar in her curious English: 'Olga is the whole time grumpy, sleepy, angry to put on a tidy dress.'

Though the second eldest daughter, Tatiana, was, in Gleb's view, more cheerful and active than Olga, she was impeded by what he called an executive mind. Her put-upon siblings referred to her as 'the governess'. As Yevgeny Kobylinsky, one of the Provisional guards, put it: 'Tatiana had no liking for art. Perhaps it would have been better for her had she been a man.'

The third daughter, Marie, was, according to Gleb, 'a typical Russian beauty, rather plump and with cheeks red as apples', but his favourite was clearly the youngest, Anastasia. Gleb was convinced that Anastasia felt unwanted: she was, after all, the fourth daughter in a family known to be desperate for an heir. This he regarded as more than an excuse for her notorious behaviour.

Anastasia aged about four

Anastasia as a little girl

Anastasia in the Grand Duchesses' study

He managed to paint a generally positive picture of her as: 'Witty, vivacious, hopelessly stubborn, delightfully impertinent and in general a perfect *enfant terrible*... she undoubtedly held the record for punishable deeds in her family, for in naughtiness she was a true genius.'

Some of her misdemeanours were indeed harmless. When the saluting cannon on the Imperial Yacht fired at sunset, she would rush into a corner, put her fingers in her ears and stick her tongue out in mock terror. Other times she would climb trees and refuse to come down. However, she once knocked Tatiana unconscious by hitting her with a rock rolled into a snowball. Princess Nina Georgievna later declared that Anastasia was 'considered nasty to the point of being evil'. The young Grand Duchess would apparently cheat, kick and scratch to get her own way. She was a 'frightfully temperamental' girl who was 'wild and rough' and resented any challenge. One of her English nannies was obliged to tie her to a chair when she refused to stop getting on the table. Her English tutor deemed her the only ungraceful member of the Imperial Family.

And then there was the Tsarevich; Gleb could find no excuse for the young heir's bad behaviour. Alexis was known for laughing openly at his stout sailor bodyguard, Derevenko, calling him 'the Fat One'. He would shout: 'look at Fatty run', as the sailor struggled to keep up in public processions. The boy's table manners were execrable, as Grand Duke Konstantin recalled in his diary: 'He wouldn't sit up, ate badly, licked his plate and teased the others. The Tsar often turned away, perhaps to avoid having to say anything, while the Tsarina rebuked her elder daughter Olga, who sat next to her brother, for not restraining him.'

Catherine Mikhailovna Frolova-Bagreeva, whose family had a small dacha down the hill from the Imperial residence at Livadia, recalled of Alexis: 'He liked to greet people who bowed to him with a bloody nose by hitting them in the face as they bowed. I remember one day his sailor-nanny taking him by the hand so that he couldn't greet people with a bloody nose, and so the Heir greeted us, in public, with very bad language.'

Probably relishing the fact that Alexis was worse behaved than his beloved Anastasia, Gleb readily added his own criticism: 'While I fully shared the general devotion to him, his manners seemed to me considerably worse than those of his sisters, and his restlessness rather depressing.'

Alexis and one of the Grand Duchesses

Nonetheless, aged nine, Alexis showed an unexpectedly sensitive side, refusing to sign an order for Gleb to do some artwork. The request, which Alexis handed to Dr Botkin, was 'to illustrate and write the jingles under the drawing'. But when Dr Botkin jocularly asked him to sign it, Alexis replied gravely: 'I can't send that paper to Gleb with my signature on it, for then it would be an order which Gleb would have to obey. But I mean it only as a request and he doesn't have to do it if he doesn't want to.'

Entranced by tales of the antics at the palace, Gleb must have regarded his own home life at Tsarskoye Selo as humdrum. The routine of the Botkin children's day – one hour of grammar, one of geography and one of locomotives – was such that the appearance of the Grand Duchesses' horses created a major disturbance. The sighting would be followed by an announcement that the horses were being taken to the palace. 'This means they (the Grand Duchesses) will soon be passing our house so we will run to the windows and exchange daily greetings. If the Tsar drives behind in a second carriage and notices our salutations, it is an event to be discussed for the rest of the day.'

***

It was hardly surprising that Gleb remembered the minutest detail of his first proper meeting with the Imperial Family in 1911. Then aged eleven, he had travelled to Sebastopol with his siblings to join their father, who was already installed on the Imperial Yacht, the *Standart*. At the station they were met with the news that their father was ill, but that the Tsarina had requested they come on board. The group duly made their way to the pier but then had trouble procuring a cutter to take them to the *Standart*.

After several refusals from one Imperial officer, the Grand Duchesses themselves saved the situation by sending their own cutter to pick up the group. Gleb blamed the difficulty on the the young Botkin's German governess, whom he brutally described as having a nose like a duck's beak and a Chinese pagoda of red hair. He denounced her picturesquely as 'the incarnation of a public menace'.

When they finally got on board they were greeted by Grand Duchess Olga. Gleb made much of his worries about kissing Olga's hand: failure to do so would, he was convinced, amount to 'revolutionary demonstration'. But he made even more of her skill in overcoming his worries: 'while all those agonising thoughts were whirling through my brain, the hand of Grand Duchess Olga came up to my lips in such easeful, convenient manner, that I kissed it with all the ease of an experienced courtier!'

The children rushed to their father's bedroom, where they were joined by all five of the Imperial children. Gleb's first mortifying discovery was that he could barely understand a word they said. 'The Grand Duchesses and the Tsarevich spoke not only fluently but so rapidly that at first I was hardly able to understand them. In addition to this they had an accent which seemed English when they spoke in Russian and

Russian when they spoke in English, and in actual fact was an accent quite their own.'

Seeing the sisters properly for the first time, Gleb admitted that he was immediately captivated by Anastasia, then aged ten. This, he insisted, was not entirely to do with her general appearance: 'For Anastasia was less beautiful than her sisters. She was small in size and her features were irregular. Her nose was rather long and her mouth quite wide. She had a small straight chin which lacked almost entirely the usual curve under the lower lip.' But he could not, finally, prevent himself from adding lyrical details about her hair and eyes. Anastasia's hair was 'blond with a slightly reddish lustre, wavy and soft as silk. In childhood she wore it loose, with a large ribbon perched on the top of her head, which looked like a giant butterfly just ready to fly away... her eyes – blue luminous eyes, always sparkling with humour – were truly beautiful.'

The children were joined in the room by the Tsar and the Tsarina. According to Gleb, the Tsar's eyes were also

The Grand Duchesses

Alexis swimming

beautiful: 'I have never met a person, who was introduced to the Emperor for the first time, who did not immediately comment on the beauty of his eyes.' Although the Tsarina had a formidable reputation – courtiers were known to take drugs to calm themselves before audiences with her – she was evidently more relaxed on the *Standart*. As Gleb put it: 'She was always most pleasant and affable in her attitude to children.'

The two young boys, Gleb and Alexis, immediately began exchanging information about military regulations and uniforms. As the conversation acquired a competitive edge, Gleb was chagrined to discover that he knew less than Alexis about the Navy. He recalled: 'Nothing could give him greater delight than to discover that I was unacquainted with some naval term or rule. Eventually I got even with him by discovering that he had four buttons on the trousers of his sailor-suit which, according to official regulations, had no right there.'

Having satisfactorily tackled Alexis, Gleb assailed Anastasia with a tactic for winning noughts and crosses. He recalled with pride that Anastasia could achieve no more than a draw and she once even warned Marie not to play with him; 'Beware Marie. For he plays well.'

He won a second victory when Anastasia teased him for not being able to reach an electric switch in his father's stateroom. Gleb had been trying to reach the switch, situated just under the ceiling, by standing on a chair. Pushing Gleb aside, Anastasia made Marie stand on the chair. She then stood on Marie. As she was reaching up, the chair toppled and both Grand Duchesses fell on top of Gleb. 'I had the satisfaction

The Grand Duchesses Anastasia and Marie

of pointing out to Anastasia that she had boasted in vain of her ability to turn on that switch.'

He was more gallant in his account of a game of hide and seek. At one point Anastasia had hidden herself behind a curtain but was given away by her foot, which stuck out. During the next round, Gleb was puzzled to see the foot sticking out once again; but upon throwing back the curtain he discovered there was nothing there but Anastasia's shoe. As he recalled: 'She graciously allowed me to put it back on her foot, while continuing to shake with laughter and tell me how very easy it was to fool me.'

Dr Botkin's selfless devotion to the members of the Imperial Family was not always reciprocated. In 1913, the Grand Duchess Tatiana contracted typhoid from orangeade prepared with unboiled water. Dr Botkin caught the disease from her and nearly died. He was obliged to be away from the palace for several weeks and eventually went abroad to recuperate. The Tsar and Tsarina's initial concern for the doctor soon gave way, to his dismay, to a prolonged coolness.

By the same token, it was now understood that Dr Botkin's illness on board the *Standart* would not get in the way of his work. The Tsarina made one concession: rather than wait for him to attend her, she would go to his stateroom for her medical examinations. A ritual developed around the daily visit, in which Gleb would help his father wash his hands. Whether this was because the doctor was too ill to do his own washing or because he simply wished to give his son a job is not known. In any case the procedure was watched avidly by

Anastasia. 'Father had a peculiar wash bowl made of glass,' Gleb recalled. 'Whenever it was brought out Anastasia would laugh and assure me that it was not a wash bowl but a container for curdled milk – a favourite Russian dish.'

The day after Gleb left the *Standart* to return to St Petersburg, Dr Botkin was disconcerted to find Anastasia in the stateroom ready to wash his hands: 'Where is your curdled milk container? It is time for you to wash your hands and now that Gleb is gone I am in charge of the curdled milk container.' Despite his reservations about propriety, the doctor eventually allowed Anastasia to wash his hands. She had worn him down with her persistent protests: 'If Gleb can do it for you, why can't I?'

***

The doctor's energetic son had clearly, in his turn, caught Anastasia's fancy. She may have been captivated by Gleb's neat, slightly eastern good looks, or even the manly pains he took to win games. But the most likely attraction would have been his talent for drawing animals. All five Imperial children loved Gleb's illustrated stories about his kingdom of bears. Marie would decorously try and copy the drawings while Anastasia enjoyed pestering him with indelicate story lines.

On one occasion Gleb drew a picture of a little brown she-bear in a blue skirt trying to steal a pot of honey from her mother's pantry. Anastasia was very excited by the image: 'Fie what a lovely little atrocity. But I hate sneaks. Do have her

Anastasia aged twelve

punished. Let that pot of honey turn over on her head and gum up all her fur.' Gleb reluctantly obliged, while later denouncing Anastasia's plotlines as 'of the pie-throwing type'.

Gleb's lack of enthusiasm for her artistic contribution did nothing to dampen Anastasia's ardour. With uncharacteristic dedication, she set about embroidering him a runner of ecru linen with blue flowers. Gleb took the gift in the right spirit, placing upon it his precious crucifixes and icons.

It was not just the Imperial children, however, who were taking an interest in the kingdom of bears. Gleb's drawings began to be discussed at Court and soon became the subject of controversy. This was less surprising than it sounds. At the time it was traditional for Tsarist watchdogs to scrutinise books, paintings and even musical annotation for messages of sedition. Gleb had created a fat Prime Minister, 'Mr Pig', who resembled Prince Orlov; more worryingly, he had depicted the Tsar of the Bears in the same pose and uniform as those of Tsar Nicholas in the famous portrait by Valentin Serov.

It is not known to what extent Gleb realised his drawings were controversial. But if he relished the attention they created, his father did not. After being subjected to disapproving murmurs from several well-wishers, Dr Botkin decided to put the matter to rest by taking Gleb's pictures to the palace for official approval from the Tsar and Tsarina. The couple were impressed rather than disturbed by the drawings, though the Tsarina's prognosis of how the 'plain people' would view them shows characteristic lack of judgement. 'These picture books must be published. Of course, they couldn't be published in Russia; people would think them offensive. But they certainly could be published in Germany.'

The Grand Duchesses pre-revolution

Although at this point in his life the young Gleb clearly shared his father's awe of the Tsar and Tsarina, over the next few years he would become increasingly aware of growing revolutionary unrest. He would have begun to wonder whether the Russian Court was as unassailable as it had once appeared.

In 1912 the charismatic Prime Minister, Peter Stolypin, was murdered in front of the Tsar at a gala performance in the Kiev theatre. Dr Botkin had just concluded a conversation with the Prime Minister, an old friend, when the assassin pulled a pistol from his pocket. Botkin caught Stolypin in his arms and watched in anguish as the dying man made a sign of the cross in the direction of the Tsar's box and whispered a prayer: 'May God save him.'

Years afterwards, in exile in Siberia, Dr Botkin told Gleb he came to believe that Stolypin had been shot by government agents. He could not explain otherwise how the Imperial couple had received the news of the great statesman's death with such 'astonishing calm'. He would not have been surprised afterwards to hear the cool words with which the Tsarina welcomed Stolypin's successor: 'Believe me, one must not feel sorry for those who are no more. I am sure that everybody does only one's duty and fulfils one's destiny, and when one dies that means that his role is ended and that he was bound to go since his destiny was fulfilled... I am sure that Stolypin died to make room for you, and this is all for the good of Russia.'

Stolypin had fallen from favour after banishing Rasputin

from the court. The Imperial couple preferred Stolypin's successor, Ivan Goremykin, an elderly minister who believed that ministers should not aspire to any higher role than that of Tsar's servant. The English Ambassador, Sir Arthur Nicolson, was amazed when he met Goremykin, 'an elderly man with a sleepy face and Piccadilly whiskers' who reclined on a sofa piled with French novels.

But in 1914 Goremykin became something of a hero in the Botkins' house when the doctor described a meeting called by ministers still hoping to avoid war. A telegram had been received from the Kaiser suggesting several compromises Russia might make; Goremykin had been asked to preside over the ensuing heated discussion. Dr Botkin told his family that Goremykin slept through the whole meeting, then opened one eye and said: 'And thus gentlemen I shall report to His Imperial Majesty that you have decided unanimously in favour of a declaration of war.' Botkin, at any rate, was impressed: 'He may be old but he is wise and a real patriot.'

Gleb always remembered in minute detail the evening he heard that war had been declared. He and his brother, Yuri, and sister, Tatiana, were at the open window of their drawing room. He gave a poetic description of the scene: 'It was the hour of sunset, the air was still and fragrant, and a bird sang peacefully in a lilac-bush under the window.' Through the birdsong, the children suddenly caught the sound of hundreds of voices singing 'God Save The Tsar'. The voices came from the barracks of the Tsar's Own Infantry. At the end of the anthem, the soldiers cheered and the drums rolled.

Shortly afterwards, Dr Botkin appeared on the doorstep with his stark announcement: 'Children, it is war.' The poignancy of the moment was completed as the family turned to the corner to face an icon.

Later that evening a naval captain whom the Botkins barely knew called by to share his patriotic fervour. There was no doubting the captain's loyalties, despite his name: Baron von der Osten-Sacken-Tettenborn. 'I declare hereby that Germany must be crushed, crushed, *crushed*,' he growled. An impromptu choir was formed to sing 'God Save The Tsar' as Gleb's brother, Yuri, drummed his fists on the table top.

But there was vinegar in the honey. The Botkins had an elderly retainer called African who boasted mutton-chop whiskers and gold-laced livery. Gleb later remembered him as resembling a relic of the days of Peter the Great. The prospect of war threw African into paroxysms of horror; he rushed into the drawing room ringing his hands. 'Little fathers, little fathers we are lost! Russia is doomed! We are all doomed.' Gleb confessed that, for years afterwards, he could not think of African's prophecy without a shudder.

The two elder Botkin boys, Dmitri and Yuri, immediately joined the army. Dmitri became a lieutenant in a Cossack regiment and was sent to the Eastern front where he was killed four months later. Yuri, meanwhile, fell victim to a mysterious illness and was hospitalised. He became a prisoner of war after his hospital was captured by the Austrians. Though he eventually returned home, he remained a semi-invalid, bearing almost no resemblance to the boy he had been.

Dr Botkin was devastated by the death of his eldest son. 'He grew more and more orthodox in his religious conceptions and developed a veritable abhorrence of the flesh,' Gleb recalled. Perhaps it was fortunate for him that, as a doctor, he was distracted by an ever-increasing workload. Trainloads of the injured were now arriving regularly at Tsarskoye Selo from the front. The doctor immediately set about converting the Botkins' modest house into a small hospital with two rooms.

According to Gleb, the heavy casualty rate was beginning to have a catastrophic effect on morale. Even at the outset of the war, Gleb had noted the contrast between the attitude towards the Tsar of the crowds in St Petersburg and Moscow. While the crowd at the Winter Palace had dropped to its knees and sung 'God Save The Tsar', the atmosphere in Moscow had been decidedly cooler.

With characteristic quirkiness, Gleb put the increasing national malaise down to a preponderance of Russian generals with German names. At one point a Russian army corps was confronting a German army corps – each of them commanded by a General von der Brinken. On another occasion a General von Grunwals was arrested by a policeman in St Petersburg for speaking German in the street. Though he was instantly released, he was ordered to pay a fine of 2,000 roubles. He apparently grumbled afterwards: 'What language does that accursed idiot want me to speak, when German is the only language I know?'

In December 1916 Rasputin was murdered by the Russian

aristocrat Prince Felix Yussoupov, with the help of a Romanov cousin, Grand Duke Dmitri. The pair poisoned and shot Rasputin before throwing him into the Neva. The growing influence of the colourful holy man had been viewed with dismay by the Russian aristocracy, who blamed him for the failing popularity of the Imperial Family.

The involvement of the Grand Duke had chilling significance for the Imperial Family. During the final month of his life Rasputin wrote a testament: 'Tsar of the land of Russia, if you hear the sound of the bell which will tell you that Gregorii has been killed, you must know this: if it was your relations who have wrought my death then no one of your family, that is to say, none of your children or relations will remain alive for more than two years. They will be killed by the Russian people.'

Though he had disliked Rasputin so intensely, Dr Botkin was deeply disturbed by the news of his death. 'Rasputin dead will be worse than Rasputin alive,' he warned his son. 'Moreover, what Youssoupov has actually done is to fire the first shot of the Revolution. He has shown others the way – when a demand is not granted, take the law in your own hands and shoot'. Six months later Gleb saw a picture of Youssoupov decorated with a wreath of laurel in the window of an official building. It bore the inscription: 'Youssoupov, the hero of the Revolution.'

By this time the Tsarina had long forgotten her resentment at Dr Botkin's protracted bout of typhoid. She now declared him the only person in whom she could confide. There must have been an element of pride in his voice when he described the Tsarina's state of mind to his son. 'She refused to see anybody, and desired to talk to me only. When I came into her room she said, "I am all alone. His Majesty is at the front and here I have no-one I can trust".'

During the first days of revolution, in March 1917, the Imperial Family was placed under house arrest. Retainers were given the chance to leave or stay; if they stayed they lost virtually all contact with the outside world. Father Vassilieff was among the first to go, claiming that he had suffered a nervous shock. Dr Ostrogorsky, the specialist attending the Grand Duchesses, sent word that he 'found the roads too dirty' to get to the palace.

There were betrayals even within the family. One of the Tsar's first cousins, Grand Duke Kyril, led the Marines of the Guard to the Duma where he proclaimed himself 'a free citizen of a free Russia'. Years later, Gleb remarked bitterly: 'Today he (Kyril) lives peacefully in Europe styling himself "Emperor of All The Russias" distributing titles and decorations among his adherents and writing nonsensical manifestos in which he sheds crocodile tears over the "radiant memory" of his "beloved cousin, the martyred Emperor Nicholas".'

For the faithful Dr Botkin there was never any choice but to remain with the Imperial Family; over the last few weeks he had been particularly indispensable as four of the five children were now suffering from measles. At the outset of the Revolution, he was apparently calm as he delivered news of the Tsar's abdication to his own children. The name of St

Petersburg had been changed to the Russian Petrograd. 'Petrograd is in the hands of the revolutionaries, and a provisional government has assumed power. The poor Empress! All the children sick, the government overthrown and in ignorance of the whereabouts of His Majesty.'

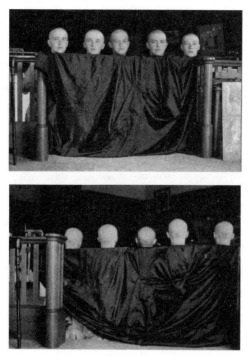

The Romanov children with the measles

Before the Tsar's abdication, the Tsarina had resorted to sending her husband a frantic message of warning: 'Clearly they don't want to let you see me so above all you must not sign any paper, constitution or other such horror – but you are alone, without your army, caught like a mouse in a trap, what can you do?' The warning was carried by two Cossack soldiers, carefully sewn into their uniforms.

Dr Botkin's assistant doctor, Vladimir Derevenko, whom he had brought in to help with Alexis, also elected to stay at the palace, but with an unremitting bad grace. Gleb had always been critical of Derevenko's pedigree: 'a capable surgeon but of peasant stock, which showed all too clearly in his manners and speech'. Now Derevenko pursued the beleaguered Dr Botkin up and down palace corridors shouting: 'Some job you've found for me, I'm telling you.'

On the streets of Tsarskoye Selo, Gleb gained a slightly broader picture of the worsening situation. He remembered hearing first that machine-gunners from Tsarskoye Selo were ordered to proceed to Petrograd to suppress disorder, then that soldiers had rebelled and murdered their commander. He heard of the families of the Tsar's policemen being set upon; in one case a four-year-old girl died after having a fork thrust down her throat.

In the end Dr Botkin himself was sufficiently alarmed by news of an approaching mob to tell Gleb and Tatiana to move away from the palace grounds and stay with an elderly lady in the centre of Tsarskoye Selo. As it happened, the mob turned back to Petrograd after being beaten back by snow. But Gleb recalled that, as he sat down to dinner, a trembling butler dashed into the dining room to tell them that the whole garrison in Tsarskoye Selo had mutinied. The household was kept awake all that night with the noise of gunfire and shouting. Gleb wandered out in the morning to find himself besieged by drunken soldiers running, howling, shrieking and waving red banners. He made the valiant decision to wear his school-cap, with the Tsar's initial and crown, and accosted a young recruit who offered an explanation for the riots: 'General Ivanov is marching on Tsarskoye Selo with a whole division of loyal (monarchist) troops. They'll hang every one of us so we may as well do some shooting in the meantime.'

Gleb subsequently became preoccupied with what he regarded as a typically Russian trait: if you have already sinned and there is no redemption, you might as well sin some more. Years later, he wrote a curious novel, *The God Who Didn't Laugh*, in which his hero, Tosha, says: 'Why not doom oneself? Why not utter some blasphemy against the Holy Ghost and be done with it? Even as it is, there seems to be one chance out of a thousand of ever getting to Heaven. In this way, one could at least be happy on earth, and help others also to be happy.'

During a lull that followed the uprising, the siblings returned to their home – Gleb noting with wry amusement that one mob, shouting 'To the Palace', had actually been besieging a large department store. Dr Botkin arrived for what would be his last visit to the family home in his customary Court carriage with a liveried coachman on the box. Gleb found the sight reassuring, while admitting that the carriage now looked incongruous. The soldiers the carriage passed on the street were so aghast they made no attempt to stop it. Dr Botkin now told his family that the Imperial couple's idea was to get the family out through Finland. 'Don't be alarmed in case you should hear of our sudden disappearance. I may not be able to comunicate with you again. If we succeed in escaping abroad you shall of course follow us at the first opportunity.'

Once Dr Botkin had elected to remain with the Imperial Family under house arrest, he was no longer allowed to leave the palace. Gleb, however, was allowed to apply for permission to visit him; he recalled waiting his turn at the palace gate. A palace cook was trying to kiss his little daughter through the iron bars. 'He was weeping bitterly and kept saying: "I can understand about the masters but why are we plain people made to suffer? What am I guilty of?".'

At the gate, Gleb was challenged by a sentry who wanted to know why he wore an Imperial crown on his cap. Gleb, with characteristic bravura, asked in return why the sentry wore Imperial crowns on his coat buttons. He added cheekily: 'You have eight buttons on your overcoat, each button with one Imperial double eagle and each eagle with three Imperial crowns. That makes 24 Imperial crowns on your person. So, before annoying me, go and cut off the buttons from your overcoat.'

Father and son met in the guardhouse. They were not allowed to touch each other and were forbidden from speaking any language other than Russian: the French they habitually spoke was outlawed because it could not be understood by the guards. The weeks under house arrest had already taken their toll; Gleb noted with dismay that his father had aged. Dr Botkin told his son he had been particularly upset about the treatment of the Tsar and Tsarina. The Imperial couple, though now theoretically reunited, were not permitted to live in the same rooms; they met only at meal-times, in the presence of a revolutionary officer.

The doctor himself was watched at all times. During his regular examinations of the Grand Duchesses, still recuperating from measles, the guards hovered in the bedroom doorways: this was a concession as, at first, the guards had insisted on listening and watching next to the beds.

Dr Botkin's own nerves had been particularly strained by the arrival at the palace of the father of the Tsarina's friend, Anna Vyrubova. Vyrubova's father had escaped from Petrograd with just an icon and a toothbrush. Already an unpopular figure, his particular *faux pas* on this occasion was to use the palace phone to ring the office of the newly formed Duma and swear allegiance to the Provisional Leader. Speaking at the top of his voice, he proclaimed that he spoke not just on his behalf but also that of his daughter.

In fact his daughter took a dim view of the Provisional Leader, Alexander Kerensky, whose subsequent visit to the palace she recalled vividly: 'I beheld a small, clean-shaven, theatrical person whose essentially weak face was disguised in a Napoleonic frown.' At the time of Kerensky's visit, Anna was claiming to be recovering from measles. She had risen for lunch, but rushed back to bed at the sound of the Leader's approaching footsteps. Kerensky was not daunted. Anna recalled her horror as he barked orders from her bedside: 'Standing over me... the man booms out: "I am the Minister of

Justice. You are to dress and go at once to Petrograd". I answered not a word but lay still on my pillows. This seemed to disconcert him somewhat for he turned nervously: "Ask the doctors if she is fit to go."' She was mortified to hear herself condemned to leave, with clean bills of health from both Botkin and Derevenko. She later huffily attributed the doctors' pronouncements to 'craven fear'.

Meanwhile, life in Tsarskoye Selo was becoming increasingly difficult for the seventeen-year-old Gleb. He was warned repeatedly that the Provisional Guards planned to shoot him and he courted hostility by continuing to wear his school-cap. He was probably relieved when the offer arose for him to escape with friends to the countryside of Kazan for the summer. The Revolution was only just beginning to take hold in the rural regions and though on this particular estate peasants were indeed threatening to kill the landowners – and their guests – Gleb deemed the conflict no more threatening than a game of cowboys and indians.

Nonetheless, it was during these months that Gleb first decided he wanted to leave Russia. He found that he did not feel part of the country; he inclined, he now realised, more towards Western Europe than Russia. This was not unusual. The aspirations of the Russian gentry of the time were predominantly French. Children were forced to speak French and occasionally even forbidden from speaking Russian. Because of this, the gentry and peasantry in Russia were almost like two different races. When, after the Revolution, French-speaking aristocrats were forced on to the streets, they found themselves unable even to beg in a language that could be understood by the people. Gleb recalled his changing views with dismay: 'The moment I found myself face to face with the mass of the Russian people, I discovered, with some bewilderment, that I did not belong to them at all!'

But, however much he wished to leave, Gleb's first obligation was to his family. While still in Kazan, he heard that his father and sister had followed the Imperial Family to Tobolsk in Siberia. He ascertained that, in order to travel from Kazan to Siberia, he needed to get permission from the Governor-General of Kazan. The Governor-General turned out to be Pavel Korovichenko, the man who had treated the Imperial couple so cavalierly when they had been under house arrest at the palace. Gleb felt he had little hope of gaining favours from Korovichenko. But, as it turned out, Korovichenko proved extremely helpful, gladly writing a letter stating that Gleb was on a mission for the new government.

The worsening treatment of the Imperial Family in the last months of their lives was such that, in the end, Korovichenko came to be regarded as one of the more benevolent guards. Indeed, after the October Revolution, he refused to have anything to do with the Bolsheviks. For this he was arrested in his own office, tied up and trampled to death by drunken soldiers, each paying ten kopecks for the privilege. Gleb was shocked by the icy calm with which the Tsarina received the details of the former guard's death. 'It may be best for him. Perhaps the torture he has suffered will diminish the punishment which God will inflict upon him for the misery he has caused us.'

Gleb's refusal to be parted from his school-cap created problems on the journey to Siberia. Every time the train stopped, the revolutionary militia would crowd into the carriages asking for papers. When they spotted Gleb's incriminating cap they would surround him, bayonets at the ready. As soon as he produced Korovichenko's letter, however, they would stand back and salute.

When Gleb finally arrived in Tobolsk, he was met off the steamer by his father and sister and taken to the Botkins' two-room apartment opposite the Governor's House, where the Imperial Family were imprisoned. Looking out of the window for the first time, Gleb saw a harrowing sight, one which would haunt him for the rest of his life: the four Grand Duchesses walking aimlessly around in a dirty courtyard comprising a piece of road sealed off by a ten-foot wooden fence.

Later he would watch impotently as soldiers shouted insulting remarks or wrote obscene inscriptions on the inside of the fence. Gleb was disparaging about the Provisional Guard, Vasily Pankratov, who was in charge of looking after the family. He reported that Pankratov would deliver lectures in the town every day, 'sobbing loudly like a frenzied woman' and making much of past grievances: 'All I did was to kill a police officer on duty because he talked rudely to my sweetheart... The Tsar had no mercy; he kept me in jail for twelve years then sent me to Siberia.'

Gleb soon began drawing again for the Imperial children. His kingdom had now, of course, undergone a revolution and the revolutionaries were gamely depicted as unattractive monkeys who came to a bad end. Gleb was thrilled to hear that the Tsar was enjoying the drawings and that he was impressed by the range of uniforms. At this point, Gleb started exchanging poetry with Olga. He later recalled a dark prayer written by Olga in which she asked God for nothing at the moment of death but 'the inhuman force to pray meekly' for her murderers.

At this curiously nebulous time of his life, Gleb thought of joining the priesthood. He had been drawn to the idea once before, and, after the outbreak of the war in 1914, had asked the advice of his mentor and confessor at Tsarskoye Selo, Father Anatoliy Dimitriev. At that point, Father Dimitriev had advised him to wait before making his decision. Both of them realised that, if the war continued, there was every likelihood that Gleb, then just fourteen, would feel torn between the priesthood and the army.

But, after the first revolution in 1917, Father Dimitriev evidently felt the time was ripe for a second discussion. He came to visit Gleb at the Botkins' house in Tsarskoye Selo: 'Do not waste your time bemoaning what you have lost. It might be that you have lost nothing at all... you should prepare yourself for the priesthood.'

Now it was Gleb who disagreed; he told Father Dimitriev that he was filled with an un-Christian hatred for the revolutionaries. He added that he was angry with the Orthodox Church, which he felt had capitulated. Up until 1917, it had been understood that all good Christians were monarchists. There were now priests willing to substitute 'Provisional Government' for 'Tsar' in the prayers. Others had even asked for permission to appear at civil funerals in robes of a revolutionary scarlet. Though Father Dimitriev had not been able to offer a convincing defence, he kept repeating his belief that Gleb would change his mind.

Father Dimitriev's prediction for Gleb came true just months later. Gleb had become less cynical about the clergy, convincing himself that they would one day rise up against the revolutionaries. He combined this hope with a feeling that the Orthodox Church was all that was left of pre-Revolutionary Russia: 'If I had to remain in the country, then it was obvious that I should not feel happy anywhere but in the Church.'

Dr Botkin was thrilled with his son's decision. So was the Tsarina, who later gave Gleb, as a Christmas present, a book on theology; the personal inscription read simply: 'To Gleb from Alexandra'. Shortly before that Christmas of 1917, the Tsarina asked Pankratov whether Gleb and Tatiana could share the Imperial Family's festivities. His reply was disingenuous: 'I consider that the grief of a second separation will be much greater for your children and Dr Botkin's than the joy they may feel at spending one day together.'

Meanwhile, the news from the front was ever more gloomy. Days after the Bolshevik coup in October, peace negotiations with Germany had begun at Brest-Litovsk. In March 1918, the negotiations were completed. The Tsarina, maliciously labelled a German sympathiser, declared that she could not think of Brest-Litovsk without a pain in her heart: 'All one's feelings have been trampled under foot.' The Tsar confided, as usual, in Botkin: 'Had I known it would come to this, I would never have abdicated.'

During these dark days, the Grand Duchesses took it upon themselves to keep the family spirits up. Dr Botkin gave an enthusiastic description of the girls' tactics to Gleb: 'Every time the Tsar enters the dining room with a sad expression on his face the Grand Duchesses push each other with their elbows and whisper: "Papa is sad today. We must cheer him up". And so they proceed to do so. They begin to laugh, to tell funny stories, and, in a few minutes, His Majesty begins to smile.'

Gleb recalled that Anastasia was usually the cheer leader on these occasions, delivering 'an astonishing supply of somewhat shady anecdotes, goodness knew where collected, which, at times, shocked my father'.

In an effort to raise morale, the children's two tutors, Gilliard and the Englishman Sydney Gibbes, staged plays which the children performed before their parents. On one occasion, during the performance of a play called *Packing Up*, Anastasia turned her back ostentatiously on the audience. Her gown then mysteriously rose, exposing, as Gibbes recalled, 'her sturdy legs and bottom encased in the Tsar's Jaeger underwear'. Gibbes, in some embarrassment, always insisted that the gown had been caught in a draught. Gleb, though more decorous in his account, was under no illusions, accusing Anastasia of 'deliberately losing at the most dramatic moment a much needed piece of her apparel'. In any case, the Tsarina, a

German at heart, was delighted. As Dr Botkin reported: 'I have never seen Her Majesty laugh so heartily and so cheerfully in my life. I thought she would fall off her chair from laughter.'

Towards the end of April, Dr Botkin was separated from his children forever. The Imperial Family had been told they must travel to Moscow so that the Tsar could be put through a trial. Alexis was too ill to travel, so the family decided to split: the Tsar, Tsarina and Marie would travel first, with the rest of the Imperial children following as soon as Alexis had recovered.

The doctor elected to leave with the Imperial couple and wrote a farewell note to his children on his last night in Tobolsk. The note was strangely buoyant; the doctor was convinced that the trial was no more than a showcase and that the Imperial Family would soon be enjoying exile in England. As soon as he was settled, he assured his children, they would all be reunited. He was adamant that Gleb must spend at least a year in England before carrying out his plan to enter the Academy of Theology. Gleb and Tatiana cheerfully packed their father's case; Gleb was struck by the incongruity of the surrounding snowy wastes of Siberia and his father's new tennis flannels and white tennis shoes.

For a few days Gleb and Tatiana felt relatively sanguine, but then they heard from Grand Duchess Olga that the roads from Tobolsk had proven terrible and that in consequence the illness-prone doctor had suffered an attack of liver-colic.

A week later they heard altogether worse news – that the party had been stopped at Ekaterinburg. Back in Tobolsk, the benevolent commandant, Colonel Yevgeny Kobylinsky, was now replaced by a dissolute guard called, according to Gleb, Haritonov: 'A coal-stoker with an appearance and manners in harmony with his calling.' Gleb recalled Haritonov moving into his house accompanied by a bevy of prostitutes wearing nurses' uniforms. Every night Gleb sat up by the front door of his apartment listening to drunken orgies, devising plans by which he could protect his sister's honour.

Meanwhile, across Russia, the terror conducted against the Russian Orthodox Church was intensifying; bishops and priests were being murdered by the thousand. Giving his account of the persecution, Gleb offers characteristically lurid detail: the Bolsheviks' favoured way of desecrating churches involved persuading prostitutes to sit naked on communion tables while they staged orgies in the sanctuaries.

As Easter approached, the Bolshevik leaders in Tobolsk prohibited all religious festivals and processions. The local Bishop, Hermogen, was threatened with execution should he break the prohibition. He promptly led a procession through the streets of Tobolsk, carrying church banners and singing hymns. Mounted Bolsheviks watched the procession but were too afraid to intervene. Gleb watched the procession pass his house; he was struck by Hermogen's appearance: 'His golden mitre, shining with jewels, was pushed low over his eyes; and those eyes, sunk deep in their sockets and raised to heaven in a strange unearthly ecstasy, alone were full of life – but not of this life.'

For two days, thousands of Hermogen's followers camped around his palace to protect him from the Bolsheviks. But the moment the followers dispersed, the Bolsheviks arrested Hermogen and took him several miles outside town. They tore off his clothes and for two days forced him to roll stones up the river bank while hired prostitutes shouted insults at him. Then the commissar tied a huge stone to his neck and lowered him by his hair three times into the river – before finally letting him drown.

Gleb's shock when he heard of Bishop Hermogen's prolonged agony can only be imagined. What is certain is that he decided, shortly afterwards, to commit himself further to the Russian Orthodox Church. With his bullish streak, he was probably encouraged by the increasing dangers he would now face. He agreed to assist a local clergyman, Bishop Irinarch, at services. In return, the Bishop would help him with his theology studies. Years later, Gleb would recall his feelings as he attended the requiem finally held for Bishop Hermogen. At every moment he expected Red soldiers to pour in and kill all those taking part: 'I felt I was transferred to the first century of Christianity.'

At this point in his life, the eighteen-year-old Gleb would have been struggling to come to terms with the collapse of the world in which he had grown up. Before the Revolution, some Russian aristocrats had been disapproving of the Imperial Family, feeling it had grown too remote. Some even accepted the necessity of revolution, handing over possessions to the new regime. Dr Botkin and his son Gleb, however, could see little beyond the indignities and privations endured by a family they had grown to love. During that freezing May in

Tobolsk, Gleb's concern for the Imperial Family showed no sign of lessening, despite daily reminders that his own life was now in grave danger. On one particularly ominous night, Gleb sat awake listening to the ticking of a clock; he found a curious consolation in the thought that, after his death, the clock would still be ticking.

The three remaining Grand Duchesses and the Tsarevich were due to leave Tobolsk for Ekaterinburg on 20 May. Three days before they left, the guards surrounding the Governor's House were replaced, to Gleb's disgust, by the 'most frightful-looking, dirty, ragged, drunken cut-throats'.

The new commissar, Nikolai Rodionov, told Gleb and Tatiana that they had 24 hours to leave their apartment. Though Gleb and Tatiana swiftly found furnished rooms in the town, they were less fortunate in their quest for 'toilet rooms'. Gleb complained bitterly that the citizens of Tobolsk appeared to be perfectly happy with sheds in the yard. These sheds were never cleaned, he insisted, and in the depths of winter would plunge to 58 degrees below freezing.

Conditions in the Governor's House, meanwhile, were worsening. Guards were now posted inside the house, along the corridors. They spoke to the Grand Duchesses in what Gleb described as 'a most insulting tone' and forbad them from closing the doors of their rooms, even at night.

Gleb heard that a boat had been chartered to take the Imperial children to Tiumen. The party would then travel to Ekaterinburg by train. He and Tatiana had expected to travel with the Romanovs, but heard no word from Rodionov.

Finally, in desperation, the two young Botkins went to see him. Gleb later noted that Rodionov was dressed in pre-Revolutionary uniform; the only concession he had made to the Revolution was to remove his shoulder straps. He was, improbably, 'very elegant'. Gleb recounted every detail of the unsavoury encounter as Rodionov cast his eye over Tatiana, asking: 'Why should such a handsome girl as you are want to rot all her life in prison, or even be shot?'

Rodionov warned the pair that, should they travel to Ekaterinburg without a special permit, they would simply be sent back to Tobolsk. The Botkins readily accepted his predictions about the bureaucracy, but they completely dismissed his suggestion that the Imperial Family would be shot. Tatiana responded with inappropriate hauteur: 'You don't appear to know the facts of the situation.'

In the end, the siblings decided it would be dangerous and futile to travel to Ekaterinburg. The day before the Grand Duchesses and the Tsarevich were due to leave, Gleb went to the Governor's House hoping to catch a final glimpse of the Grand Duchesses. He was rewarded with the sight of Anastasia in one of the windows. She smiled and waved at him and he immediately stopped and took off his cap.

Unfortunately he was spotted by Rodionov, who left his post to storm out on to the street: 'Nobody is permitted to look at the windows of this house. Pass on, pass on, comrades,' he roared at the passers-by that continually gathered outside the walls. He turned to the sentries: 'Shoot everybody who so much as looks in this direction. Shoot to kill.' It was not clear, according to Gleb, whether Anastasia heard Rodionov's order or the cries of the fleeing crowd but, as she carried on smiling, it seems unlikely. Before turning into a side street, Gleb bowed to the Grand Duchess for the last time.

***

Soon after the Imperial children had left Tobolsk, Bishop Irinarch found an apartment for the young Botkins in the house of the former District Attorney. The Bolsheviks continually searched the house and Gleb recalled with anger the debilitating effect of living under threat of execution for possessing an icon or an extra cake of soap.

As the Bolshevik grip on the area tightened, people were expected to register and failure was punishable by death; those found to be on a list of 'undesirables' were put to death. The day before they were due to register, Gleb and Tatiana found out that their names, together with that of the District Attorney, were now on the death list.

Gleb and the District Attorney disagreed as to how they should act. While Gleb was prepared to fight his persecutors to the death, the District Attorney was for throwing himself under the protection of nuns at a nearby convent. But if Gleb was disappointed by the District Attorney's proposal, he was disgusted by the reaction of the president of the local Tsarist Front Alliance. The president visited Gleb briefly before fleeing to a forest disguised in a woman's raincoat and a black hat with an ostrich feather.

In the end, neither Gleb nor the District Attorney were put to the test. The following day the Red soldiers themselves fled. For three days Tobolsk was jubilantly without government before the White Army arrived, comprising 80 officers with 80 rifles and one machine gun.

It was the leader of the White Army who had the corpse of Bishop Hermogen formally laid to rest under the floor of the cathedral at Tobolsk. The funeral service lasted a full eight hours; the stone that had been attached to the Bishop's neck when he drowned was placed on a small altar over the tomb. Both Gleb and Bishop Irinarch noted that Hermogen's body had undergone almost no decomposition. Neither of them wanted to accept that a miracle had taken place, but neither could offer any explanation. The body did not smell and there were no visible signs of decay beyond swollen eyes and a missing tuft of beard.

Gleb now decided to travel to Ekaterinburg – also under White rule – to find out what had become of his father and the Imperial Family. Before leaving, he saw the children's Swiss tutor, Pierre Gilliard, in the street. Gilliard told him he had been separated from the children at the Ekaterinburg railway station and sent back to Tobolsk. He told Gleb that nothing was known for certain about the fate of the Romanovs. The tutor had heard from one source that the Tsar had been killed but from another that the family had been released and were living as ordinary citizens in Ekaterinburg.

Gleb eventually managed to find himself a seat on a box of explosives in a munitions train bound for Ekaterinburg.

Walking from the station, he met the Tsarevich's doctor, Derevenko, who had mysteriously been released and allowed to start practising again. It has since been suggested that the doctor struck up a deal with the Bolsheviks. Derevenko told Gleb that the House of Special Purpose was empty but that the cellar was apparently covered in blood. Gleb made his way immediately to the house, but, overwhelmed with apprehension and anxiety, he was unable to enter. He could not share Derevenko's conviction that the bloody cellar was a canard.

Ipatiev House or the House of Special Purpose

Though little further in his researches, Gleb felt he must now return to Tobolsk to look after his sister. As it turned out, Tatiana would shortly cease to be her brother's responsibility. She told her brother, upon his return, that she was to marry Konstantin Melnik, a young man whom the Botkins had known before the Revolution. Konstantin had been a particular favourite of Dr Botkin, the doctor had even told Gleb that he always hoped Konstantin would marry Tatiana. The Revolution had not damaged Melnik's eligible bachelor status. He now received a decent salary acting as chief of police for the new White government.

Gleb, meanwhile, embarked on a more precarious existence as a novice studying theology at the local monastery. It was a full seven months before he received a letter from Derevenko to say that it had now been confirmed that the whole of the Imperial Family, with Gleb's father, had been murdered in the bloody cellar of the House of Special Purpose in the early hours of 17 July 1918.

Thrown into despair by this painful news, Gleb became consumed by a desire to leave Russia. He was enraged by what he saw as the betrayal of the Romanovs by the Russians. He was horrified by the number of Whites now presenting themselves as antimonarchist: a feeling later exacerbated by his conviction that the Whites' investigations into the murders were mishandled.

Gleb claimed there were disruptions and consequent delays because the Whites' investigator, Nikolai Sokolov, lacked the steel for the job. At the slightest hint of trouble, Sokolov would apparently pack his bags and head to Vladivostok.

Gleb's unforgiving attitude towards Sokolov may have had something to do with the investigator's lifelong insistence that none of the Romanovs had survived. So sure was Sokolov of his facts that he refused to follow up claims that various members had been seen after the shootings. But this may have been just as well: Gleb himself admitted that, at that point, Siberia was swarming with impostors.

Rasputin's son-in-law, Boris Soloviev, ran a business conning local millionaires into giving him money to help surviving 'grand duchesses'. The hapless merchants were allowed to kiss the hand of their 'grand duchess', in fact a local courtesan, before she boarded the steamer. The courtesan would then scuttle down a second plank and be safely back on land before the last whistle had sounded.

Even before the shootings, claimants had begun to appear. The Imperial children's English tutor, Sydney Gibbes, recalled the Grand Duchess Tatiana reading the *Daily Graphic* in Tobolsk and being fascinated by an account of her 'escape' to New York.

After the shootings, a third Tatiana appeared alongside troops at the front; she was a handsome prostitute and was apparently feted by many White regiments. A fourth Tatiana was reported in 1920 as having escaped to America and settled down with a waiter in Birmingham, Alabama.

***

But the key claimant was, of course, Anna Anderson. Her recollections, though hazy, went right back to the fateful night of the shootings, 16-17 July 1918: 'I have gone through every-thing, dirt and all, everything,' she would habitually protest, when asked questions. She never referred to the exact date of the shootings, preferring to leave it at 'month of July is the worst for me'.

She did, however, have a disconcerting knack of issuing interpolations when she felt 'wild imaginations and selfish motives' were getting the upper hand. A police inspector once remarked in her presence that she had been wearing soldiers' boots on the last night in Ekaterinburg. She cried out: 'What is that man thinking of! It's crazy... We weren't supposed to be going anywhere, just into another room; we didn't need to put on boots.'

Anna claimed to have been rescued in the chaos following the shooting by two brothers called Alexander and Serge Tschaikovsky. It was later claimed, by Gleb, that she must have meant the Polish guards and factory workers Nicholas and Stanislaus Mishkevich. The brothers had given up work at the Zlokozov Factory to begin guard duty at the House of Special purpose on 11 June.

In a rare, expansive mood, she later related to one of her supporters: 'It was a dreadful mix-up, then he (Alexander) saw that I was still alive. He did not want to bury a live body and he escaped with me under greatest dangers.' The two brothers, now possibly accompanied by their mother and sister, apparently bundled their 'grand duchess' into a farm cart and took her west among thousands of refugees. She claimed to have been slipping in and out of consciousness and to remember only the bumping of the cart; her estimation of the length of the journey was characteristically vague: 'weeks and weeks'.

According to Anna, the family ended up in Bucharest and there settled in a gardener's cottage in a street called Svienti Voyevodo. The road has never been located, though her supporters were quick to point out that the name resembled Sfintii Voyevozi, a street with a side entrance to the German Embassy. Her supporters also tracked down a German military officer who swore it was widely known that the Grand Duchess Anastasia was living in Bucharest under the protection of the Germans. One of her most avid supporters, the historian and genealogist Ian Lilburn, keeps an old map of Bucharest in his Knightsbridge house and readily pinpoints the street.

Anna claimed to have spent a year in Bucharest, mostly in bed. 'I was only out of the house twice... I saw nothing in Bucharest.' About the gardener, in whose cottage she lived, she was equally vague: 'He was Russian... He was not young and he was not old.' She claimed that the Tschaikovskys lived on the proceeds of the jewellery she had sewn into her clothes. Unfortunately she also apparently became pregnant; Alexander Tschaikovsky, she complained, was, like so many of his class, 'hot'.

She said she gave birth to a son who was immediately put up for adoption. She was anxious to keep the pregnancy quiet because she was worried she would be accused of gaining her freedom from the Bolsheviks by offering sexual favours. She claimed to have subsequently married Alexander Tschaikovsky in some kind of Roman Catholic service, though no record exists of any such ceremony. 'I never went into the street; once for the wedding I was put into a car, I did not look out. I was frightened. The church, yes, it was large.'

But she kept Tschaikovsky's name and for years was known as Anna Tschaikovsky. She said Tschaikovsky was shot one day while out looking for food; no record exists of his death, but she claimed to remember seeing his body in a coffin. 'They may have robbed him,' she commented. 'The Roumanians are quick with the knife.'

She related how she then decided to contact her mother's sister, Princess Irene of Prussia, in Germany. Her 'brother-in-law', Serge, agreed to travel with her to Berlin: 'Many places we were afraid they would ask for the passport,' she claimed to recall. 'Sometimes I travelled on the train and sometimes I walked.' When they arrived they had difficulty finding a cheap hotel; though they eventually found one, Anna never remembered the name: 'Everything was so new to me.' Serge went out on a mysterious mission and failed to return. Anna claimed she went out to look for him, setting off in the direction of the Netherlands Palace, where she hoped to find her aunt.

This momentous night has frequently formed the climax in a torrent of films and books telling the story of Anna Anderson. The scene is usually embellished with frost and fearsome winds; in fact, on the evening of 17 February 1920, the temperature was about 35 degrees Fahrenheit.

***

Early in 1919, Gleb wrote to his uncle, Victor Botkin, in Vladivostok, begging for help. He told Victor he was desperate to leave Tobolsk and soon a telegram arrived inviting Gleb Botkin, Tatiana and her husband, Konstantin Melnik, to go to him. The Melniks, satisfactorily established in Tobolsk, were reluctant to leave. Though they did eventually agree to go, they may well have felt their hesitation was justified. The journey was long and hard. The first leg involved inching the 200 miles to Tiumen on peasants' sleighs; the last leg involved a packed train from Omsk, with decaying corpses of Reds strung from wires alongside the tracks.

When they finally reached Vladivostok, Gleb found the city suited him well. He lived happily there for several months, working as a censor with the Inter-Allied Military Censorship and secretary to the Bishop of the Regiments of the Holy Cross and of nine Cossack armies. He wrote and published poems, articles and short stories. But in February 1920 the Reds invaded Vladivostok and Gleb found himself once again under threat of execution, obliged to spend every night in a different place.

He eventually managed to escape on board a Japanese ship. Suffused with gratitude and relief, he afterwards declared heaven would not be an entirely new experience. For the first time in three years he felt absolutely free. He was certainly unencumbered with material wealth; he had no money and just one possession: a handkerchief.

In Japan, Gleb was appointed secretary of the diplomatic mission of the White Government in Siberia. He held the post until the White Movement was liquidated in 1922. He met and married a widow, Nadine Mandragy, daughter of a former president of the Russian Bank, and then worked with his father-in-law setting up a business in Yokohama. Nadine had been widowed when her first husband, a lieutenant of the Imperial Bodyguard, was killed on the German front in 1915; the couple had had a daughter, Kyra.

In his memoir *The Real Romanovs*, Gleb offered no detailed description of his wife. A picture emerges by default, however, of a strong woman who successfully raised five children – she had four with Gleb – in challenging circumstances, not least her husband's lifelong obsession with the Romanov legacy. It was just eight years after his marriage that Gleb first met Anna Anderson. He was immediately convinced that she was the young Grand Duchess Anastasia and became fiercely committed to her cause. Nadine was sufficiently strong-minded to accommodate her husband's preoccupation. She herself never met Anna. 'She was kind of never invited,' as Gleb and Nadine's daughter, Marina Schweitzer, put it.

***

During his period in Japan, Gleb attended a service for the Imperial Family in a Russian cathedral in Tokyo. In Russia he had had trouble persuading priests to take part in such requiems, yet the service in Tokyo was packed. He recalled commenting upon the size of the crowd to a Baltic Baron from Russia.

The Baron's response was grim: 'Now they come in crowds. A year ago, none of them dared to even approach a church where a service for Their Majesties was being held.' Gleb asked the Baron what he thought would happen if the Tsar were suddenly to reappear. The Baron replied that he felt most of the congregation preferred the Tsar dead: 'They would do their best to murder him again.' Gleb put in a wry addendum, with an obvious allusion to Anna Anderson: 'How often... I was to remember these prophetic words!'

In 1922, when his father-in-law's business venture failed, Gleb decided to leave Japan for America with Nadine, their son Eugene and Nadine's daughter, Kyra. He soon established himself in New York, perfecting his English sufficiently to write and publish short stories, finally becoming art editor at an educational publishing house. He devoted his evenings to writing novels, destroying ten before he had his first published in 1929. *The God Who Didn't Laugh* bristled with savage attacks upon absurd aspects of formal religion; it was clear that, after all his vacillations, Gleb had made the right decision in rejecting one bishop's suggestion that he stay in Japan to be ordained.

It is impossible to tell how much *The God Who Didn't Laugh* is autobiographical, but Gleb certainly depicts his hero,

Tosha, as a romantic who dreams, as a boy, of becoming a priest of Aphrodite. Like Gleb, Tosha is born in about 1900; he is raised in St Petersburg and undergoes a turbulent spiritual journey.

In what seems an autobiographical touch, Tosha suffers from a deadly combination of weaknesses: an interest in women and an inability to suppress his sense of humour. One of his priests describes to him how the sins attached to sex and laughter are linked. 'The sight of a woman's naked body, especially of certain parts of it, the mention of certain sinful pastimes and so on, always provoke laughter... a real Christian should never laugh or smile just as Christ Himself never laughed or smiled.'

Towards the end of the novel, it comes as no surprise that Tosha denounces ordination as a sort of death. 'It was an endless list of renunciations. The world, with all its joy and beauty, power, personal property, parents, relatives, love, ambition, dignity, all even most elementary human rights, all hopes, aspirations, desires and instincts – in short everything which distinguishes a living being from an unconscious plant.'

However the last paragraph of *The God Who Didn't Laugh* seems to leave a question mark in the air. Tosha has announced his intention of leaving the Church. 'He bowed in silence and hurried out of the room, feeling as if he had just broken something very precious, something that he was going to miss for the rest of his life.'

While Tosha's refined sensibilities are overdone and the tone sentimental, the story of his spiritual journey rings true. Gleb combined a deep need for a spiritual element to his life with an inability to conform to an orthodox religion. The origins of his interest in Aphrodite are referred to by one of the fictitious novices: 'The day you renounce Christ you will find some other divinity, and most likely it will be Aphrodite.'

It is inconceivable that, as a young man, Gleb was not deeply affected by the terrible events unfolding around him. His awareness of the absurdities of pre-Revolutionary Court life would in no way have mitigated his horror at witnessing their bloody end. Gleb gives what were undoubtedly his own impressions of revolution in *The God Who Didn't Laugh*: 'An abyss that suddenly opened under their feet and swallowed everything and everybody... Hell brought to earth. Infinite anguish, shame, despair, misery. A nightmare, a dreadful nightmare...'

With his strong moral sense and bullish tendencies, he would have found it particularly painful to look on, helpless, while horrific injustices were perpetrated all about him. But perhaps, as Russia fragmented into warring tribes, he comforted himself with the thought that he had not lost his capacity for independent thought.

By the time he reached his late twenties and was settled in America, Gleb would have been more than ready for an active role in some moral crusade. The cause he eventually embraced was linked, gratifyingly, to the murders of his beloved father and the Imperial Family. Its popular appeal was open to question, but that would not have been a deterrent to a maverick thinker. Maybe part of Gleb rejoiced to find a cause so controversial that he sometimes appeared to be its sole supporter.

CHAPTER THREE
Anna in Germany, 1920-1927

The fuzzy, uncorroborated details of Anna Anderson's escape from Ekaterinburg give way to indisputable fact with a police report written on 18 February 1920. A Sergeant Hallman of the Berlin city police recalled seeing a female figure fall into the Landwehr canal. He related how he tore his coat off and dragged her on to the bank. She had no identification. Her coat and dress pockets were completely empty, there were no labels in her clothing and she had no handbag.

Anna is now on surer ground. Her account of her jump from the bridge is full of piquant detail. 'Now I wondered even more what on earth was going to happen to me. I was wholly without help. From a park I came to a canal, with a road on each side of it, joined by a bridge. There were trees along the canal banks which were quiet and deserted... I never thought about it being cold if I jumped in, I thought instead that it would completely envelop me with its white mist and then everything would be over: the pain in my head, my despair and my loneliness. Then I should no longer need Tschaikovsky, nor Aunt Irene; and after death I should meet my parents again, meet again my sisters and little brother.'

At that point there were half a million émigrés in Germany; the Germans were anxious to repatriate as many as they could. The mystery woman was taken to the Elizabeth Hospital where she was questioned for six weeks but would say nothing. She was then transferred to the Dalldorf asylum outside Berlin. She was registered as Fraulein Unbekannt – 'Miss Unknown'.

Anna in hospital in Berlin

Little detail is known of the real lead-up to what was later portrayed as the Grand Duchess Anastasia's suicide attempt. But it is now known that the woman pulled from the river was a Polish peasant, Franziska Schanzkowska. Franziska was actually five years older than Anastasia: born on 16 December

1896, in the Prussian province of Posen, on the Polish border.

Two hundred years before, the Schanzkowski family had belonged to the lesser Polish nobility, but by the end of the nineteenth century, the social status of the Roman Catholic family had fallen and the Schanzkowski men were simply farm workers. Franziska's father was an alcoholic who died when she was still very young; she was one of two children of her father's second marriage. Her older half-brother and sisters had been given a strict religious upbringing while she and her brother Felix were left to their own devices.

The young Franziska apparently considered herself a cut above her siblings. While the entire village worked, bringing in the hay at harvest-time, Franziska would lounge in a cart, reading a book. A niece, Waltraut Schanzkowska, later said: 'My Auntie Franziska was the cleverest of the... children. She didn't want to be buried in a little one-horse town. She wanted to come out into the world, to become an actress – something special.'

One of her former teachers, Otto Meyer, questioned on 22 April 1927, said that she had left his school in November 1910. He added that the following year she was dismissed, aged fifteen, from a school at Tanzen. He himself was not impressed with her academic prowess. 'There cannot be the question of any knowledge of Russian or English. That she has learnt them later I think impossible, as I considered her rather limited than intelligent.' His comments would later be picked up as favourable testimony amongst Anna Anderson's supporters.

In 1914, shortly before the beginning of the First World

War, Franziska left for Berlin, apparently to pursue her dream of an acting career. She worked as a waitress, then met a young man and became engaged. Her fiancé was called up for military service and died on the Western Front in 1916. Franziska meanwhile began working in a munitions factory where, soon after her fiancé's death, she let a grenade slip from her hands on the assembly line. It exploded, blowing apart the foreman standing next to her; she herself suffered splinter wounds on her head and other parts of her body. The treatment she subsequently received in a sanatorium helped her over her physical injuries, but did little to repair the psychological damage. Franziska was finally declared 'not cured, but not dangerous' and discharged; she was taken in by a family called Wingender, almost as a charity case. The next period of her life she spent in and out of sanatoria, swallowing pills and complaining of headaches. Her favourite pastime was lying in bed, reading history books from the local library.

Otto Meyer said that from 1919 to 1920 Franziska worked in a brewery in Buetow washing bottles. A man from Buetow later testified that he remembered Franziska distinctly and that he was bemused by the photographs of Anna Anderson, as they did not look like her; he said Franziska's mouth had never been so broad or turned down. Meanwhile Otto and his wife disagreed as to the likenesses: while they both thought the photographs of Anna resembled Franziska, Mrs Meyer thought they looked more like her sister, Juliane.

In February 1920, her brother, Felix, received a last message from Franziska, sent on his birthday, 17 February; the message arrived two weeks later. As Felix said in a statement three months afterwards: 'I remember this very exactly. My sister excused herself for sending it so late by much work.'

Franziska

Felix's daughter later claimed that her father regularly confessed that he knew Anna was really Franziska. However it has been pointed out that this young woman received payment for her claims. The daughter of Franziska's sister, Gertrude, meanwhile refuses to help with any investigation. She lives in fear that the Schanzkowski family will one day face litigation over the antics of her errant aunt, Franziska.

Anna Anderson's supporters have not been fazed by the vagaries of the Schanzkowskis. Over the years they have contested that there is no proof Franziska was ever wounded in an explosion. They contest, more crucially, that Franziska was a full three inches taller than Anna Anderson.

***

At the Dalldorf, Anna had succeeded in attracting the attention of another inmate called Clara Peuthert. Clara had lived in Russia as a dressmaker or laundress before the First World War. She claimed she had supplemented her income in Russia by serving the Germans as a penny agent, passing on high-class gossip. When she became famous as one of Anna's supporters, she would display a certificate, to anyone who was interested, attesting to the fact that she was 'not mad, only pathological'. She was admitted to Dalldorf at the end of 1921 after accusing her neighbours of stealing her money. Anna later insisted that Clara was only in the asylum because of her fits of temper.

Clara befriended Anna, then still referred to as Miss Unknown, and the pair began to enjoy mysterious exchanges. Clara would begin: 'Your face is familiar to me, you do not come from ordinary circles.' At which point Anna would put her fingers theatrically to her lips.

The climax came when a copy of the *Berliner Illustrierte Zeitung,* of 23 October 1921, headlined: 'The Truth about the Murder of the Tsar', was brought into the asylum. Beneath a portrait of the Grand Duchesses ran the caption: 'Is One of the Daughters Alive?' Clara apparently ran to Anna's bed brandishing the magazine: 'I know who you are. You are Grand Duchess Tatiana.' Miss Unknown at first turned to the wall, refusing to speak, but later had second thoughts, revealing to Clara that her grandmother was living in Denmark and there was an aunt, Irene, in Berlin.

From the evidence of photographs Anna seems to have

borne little resemblance to any of the Grand Duchesses. Her mouth was wider and her jaw squarer than those of Tatiana or Anastasia. Her brow also appears broader and more Slavic-looking than either of the sisters'. Her eyes were captivating, but in a different way from the Grand Duchesses'. In the end, perhaps Clara was persuaded less by physical resemblances than by the somewhat grand air which set Anna apart from the less fortunate inmates of Dalldorf.

Much excited by Miss Unknown's revelations, Clara left Dalldorf on 20 January 1922 and set to work to prove the identity of the Grand Duchess Tatiana. She wrote two letters to Irene of Prussia – neither was answered. She reinforced her case with an assurance that she herself had seen the Grand Duchess three times in Moscow before the Revolution. Miss Unknown evidently baulked, at this point, from making the further confession: that she was not Tatiana but Anastasia.

One of Clara's first converts was a Russian refugee with a suitably smart name: Captain Nicholas von Schwabe. She came across Schwabe selling monarchist propaganda at the Russian Embassy church on Unter den Linden. He had been a staff captain of the personal guard detachment of the Dowager Empress. He wore a swastika round his neck and was, apparently, anti-semitic, though, in 1922, the two were not necessarily connected. Clara immediately singled him out, approaching him with dramatic circumspection: 'Can I trust you? In a lunatic asylum near Berlin, there is a person interned who very much resembles the Grand Duchess Tatiana. I myself am even convinced that she is. I believe this on account of her social manners, the noble cast of her features and her well-shaped hands.'

Schwabe went to visit her. He too was convinced; he found her regal nod, a gesture of dismissal, particularly convincing. He wrote a note on the flyleaf of a Russian Bible asking her to trust him and promising to serve her. In a gesture foreshadowing decades of abuse lying ahead for her supporters, most of whom took it as the ultimate proof of her grandeur, Anna wrenched the page from the book and ripped it to shreds.

Another early champion was Zinaida Tolstoy, who had been a friend of the Tsarina at Tsarskoye Selo. Anna was at first extremely reluctant to see Zinaida, gripping the bedclothes over her head. Eventually, doctors had to be called to help with the ensuing tussle. Anna need not have worried; Zinaida proclaimed afterwards that she must be Tatiana: she had the eyes of the Tsar.

Despite this early triumph, Anna retreated under the blankets once more when the Tsarina's lady-in-waiting, Baroness Buxhoeveden, visited some weeks later. Eschewing the help of the doctors, the impatient Baroness tore off the blankets herself before snorting, 'She's too short for Tatiana.' Anna returned the compliment with tales of the Baroness's treachery. She declared that the Baroness had gained her freedom in 1918 by exposing a plan to free the Romanovs to the Bolsheviks.

But Anna's counter-attack did little to lessen the blow inflicted upon her supporters by the Baroness's denouncement.

It was probably the feeling of trouble brewing that induced Anna to issue a further announcement: 'I never said I was Tatiana.'

The stalwart supporters had no choice but to accept that their protégée was not Tatiana. However they refused to give up the idea that she was a grand duchess. The question now was simply which of the three remaining sisters could she be? A friend of Schwabe hit upon a solution. He proposed presenting the invalid with a list of the Grand Duchesses' names: she was to cross out the names that were not hers. After some deliberation, she left one name free: Anastasia.

***

It is difficult to know to what extent Franziska was able to gauge the effect of this decision upon the rest of her life. It is certain that, as Franziska, she had reached a point where she saw no future; as a grand duchess, her life would be filled with glamorous possibilities. Maybe she saw a revival of her hopes for an acting career, or perhaps she was already employing her acting skills.

As she contemplated her past, with its more tawdry tragedies, Franziska would surely have been drawn to the dramatic and uplifting story of the Grand Duchess who triumphed over terrible odds. The choice of Anastasia, in particular, would have been an appealing one. She would have been aware of the pathos attaching itself to Anastasia as the youngest of the four pretty daughters.

However, there is no proof that Franziska entertained all or any of these thoughts. There is every likelihood that she simply dimly grasped the idea that her life, and the lives of everybody around her, would be richer were she Anastasia. A fantasy soon solidified into belief.

With the identity of his grand duchess settled, Schwabe felt his next duty was to find her a suitable home; her residency at the Dalldorf asylum was damaging to her image. A Baron Arthur von Kleist, who had been a Tsarist district police officer in Russian Poland, approached Schwabe offering to help. He and his wife Maria nurtured an unlikely hope that if they adopted Anna they would advance from the fringes of Russian high society to its heart.

The Baron and Baroness visited Anna at Dalldorf over several months in an attempt to persuade her to move to their apartment. Making full use of the contrary trait that was to stand her in such good stead, Anna put on a great show of spurning their overtures. But she finally decided they had shown themselves sufficiently willing and, in May 1922, Anna left Dalldorf with a cryptic comment to a member of staff: 'Soon probably, we won't be seeing each other any more and I will be alright, but the mad rush is beginning again.'

Her predictions of a mad rush turned out to be peculiarly apposite. The Kleists' apartment became a mini court in exile for White Russians. Indeed the Baron created some controversy when he tried to keep coarser figures, like Anna's old friends Schwabe and Clara, at bay. While the Kleists were undoubtedly spending money on parties, they had no fear of being left out of pocket: the buoyant Baron had put together an agreement stating that he would receive 50,000 crowns upon Anna's recognition by the Dowager Empress.

Anna Anderson at the Kleists

But Anna proved an ungracious guest. She readily agreed to be called Anna, a shortened version of Anastasia that she herself had suggested. But she was less pleased with the bolder suggestion that she should wear linen embroidered with the Imperial crown and the name 'Anastasia'. Far from appreciating the high life offered by the Kleists, she ran away. She was found several days later by one of Schwabe's friends who, remembering her love of animals, located her in the Berlin zoo.

Refusing to return to the Kleists and now claiming the Baron had made improper overtures, Anna finally agreed to live with a police inspector called Franz Grunberg outside Berlin. 'Feeling that there was a historical mystery here comparable to that of *The Man in the Iron Mask*, I decided to take the young lady for three weeks to my estate,' the inspector recalled.

Anna began to feel comfortable and now dreamt, she later insisted, of her childhood friend Gleb Botkin. 'After a long time I again took up a drawing-block and drew the animals which leapt around in the meadow. I found myself thinking of Gleb Botkin who could do it so much better than I, and whom I had last seen at Tobolsk.'

It was at Grunberg's house that the meeting between Anna and her 'aunt', the Tsarina's sister, Princess Irene, took place. It was Irene whom Anna claimed she had been so desperate to find the night she threw herself into the Landwehr Canal. The Princess was not impressed. 'I saw immediately that she could not be one of my nieces. Even though I had not seen them for nine years, the fundamental facial characteristics could not have altered to that degree, in particular the position of the eyes, the ear, etc... At first sight one could perhaps detect a resemblance to Grand Duchess Tatiana.'

During dinner Anna had simply left the table and gone to her bedroom. She later claimed her departure was not to do with social pressures but because she realised she had been tricked: she had not been told that her aunt was to be among her fellow guests. The Princess was prevailed upon to follow her, but Anna refused to speak to her. Anna later defended herself, describing her feelings at the dinner: 'I was not rude.

Really not. It was like this, I was ill, I had to get up, the room was dark, then a lady came. I knew the voice and was listening but didn't know because the name was different. Then at table the face was familiar but I didn't know, wasn't sure, then I recognised Aunt Irene. I was feverish and excited, went into my room. Aunt Irene came after me, spoke and asked so many questions I stood at the window and because I had to cry I turned my back to her; I did not want to turn around, but not because I was rude. I was crying.'

Undaunted, Grunberg then arranged a meeting with the former German Crown Princess, Cecilie of Prussia. She also was unimpressed. 'There proved no opportunity of establishing her identity (however) because it was virtually impossible to communicate with the young person. She remained completely silent, either from obstinacy or because she was totally bewildered, I could not decide which.'

She did have minor successes. Marianne Nilov, the widow of the commander of the *Standart*, was convinced Anna was Anastasia. She swore, like Zinaida Tolstoy, that she saw a family likeness in Anna's eyes. 'She told us she thought she was looking at the Tsar's eyes,' recalled Mme Nilov's niece, 'and then she heard a little laugh which she recognised at once. Anastasia had a very distinctive laugh.' One woman who met her at Grunberg's place was keen to point out that Anna never left the house without gloves and was expert at deferring to her elders: 'She never spoke to anybody without the proper salutation and she never forgot a title.'

But her supporters were beginning to fall away. Zinaida

Tolstoy was among the particularly stalwart group who had stuck by Anna through her early transition from Grand Duchess Tatiana to Anastasia. Indeed, Zinaida's support seemed assured when she witnessed Anna throwing herself upon a sofa, sobbing loudly, on hearing a piece of music last heard at Tsarskoye Selo. So affected had Zinaida been by this display that she immediately wrote to the Tsar's sister. However, upon receiving crisp replies with details of Anna's adventures in Bucharest, Zinaida changed her mind. Her explanation was bald: 'A Grand Duchess cannot have a baby with a private soldier.'

Kleist also lost heart upon receiving a severe letter written on behalf of Princess Irene's husband: 'His Royal Highness... has requested me to inform you that he as well as his wife, after the latter's visit to your protégée, have come to the unshakeable conviction that she is NOT a daughter of the Tsar, specifically not Grand Duchess Anastasia.' Kleist had previously suffered a disappointment when Anna had told him that her baby had been born on 1 December 1918. If the date was correct, the baby would have been conceived in February 1918, five months before the shootings. Gleb later breezily dismissed the confusing date: 'She had a habit, when annoyed, to give purposely impossible answers.'

At this stage, Anna was even managing to antagonise her most stalwart champions, Schwabe and Clara. At one point, a young man, allegedly her shadowy brother-in-law, Serge Tschaikovsky, turned up at Clara's flat. Clara took him to see Schwabe; if Serge could relay the story of her escape from

Ekaterinburg, Anna's identity might be established once and for all. Unfortunately, after one brief discussion, the pair managed to lose not only Serge, but a letter and photograph he gave them. When she was told of the visit, Anna accused Schwabe, improbably, of destroying evidence and, more importantly, of doing away with Serge. Schwabe eventually got his own back, immersing himself in extensive lecture tours during which he denounced his earlier protégée as a fraud.

Anna and Clara began to have arguments, the most furious of which revolved around Anna's reluctance to become involved in any sort of campaign. At this point Anna may have felt it unwise to overplay her part. But Clara was not plagued with any such doubts; she was thoroughly enjoying her new-found role in the limelight and resented what she saw as Anna's ungrateful lack of co-operation. After one particularly furious row, Clara threw her bodily out of her flat and locked the door. Her impoverished neighbours, the Bachmanns, took her in after hearing her crying on the landing.

In January 1925 Anna moved back with Inspector Grunberg; she now divided her time between his country property and town house. However, after five months, the hapless inspector decided he could no longer manage her. Without establishing whether she had anywhere to go, he set her a departure date: 3 July 1925. He described his disillusion to one of Anna's supporters: 'Half a year I bother with that creature and I do not get on – nothing can be got out of her... And since she has been naughty to the Princess Heinrich (Aunt

Irene), I am quite upset. Just the same as the Iron Mask and Kaspar Hauser, nothing can be got of her.' He salved his conscience with an improbably effusive reference: 'Having lived with her for months, I have come to the firm conviction that she is a lady from the highest circles of Russian society and that she is most probably of princely birth. Every one of her words and movements reveals so lofty a dignity and so absolutist a bearing that it cannot be asserted she has acquired these characteristics in later life.'

Luckily for Anna another champion appeared, in the form of Harriet von Rathlef-Keilmann. Harriet had heard of Anna's plight through a prominent philanthropist, Dr Karl Sonnenschein, who took a special interest in Berlin's Russian refugees. Harriet made much of her Bohemian existence as a sculptor and writer of fairy tales. She now set about devoting herself to Anna's struggle with an almost unnerving fervour. She took an immediate dislike to Grunberg. In a statement dated 20 June 1925 she wrote: 'Impression: primitive, noisy, official... I had to ask him to lower his voice.' Harriet set great store by the name of Anastasia, which means 'the resurrection'. She was further thrilled to discover that Anna boasted double life lines on both hands.

A Russian émigré, Harriet declared herself impressed by Anna's resemblance to the Tsarina and the Tsar's mother, the Dowager Empress. She was evidently prepared to overlook her new friend's frequent outbursts of tears, giving an early appraisal of Anna's manners almost as enthusiastic as Grunberg's: 'Her courtesy was, as it seemed to me, heartily conventional, and her good breeding showed in everything.' Harriet was thrilled to discover that, though Anna refused to speak Russian, she understood the Russian for 'Have you a pencil?' Anna's detractors made much of her reluctance – or even inability – to speak Russian: her supporters maintained that the language had too many bad associations for her.

Harriet von Rathlef and her family

However Harriet's first exchange with Anna was not promising. She was accompanying Anna from Grunberg's town house to her new residence: a hospital called St Mary's. Anna asked Harriet about her work as a sculptor, then told her that she used to paint. 'What was your teacher's name?' Harriet asked. Anna's hand flew to her eyes and her voice dropped an octave: 'That I can no longer say.' Harriet had more luck subsequently, establishing the Grand Duchess Tatiana's preference for riding her horse astride and the fondness all four sisters shared for a cigarette: 'We were not allowed but secretly, especially Tatiana. She was already quite cunning.' In a buoyant and perhaps misguided statement about her new friend, Harriet wrote, under 'Special Marks: As to her character: I have never heard her say one bad word about another being.'

With Harriet's assistance, Anna gathered a new band of supporters who swore by her 'infinitely aristocratic hands', the 'long expressive fingers', the 'perfect neck' and a 'certain haughty grace'. The aura of grace caught by one was at variance, however, with the impression of another that she was like a 'young deer ready to butt'.

From memoirs of the Russian court, Harriet eagerly assembled a list of the Grand Duchess Anastasia's distinguishing marks: a scar on her shoulder blade, a scar surrounding the base of the middle finger of the left hand, a scar on her forehead. She managed to match these with marks on Anna. There was later much arguing about scars. Anna's one-time landlady, Mrs Wingender, sniffily attributed her former lodger's stiff finger to a cut sustained while washing crockery.

Harriet's findings were reinforced by the observations of the Russian-born Dr Serge Rudnev, then treating Anna for a tubercular infection. He noted a congenital malformation of the feet called *hallux valgus*, from which the Grand Duchess Anastasia and all her sisters had suffered. Dr Rudnev later became an important witness because he swore he had seen Anastasia and Tatiana throwing paper pellets out of a palace window in Moscow on the day that war was declared. At one point he asked Anna whether she remembered what she was doing that day. He was thrilled by her bafflingly apposite reply: 'Shame, shame my sister and I were playing the fool and pelting passers-by with little paper balls.' Actually, it seems that on the day war was declared the family were still in St Petersburg. They did, however, travel to Moscow days later, on 17 August.

A psychoanalyst, Professor Karl Bonhoeffer, examined Anna while she was at St Mary's Hospital. He offered more testimony in her favour. 'The curious amnesia is a result of a more or less deliberate engagement of the will. It is probably a case of loss of memory by auto-suggestion, arising from a desire to suppress what she has experienced – the possibility must at least be conceded that this (auto-suggestive) influence might have developed in the daughter of the Tsar.'

Bonhoeffer established that she could neither count nor tell the time. 'The patient is not suffering from a mental illness in the true sense; on the other hand, she does exhibit signs of a psychopathic constitution, evidenced by her emotional excitability, her tendency toward changes of mood, especially toward depression, and by the peculiar disturbance of the memory... It has been asked if there can be any question of hypnotic influence on the patient by some third party. That is to be denied, as is the other supposition that this is a deliberate fraud.'

Harriet now felt the time was ripe to appeal to the Tsarina's brother, Grand Duke Ernest Louis of Hesse. In later years it was said that the Grand Duke refused to recognise Anna as Anastasia because she claimed he had visited the Russian Court during the First World War, in 1916. A visit of this kind would have been treasonous.

Grand Duke Ernest and his family

But Anna had described the event in some detail: 'He came to arrange with my mother and father a treaty. He came under an assumed name, but all of us children knew him because we had seen him before. I heard my mother talk about it. We were great friends together and we all knew what was going on at home.'

If Grand Duke Ernest was intent on discrediting Anna, his nephew, Prince Waldemar of Denmark, now began to take up cudgels on her behalf. On 3 July 1925, Prince Waldemar wrote to the Danish Ambassador in Berlin, Herluf Zahle, asking him to proceed 'privately' with an inquiry. Zahle was an eminent diplomat who had been president of the League of Nations. He was to become one of Anna's most important supporters. In later years, even at her most grudging, Anna acknowledged the debt she owed Zahle. His wife, Lillan, she pronounced 'the finest lady on earth'.

The Prince's letter was carried by hand to Zahle by Alexis Volkov, the former personal servant and groom of the chamber for the Tsarina. Volkov had survived the Revolution only after pulling off a dramatic escape from his Bolshevik captors in a forest in Perm.

Waldemar was keen that his messenger, Volkov, should also meet Anna and write a report of his impressions. When the two men first encountered Anna, Volkov gave every impression that he believed she was the Grand Duchess. He was moved to tears as she appeared to remember the sailors who looked after the Tsarevich: Nagorny and Derevenko. He seemed to share poignant memories with Anna as they touched upon the night before the shootings, when the sisters sewed jewels into their clothes.

The detailed report Volkov wrote of the meeting was immediately sealed by order of the Queen of Denmark. The sealing gave rise to excited speculation amongst Anna's supporters. But Volkov's comment at the time indicated that he would always fight shy of committing himself publicly. 'Think of the position I am in. If I now say that it is she, and others later claim the reverse, where would I be then?' Zahle's impression, however, was unequivocally positive: Anna's detached politeness, as he put it, bespoke an 'inborn distinction'.

Zahle received immediate instructions from Waldemar to take up Anna's case formally. Prompted perhaps by the rise in status of those taking an interest, the Tsar's sister, Olga, now felt compelled to contact the Imperial children's tutor, Pierre Gilliard, who was living in Lausanne: 'Suppose she really were the little one. Heaven alone knows if she is or not.' Gilliard, who had already outed one false Alexis, lost no time; he set off instantly for St Mary's with his wife, Shura. Shura had been a nursemaid to the Imperial children and she had married Gilliard after the Revolution.

Though the Gilliards found Anna ill and disinclined to talk, Shura successfully examined Anna's feet. She was excited by what she saw, pronouncing them similar to the Grand Duchess's: 'The feet look like the Grand Duchess's – with her it was the same as here, the right foot was worse than the left.' Also apparently convinced, Gilliard insisted she move to a better clinic, the Mommsen nursing home.

Gilliard returned in the autumn with the Grand Duchess Olga herself. Though Anna was still very ill, she was sufficiently recovered to be able to engage properly with her visitors. Her first comment, which seemed plausible, was that she could not recognise Gilliard without his beard.

Her conversation with Olga ran swimmingly as they exchanged pleasantries about Kiki the cat; Kiki had been a present to Anna from Harriet. According to Anna's supporters, however, Olga's attitude changed when Anna raised the possibility of the Tsar investing money in the Bank of England. They believe Olga decided, then and there, to deny Anna's identity in order to leave the way clear to claim any legacy herself.

Grand Duchess Olga with her sons

Though the idea that Anna might one day claim a vast inheritance was rarely the motivating force amongst her supporters, it was inevitably a factor. She began the speculation by claiming that the Tsar had told her he had deposited money for her in the Bank of England. Whether the idea came to her in one of her sporadic moods of optimism or whether it was suggested to her by an over excited supporter is not known.

In any case Anna now insisted that she had discussed the legacy with the Tsar in Ekaterinburg. 'He told us four sisters that in 1914, before the outbreak of war, he had deposited five million roubles for each of us with the Bank of England in the name of an agent. Unfortunately I can no longer remember the name my father mentioned then, I think it was a German-sounding one-syllable name with an "a" in it,' she relayed tantalisingly.

A close friend of the Imperial Family, Lili Dehn, seemed to confirm the story when she recounted, under oath, uncharacteristically sanguine musings from the Tsarina: 'At least we shan't have to beg, for we have a fortune in the Bank of England.' The Tsarina had apparently spoken of millions in gold.

The money was never traced and Anna is now believed by some supporters to have been referring simply to a bank IN England. However one of Anna's lawyers believed he identified the agent. He was thought to be the banker who had acted as the Tsar's finance minister and now managed the financial affairs of the Tsar's sisters. He was an Anglicised Russian named Sir Peter Bark.

Bark's subsequent refusal to co-operate with inquiries gave rise to the suggestion that he was involved in a cover-up, even using Imperial money for his own business interests. This accusation was particularly unfair. Bark ended his days in relative penury, issuing awkward requests for money from banks which had previously employed him. When he died, in 1937, his estate was valued at just £14,126. His dealings with the Romanovs, furthermore, demonstrated almost excessive loyalty. At one point, before the Revolution, Bark took a 90 per cent drop in pay in order to work for the Tsar. When the Tsar asked what lay behind this altruism, Bark replied loftily that he preferred 'the wider field of state service devoted to the country's good... to service in the private interests'.

It is known that, while they were in captivity, the Romanovs made elaborate efforts to conserve their collection of jewellery. Gilliard was in charge of its complex distribution, assiduously maintaining a list of the jewels and the names of people to whom they were given. Among the conspirators was the nun who brought the family eggs; every day she would leave with her egg basket brimming with jewels.

But the collection was never found. The prioress of the local convent ordered the nuns never to hand over any jewels to the Bolsheviks; she herself died in police custody, taking her secrets to the grave. One couple who had received a small box of baubles took an oath never to hand it over; the husband threw himself out of a window while his wife died in agony in a police cell having broken up and swallowed an aluminium spoon.

***

Throughout the second half of 1925, both Gilliards remained convinced that Anna was the Grand Duchess Anastasia. During Shura's visit, Anna had put scent into the nursemaid's hand, exactly as the Grand Duchess had as a child. According to Harriet, Gilliard emerged from the sick room saying: 'I want to do everything I can to help the Grand Duchess...' Turning to Dr Rudnev, he said: 'What is Her Imperial Highness's condition? Can she get well?' Olga's parting words to Zahle became well known amongst Anna's supporters: 'My reason cannot grasp it, but my heart tells me that the little one is Anastasia. And because I have been raised in a faith which teaches me to follow my heart before my reason, I must believe that she is.'

Olga sent affectionate notes and a shawl, but months later denied that Anna was Anastasia. She now denounced the scar Anna boasted on her finger; in a letter to a friend she pointed out that the Grand Duchess with the wounded finger was Marie. She later wrote a sad letter to Princess Irene in which she explained how, in her view, Anna had come to know that Olga called Anastasia 'Schwibs', which was once held by Anna's supporters as strong evidence for her claim. 'For nearly four years, they stuffed the head of this poor creature with all our stories, showed her a large number of photographs etc, and one fine day she astonished everybody with her memories...

'During the four days that we spent in Berlin, Mr Gilliard and my husband saw all the Russians with whom she had stayed and they learned in this way many things of great importance. Here is one: they told them that she had learned the nickname 'Schwibs' from an officer I met in the Crimea, who later came to Berlin. He was interested in the invalid and asked her if she knew this nickname and who gave her the name; naturally she was unable to reply. But later, she suddenly said: "My Aunt Olga called me 'Schwibs'!" Everybody was astonished and made inquiries to find out if this was true.'

Some of Anna's supporters believed that Olga's change of heart came about when it dawned on her that her 'niece' was not, after all, deathly ill. With Anna's death, the matter of her identity would obviously be brought to an end: her continued existence brought with it the possibility of litigation and consequent delays in the distribution of legacies.

Money was a recurring problem for the surviving Romanovs; they knew nothing of saving, or even spending. The Tsar's mother, the Dowager Empress, took a lofty view of economy. When her Danish host and nephew, King Christian X, ordered a cut-down on fuel consumption, she huffily insisted her staff illuminate all the lights in her quarters. Olga's sister, the Grand Duchess Xenia, betrayed a similar attitude when she raced to Harrods and, with her first English cheque, spent a full £98, the equivalent, today, of more than £2,000.

Gleb later swore that he saw an uncompromising cable sent to Olga from Xenia saying: 'Do not acknowledge Anastasia under any circumstances.' In January 1926 an article appeared in *National Tidende* in Copenhagen: 'Grand Duchess Olga went to Berlin to see Frau Tschaikovsky, but neither she, nor anyone else who knew Tsar Nicholas's youngest daughter was able to find the slightest resemblance between Grand Duchess Anastasia and the person who calls herself Frau Tschaikovsky...' Anna's supporters, irritated by Olga's lily-livered retraction, declared her a poor put-upon thing: a Plain Jane who, one claimed, looked like her own cook.

In fact, as late as 1958, Olga was still changing her mind, making confusing confessions to friends in which she claimed she had, after all, recognised Anna as the Grand Duchess. She knew she was real, she now claimed, because she had known her dog's pet name. Asked why she changed her story, Olga had simply shaken her head and whispered: 'Family pressure.'

The Gilliards now also did a volte-face, claiming Anna was a fraud. Harriet, they insisted, was simply suffering from an *idée fixe*. Within two months of their visit with Olga, both were sending Harriet equivocal letters. First Shura wrote: 'Though I have not found anything either in her features or her ways that reminds me of the Grand Duchess Anastasia, I am ready to help you in your researches.' In the margin she wrote: 'The letter of the invalid (*la malade*) is touching and has moved me deeply but I have not found in it AN.' Her husband, while also pledging support for Harriet's research, picked holes in Anna's memories of Tobolsk. One memory concerned the play staged by the family, during which Anastasia had revealed her underwear. Gilliard remarked that the play was English, not French. He added further that Anastasia had not lost a piece of underwear, as Anna claimed. He pointed out that, on the second day of his first visit, he had noticed that Anna mistook his wife for Olga.

Gilliard published an article accompanied by photographs of the young Grand Duchess Anastasia and Franziska. Years later Gleb claimed the photographs had been altered, with what he referred to as 'ear drops' clumsily added on to Franziska's lobes. While Anastasia's ears were pierced, Franziska's were not. The photograph, scoffed Gleb, was captioned 'The Gradual Transformation of Franziska Schanzkowska'. Gleb and Gilliard were to become particular adversaries. In a criticism of one of Gilliard's books, *The False Anastasia*, Gleb issued a crisp response to Gilliard's description of him as living in America without definite occupation: 'As a matter of fact Mr Botkin has two definite occupations, being a commercial artist for eight years and a writer for eleven years.'

However, as was the pattern in Anna's life, no sooner did one supporter fall by the wayside than another appeared. Serge Botkin was a cousin of Dr Botkin and president of the Berlin Russian Refugee Office. While Serge Botkin never declared publicly that he believed in her claim, he confessed his private feelings to Gleb: 'Well, Madame Tschaikovsky is either the Grand Duchess Anastasia or else she is a miracle; and you know I do not believe in miracles.' It was, of course, through Serge that Gleb finally met Anna.

Now Serge Botkin and Zahle combined forces to organise an improbable holiday for Anna and Harriet in the Swiss resort of Lugano. To the secretary at the Refugee Office, Baron Vassily Osten-Sacken, fell the unhappy task of dealing with the minutiae of Anna and Harriet's holiday routine. This inevitably featured fall-outs. Anna soon turned on Harriet, complaining to a hotel maid that her friend was refusing to change her bandages: she was being treated for wounds resulting from her tuberculosis. At one point she threw her stockings at Harriet, shouting: 'You are supposed to darn them'. Baron Osten-Sacken gave a muted account of the holiday: 'I would think the two ladies have simply gotten on each other's nerves.'

The Baron was then in charge of transferring Anna to a hospital, Stillachhaus, in Oberstdorf, in the Bavarian Alps. The director of the hospital, a Dr H. Saathof, readily declared his belief in her claim. With the rest of the staff following his lead, it is hardly surprising that Anna looked back fondly on her time at Stillachhaus. Saathof gave a lyrical description of his patient: 'Her whole nature was so distinctive and, in spite of the narrow range of her intellect... so thoroughly refined that one must, without knowing anything at all about her origins, recognise her as the offspring of an old, highly cultured and, in my opinion, extremely decadent family.'

Saathof managed to link her outbursts of ill temper to what he termed the 'ingratitude of the House of Habsburg... her behaviour has reminded me frequently and in a striking way of a similar mental attitude... which it might be appropriate to describe as analogous to the "ingratitude of the House of Romanov".'

Anna at Oberstdorf

It was at Stillachhaus that Anna met Grand Duchess Anastasia's childhood friend and Gleb's sister, Tatiana Botkin. Tatiana came at the behest of Anna's former supporter, Zinaida Tolstoy, who was clearly still haunted by her encounter with Anna. Within 24 hours of their initial meeting, Tatiana was convinced that Anna was the Grand Duchess. Gilliard later claimed in an article that Tatiana had been hypnotised by Harriet; actually the two had never met. Tatiana later described her recognition of the Grand Duchess Anastasia: 'The way she turned her head, the movement of her body when she got up to leave, the gesture she used when she offered her hand, her bearing, her walk, were the same as the Grand Duchess's.'

Tatiana's friends now testify to her being a prim, almost schoolmarmish woman, not given to flights of fancy. But Tatiana later described herself as nearly suffocating with emotion when she first saw and heard Anna laughing; the laughter, she was convinced, was exactly the same as it had been nine years before. 'When Anastasia Nikolaievna laughed, she would never turn her head to look at you. She would glance at you from the corner of her eye with a roguish look on her face. It was exactly the same, the same as before,' she said afterwards.

She had brought along a photograph album with pictures of the Romanovs: 'Anyone who had seen her bent over these photographs, trembling and crying "my mother, my mother" would not have been able to doubt any longer.' When Tatiana showed her a photograph of a letter the Grand Duchess had written as a child, Anna gazed at it in disbelief: 'I should never have believed that I wrote this letter; I can't imagine it.' Tatiana herself drew no particular conclusions from this protestation; however, throughout her life, Anna's supporters were quick to cite this type of ostensibly damaging confession as further proof of her identity as the Grand Duchess.

Anna at Oberstdorf

***

Such double-bluff on the part of a claimant has often proved efficacious. Years before, in 1865, an Australian came forward claiming to be Sir Roger Tichborne, who had disappeared after sailing from Rio de Janiero in 1854.

The 27-stone Tichborne claimant, actually a butcher from Wagga Wagga, was unable to remember the school he was meant to have attended, had forgotten all his French and even managed to lose a tattoo.

So keen, however, was Sir Roger's mother for a reunion with her son that she was prepared to overlook these impediments. As she wrote before the meeting: 'I think my poor dear Roger confuses everything in his head, just as in a dream, and I believe him to be my son, although his statements differ from mine... I fancy that the photographics you sent me are like him, but of course after thirteen years' absence there must be some difference in the shape...' She was not put off when, at their final emotional meeting, her hugely inflated son called her 'Mamma', a form of address Sir Roger had never used. Nor was she worried by the tendency that he shared with Anna to hide his face under a handkerchief.

A growing number of supporters looked upon the butcher's drunken antics benignly, some even declaring that he shambled with the 'easy grace' of the upper classes. They viewed their protégé's ineptititude positively, as evidence of an uncalculating nature. The Tichborne family solicitor wrote an enthusiastic letter to the Dowager's brother: 'I am perfectly satisfied that the more you hear and perhaps the more you see the more certain it will appear to you Sir Roger is the long-lost man. I cannot express how much respect I have for Sir Roger's truthfulness and entire absence of guile.'

***

After her meeting with Anna, in 1926, Tatiana Botkin was so convinced by the claimant that she immediately wrote to the Gilliards and Grand Duchess Olga. She received peremptory notes from both parties denying that they had ever thought Anna was Anastasia. It has been claimed that Gilliard was, in any case, by this time in the pay of Anna's enemy, Grand Duke Ernest of Hesse.

But Tatiana was visited in Nice, shortly after her return, by Grand Duke Andrew, youngest brother of the self-proclaimed head of the Romanovs, Grand Duke Kyril. Anna always hated Kyril; she claimed that, as the first Romanov to break his oath to the Tsar and declare allegiance to the Provisional Government, Kyril had dealt her a personal blow. Her antipathy towards him was the reason she gave for her initial suspicion of Andrew. In fact Andrew was to become one of her great champions.

Grand Duke Andrew

At roughly the same time as Grand Duke Andrew began his investigations, Harriet published a book about her friend: *Anastasia: A Woman's Fate as a Mirror of the World Catastrophe.* The book and newspaper serialisation earned Harriet 4000 marks which she dutifully handed over to Grand Duke Andrew for Anna's use. But Anna was furious when she discovered that Harriet had written a book: she was never told that she herself was benefitting from the proceeds. So began Anna's first moments of fame, as packets of 'Anastasia' cigarettes and boxes of sweets began to appear on the Berlin streets. A song even emerged from the night clubs: *'Nobody knows who you are, little girl/ But your smile and your glance enchant me.'*

With the heightening of interest in Anna, the doctors at Stillachhaus became worried about her security. Anna had begun receiving death threats and the doctors were insisting a new home be found for her. An aristocrat with credentials almost as impressive as Andrew's now stepped forward: the great-grandson of Tsar Nicholas I, George Nikolaievich Romanovsky de Beauharnais, Duke of Leuchtenberg.

The Duke contacted Andrew to say that Anna would be welcome as a guest at Castle Seeon in Upper Bavaria. Anna received the invitation with ill grace: 'What are the Leuchtenbergs?' She finally agreed to travel, as long as Tatiana Botkin would accompany her. For the journey she would need 'playing cards, morning dresses, a rain umbrella and a parasol'.

Soon after Anna arrived at Castle Seeon, the news broke that she was actually the Polish peasant Franziska Schanzkowska. Though her supporters later claimed that all the witnesses involved were bribed, the news reports contained convincing details. The sober Zahle was one of those whose confidence in Anna's identity as Anastasia was dented.

Doris Wingender, the daughter of Franziska's former landlady in Berlin, had turned up at the offices of the *Nachtausgabe*, a German newspaper, which was then publishing Harriet's memoirs. Doris said she recognised the photograph of the claimant as Franziska Schanzkowska, who had disappeared in the first months of 1920. She said Franziska had reappeared in the summer of 1922 claiming she was living with Russian monarchists who mistook her for someone else. This, the report claimed, was during the time of Anna's disappearance from the Kleists.

Anna at Castle Seeon

Worried that she was being followed, Franziska had insisted she and Doris exchange clothes. Doris still had the clothes, including a camel's hair coat, she had been given by

Franziska. The Baroness von Kleist now identified these clothes as those of her former protégée. In what should have been a conclusive moment the Baroness exclaimed that she recognised Anna's underwear: 'That is the monogram I embroidered myself.'

But Anna's supporters were quick to point out that Doris was promised 1500 marks if her story proved correct. Harriet, of course, had an opinion on the matter, insisting that the only explanation for Franziska's disappearance was that she had died. At one point, she even declared herself convinced that Franziska had been killed by a notorious criminal gang, a claim she later retracted.

With doubts lingering, it was decided that a formal meeting should be conducted between Doris and Anna. Doris travelled with a detective and a journalist to Castle Seeon. In his subsequent report, the journalist was quick to portray Anna's warped frame of mind: 'Only rarely has anyone seen her scurrying along the lengthy, lonely corridor in the former Benedictine monastery. She shuns people, she always smells danger.' In fact, one of the reasons she was rarely seen was that, as Tatiana Botkin later recalled, Anna had no sense of space or direction and frequently became lost when she stepped out of her room into the corridors.

Anna did not receive Doris very graciously, pointing at her and shrieking: '*Das soll rausgehen!*' (that must go out) as she entered her room. One of the attendants, an English governess called Faith Lavington, wrote in her diary that she found Anna's reaction extremely suspicious. 'One would hardly treat a *soi-disant* unknown person in such a fashion. Anastasia did not even seem to trouble about the two men, she concentrated entirely on the woman.' The detective produced a photograph of Franziska in peasant clothes. One of the Duke's daughters later confessed to Faith that, though she had accused the detective of faking the picture, her heart had sunk because the likeness was unmistakable.

The older Duchess, however, dismissed the trio as nothing more than intriguers and adventurers. When she drove Doris back to Munich, the car had to cross the castle lake on a rickety bridge. It was known as Liar's Bridge because it was reputed to collapse if crossed by liars. The Duchess issued a warning to Doris as they approached the lake, but the bridge remained intact.

CHAPTER FOUR

Anna and Gleb in America, 1928-1931

It was in May 1927 that the meeting took place between Gleb and Anna. Now of course in America, Gleb had been inundated with press inquiries about the woman the *Herald Tribune* had called 'the reigning enigma of Europe'. The first article he read concerning her was written in the *New York Times* during the period when the Gilliards still believed she was Anastasia. When Gleb wrote to Gilliard, however, he found that the tutor had already changed his mind. He was ready to accept Gilliard's revised opinion as an end of the matter, until he received an emotional letter from his sister, Tatiana, saying that the claimant really was Anastasia.

He finally agreed to travel to Castle Seeon to make up his own mind. He was commissioned to write his account of the meeting for the *North American Newspaper Alliance*.

Upon arriving at the castle, he was kept waiting for several days by Anna, who refused to see him. He was intrigued, however, to hear that she was asking whether he had brought his drawings or, as she put it obscurely, his 'funny animals'.

Gleb first saw Anna the day she was making a rare foray out of the castle to meet Franziska Schanzkowska's brother, Felix. Gleb was standing in the main foyer of the castle when he saw Anna coming downstairs. She extended her hand and said: 'How do you do?' In those few seconds, he was convinced she was Anastasia. 'The shock was so great that I remained standing, unable to utter a word. She was changed of course. She was now a grown woman... she looked sick, tired, as it seemed to me frightened... As she went in her swift manner toward the car, she slightly bowed her head with an absent and benevolent smile, in that inimitable manner of royalty who know that wherever they go they are greeted from all directions and automatically return these salutations, bowing and smiling to everybody and to no one in particular.'

Anna enjoyed a second success that day with Felix Schanzkowski, though the meeting, at a nearby inn, got off to a bad start with him declaring: 'That is my sister Franziska.' Indeed Faith heard from the Leuchtenbergs afterwards that Anna and Felix were uncannily alike, sharing the same height, colouring and features, particularly, apparently, their mouths. But just as onlookers prepared themselves for an emotional reunion in the beer garden, Felix mysteriously changed his mind. Harriet's lawyer had prepared a stringent affadavit she hoped Felix would never sign, saying that he recognised his sister's hair, teeth, figure, walk, feet and hands. This he now did refuse to sign, insisting: 'She isn't my sister.' Harriet, incidentally, was also present; mindful, however, of Anna's abiding fury over her book, she felt it wisest to remain out of sight.

Felix Schanzkowski

In the end, Felix was persuaded to sign a second document including the words: 'She showed no sign either of astonishment or of the slightest fear. She behaved rather as one behaves towards a third party to whom one is just being introduced.' He declared that his sister had no deformities of the feet; removing his shoes he added that Franziska had 'pretty' feet 'just like mine'.

Years later it was claimed that Felix had been confused by Anna's smart outfit. Gleb utterly refuted this: 'I saw the Grand Duchess on the day of the confrontation and she had on the shabbiest clothes imaginable.'

Anna now agreed to see Gleb; she had been hesitant

because she had guessed he would write articles about her. But her guess probably had more to do with her awareness of the growing public interest in the Schanzkowskis than her ability, as Gleb excitedly suggested, to read his mind.

At any rate, she eventually overcame her qualms and over the following week the pair met regularly. At one point, Gleb showed her drawings he had done recently, along with some from pre-Revolutionary days. The recent ones apparently made her laugh, but those from pre-Revolutionary days troubled her. This, Gleb felt, was further evidence in favour of her claim. The deficiencies he encountered in her temperament he happily put down to her autocratic heritage. Indeed, he found her, as he put it 'witty, cheerful, charming and delightful'.

The pair enjoyed a romantic boating trip, during which Gleb rowed her across the lake. He had been in some trepidation because the Duke's daughter had warned him that Anna had to be rowed according to the regulations of the old Navy of the Guard. As it turned out, Anna found no fault with Gleb's rowing; indeed, upon their return to the castle, the couple shared a tremulous farewell at Anna's bedroom door. Gleb kissed her hand and told her that he was so happy to see her again. She apparently burst into tears and whispered: 'It was all so awful,' before in turn pressing his hand.

When Gleb proposed that Anna join him in America, she revealed herself smitten enough to agree. In his memoir, *The Woman Who Rose Again*, published in 1937, Gleb gave a lavish description of a poetic moment when her appearance was enhanced by a storm: 'The gold of her hair shimmered softly against the background of the dark, bluish clouds. Her finely carved features acquired an ephemeral quality in the weird glow of the almost uninterrupted lightning.'

Fired with enthusiasm, Gleb travelled immediately to Berlin. His first mission was to discredit what he saw as the Franziska myth. He later claimed that Franziska had been picked solely for the unlikely reason that she was the only woman to have disappeared in Berlin in 1920. He produced conflicting dates: Franziska disappeared in March; Anna had been hauled from the canal in February. Franziska, he added, was judged insane; Anna, he insisted, never was.

Gleb and Harriet's lawyer now posed as journalists in order to have several meetings with Doris. Gleb never quite forgave Doris her apartment, 'located in the worst slums of Berlin', or her choice of cafe for their first talk, 'a notorious rendezvous of the Berlin underworld'. The trio conducted their subsequent meetings, apparently, in respectable restaurants.

According to Gleb, Doris gave herself away by continually consulting a notebook; the notes, Gleb believed, had been dictated to her by the same detective who had accompanied her to Castle Seeon, Detective Knopf. Even with the notes, she was apparently caught with inconsistencies. She said at one point that Franziska and Anna both had black, decayed teeth. Gleb retorted that Anna's were all extracted; she did not have a single black tooth in her mouth.

Gleb returned to America determined to persuade the authorities to let Anna join him. But his recognition made little immediate difference to life at Castle Seeon. Anna maintained her role as a tiresome guest, beginning to argue with the Duchess over the linen, tea service, food and even flower arrangements. The Duke hoped to smooth over unpleasantnesses with a 26th birthday celebration on 18 June. This vote of confidence she apparently received graciously enough, but hostilities were soon resumed: 'Who does she think she is?' the Duchess would rant. Anna would draw herself up and snap: 'I am the daughter of your Emperor.'

The unsettling stream of witnesses arriving at the castle, meanwhile, showed no sign of slowing, nor were their verdicts in any way conclusive. Faith offered an oblique description of the comings and goings: 'A case of pull devil pull baker.' Scientists and specialists carried out inconclusive examinations of feet, ears, face and handwriting. A particular point at issue was her teeth. The Imperial dentist was shown a cast of what remained of Anna's teeth before the last ones were extracted and responded in furious disbelief: 'Would I have left the teeth of one of the Grand Duchesses in this condition?'

At one point a Professor Osti, the head of the Psychological Institute in Paris, came to see if he could make any progress with Anna through hypnotism. The Professor failed entirely to hypnotise Anna; indeed, he accused her of having strong hypnotic powers before falling into a trance himself. All this despite being, as Faith put it 'a very big bug in his line'.

One particularly unwelcome visitor that summer was Prince Felix Yussoupov, who turned up unexpectedly and demanded to see Anna. Over the years Anna seems to have cultivated a hatred of Yussoupov; she loathed him apparently as much for his alleged homosexuality as for his murder of Rasputin. She agreed to meet him in the grounds of Castle Seeon for a talk lasting just fifteen minutes. He spoke to her in French, German, Russian and English, then asked her if she would like some new frocks, as he had recently gone into the fashion industry.

According to one account, the conversation then soured when he went on to berate her for abandoning her family and she had to remind him that he was addressing 'the daughter of his Emperor'. She flounced off to her room and was smoothing herself down before her bedroom mirror when she caught sight of Yussoupov in the reflection. As she asked what he was doing, he apparently came towards her, arms outstretched and hands trembling: 'I killed Rasputin and I will kill you for what your mother did to my country. We will have you out of the way.' She ran past him, out of the door, down the stairs and managed to lose herself amongst the guests at one of the Duke's luncheon parties.

Whatever the truth of the encounter, Yussoupov roundly declared to Grand Duke Andrew that she could not possibly be Anastasia: 'If you had seen her, I am convinced that you would recoil in horror at the thought that this frightful creature could be a daughter of our Tsar.' He denounced her as 'hysterical, vulgar and common' and proposed an ill thought-out plan for all the claimants. 'These false pretenders ought to be gathered up and sent to live together in a house somewhere.'

In fact Anna was proving herself incapable of remaining on equable terms with almost anybody. She was slightly better with men, maintaining inappropriately flirtatious relations even with the elderly Duke, but she fell out with an endless succession of maidservants. Faith was almost alone in maintaining affection for Anna while recognising and acknowledging all the shortcomings of her 'Sick Lady' . She remained ambivalent about the issue of Anna's identity but offered a grimly prescient picture of her future life: 'I don't know who she is, I only know one thing, that wherever she is or in what circumstances she is, her unhappy character will always bring grief and pain upon the people surrounding her.'

At one point Faith's sister sent her photographs of the inside of the palaces at Tsarskoye Selo and Livadia. The photographs, published in the *New York Times,* were billed as the 'First Uncensored Photos from Soviet Russia'. They included pictures of a study, bathroom and drawing room as well as bedrooms. Anna apparently glanced at the photographs before turning very red and exclaiming: 'But this is my Papa's bathroom... But these are all our rooms.' She ran from her room, followed by Faith who expected a *pied au derrière.* In fact Anna recovered her composure and was soon prepared to study the photographs minutely.

Faith later insisted, without offering further explanation, that Anna managed to identify every room. As Faith described it: 'At my very innocently enquiring all about them she told me every one right, though there was not a scrap of anything to show where they came from... It was just as if she were living there again.'

Unfortunately, days before Anna was due to leave Castle Seeon, the pair fell out. Anna believed that Faith had secretly arranged an unwelcome doctor's visit. Now, whenever poor Faith knocked on the door, Anna would shriek: '*Sie können nicht herein kommen*'. In combative mode, Faith returned all Anna's gifts and, at one point, even challenged her. But she failed to win back Anna's approval and confessed herself surprisingly regretful: 'You will think me awfully sentimental but I must own that I feel it most terribly, for I gave of my very best... I feel a miserable gnawing pity and anxious solicitude still for this poor woman – a sort of feeling as if some living part had been torn right out of me.'

Faith's intense feelings about her 'Sick Lady' may well have been exacerbated by her own worries. Throughout the summer, she had fallen prey to ghostly manifestations at the castle. She complained that, in Room 16, the wardrobe began cracking at 2.30am and carried on till dawn. After one sleepless night she cursed the 'vile room' for giving her 'the jam-jams'.

***

It was perhaps as well that Gleb was making progress with his plan to transfer Anna to America. A Mrs William B. Leeds had contacted him to say that Anna would be welcome as a guest at Kenwood, her estate on Long Island. Mrs Leeds had formerly been Princess Xenia Georgievna of Russia; she was the younger daughter of Grand Duke George Mikhailovich, and a second cousin to Grand Duchess Anastasia. Billy Leeds was a millionaire son of a tin magnate.

Though she did eventually carry out her promise, the Princess initially proved mercurial, insisting that she had no money to transport Anna to America. Gleb's own position towards her was somewhat ambivalent; he gave an overly detailed description of her as unusually handsome, with the full lips of what the Russians call a 'butterfly mouth'.

In his novel, *The Baron's Fancy*, Gleb describes the hero Max's relationship with a grand duchess – obviously based on Xenia – in unmistakably flirtatious terms. Gleb clearly felt drawn to Princess Xenia as much as to Anna; but he insisted, and may well have convinced himself, that his feelings were primarily paternal. This despite his being aged only 27: barely three years older than Xenia, born 1903, and four years younger than Anna. The real Grand Duchess Anastasia, had been, of course, one year younger than Gleb. 'I mused to have these two lovely princesses, Anastasia "the little one" and "the little Xenia" – together defying and defeating the hosts of their bitter enemies. I even wrote a letter to Xenia, expressing my feelings on the subject and the devotion that she inspired in me.'

The plan for Anna to go to America was not universally popular. Gleb had antagonised Grand Duke Andrew with an article criticising the Russians' attitude to Anna. The article appeared in November 1927 in the *New York Herald*

Tribune. 'Has Gleb really not got enough instinct and tact to understand how inappropriate, even harmful, it is for a Russian to sling mud at his own people in the columns of the foreign press?' Grand Duke Andrew raged to Gleb's uncle Serge. 'If I agreed to the transfer of the invalid to America, it was solely for the reason that she would come into the hands of relations. However, after reading the article, knowing that Gleb is involved, the dangerous idea can arise that she is being summoned to America to isolate her from Europe and that everyone can then be more easily vilified.'

As Anna prepared to depart, Faith described the predominant feeling at Castle Seeon as one of concern for Anna's future hostess. 'There is a universal feeling of compassion here for poor little Princess Xenia who has no idea what she has landed herself in for.' The Duchess's daughter's feeling was less altruistic; she repeated a sort of mantra as she watched Anna's departure from a window: 'If you curse my husband, my children or this my household, then may this curse return upon you and yours forever.'

On her way to Cherbourg, Anna stopped off in Paris, where she saw Grand Duke Andrew for the first time. He was much moved by the meeting and apparently looked as though he had seen a ghost. 'I have seen Nicky's daughter, I have seen Nicky's daughter,' he proclaimed. He wrote to the vacillating Olga: 'Two days I have spent with her, have observed her carefully at close quarters and to the best of my conscience I must confess that Anastasia Tschaikovsky is none other than my niece, the Grand Duchess Anastasia Nikolaievna. I recognised her at once, and further observations only confirmed my first impression. For me there is definitely no doubt – it is Anastasia.'

The Duke of Leuchtenberg accompanied her all the way to the ocean liner. Through tears, the old man stammered his last question to her: 'Are you still angry with me because I brought so many people to see you?' She made no reply and offered no thanks for his hospitality, simply saying: 'All this is the fault of Frau von Rathlef.' She later assessed his character with customary condescension: 'He was friendly but he was weak.'

***

Meanwhile Gleb was having some success in gathering support in America. While his unrestrained commitment to his cause had undoubtedly cost him some supporters, he now discovered his heartfelt articles in the *Tribune* had captured the attention of one of the most prominent Russian émigrés, the composer and piano virtuoso, Sergei Rachmaninov. Perhaps it is not surprising that Rachmaninov took an interest in Gleb's story. Forced to leave Russia in 1917, he was consumed with nostalgia for his native land. All through their lives in exile, he and his wife spoke in Russian and employed Russian servants, Russian cooks and a Russian secretary. They consulted Russian doctors, attended Orthodox services and drank tea from a samovar.

Rachmaninov expressed his sadness in an interview he gave in June 1930 to the *English Musical Times*. 'There is however a burden which age perhaps is laying on my shoulders. It is that I have no country. I had to leave the land where I was born, where I passed my youth, where I struggled and suffered all the sorrows of the young, and where I finally achieved success. The whole world is open to me, and success awaits me everywhere. Only one place is closed to me, and that is my own country – Russia.'

The composer telephoned Gleb and invited him for dinner. Gleb was particularly surprised by the call, as Rachmaninov was said to be a rabid socialist who enjoyed insulting the newly impoverished aristocrats. The composer's unpopularity may have been linked simply to his failure to help his less fortunate compatriots. New York's Russian community relished rounding off tales of his meanness with inflated figures representing his earnings: 400,000 dollars in a single season, or so they said.

Gleb looked forward to the evening with interest; a proficient pianist, he relished, not least, the prospect of meeting the composer of some of his favourite pieces. He described his first impression of Rachmaninov in picturesque terms: 'A strange sensation it was to have the door opened by the cover of the Prelude C sharp minor, suddenly come to life.' Within a few minutes Gleb dismissed all the rumours about the composer. 'He proved a kindly, benevolent man, very conservative in his political views and altogether much more reminiscent of an old-time Russian bureaucrat than of the proverbial wild-eyed musical genius'.

While Rachmaninov confessed himself not convinced of

Anna's identity as the Grand Duchess, he was clearly entranced by the story. 'Hers seems to be one of those stories which are too fantastic to be believed, yet require even more fantastic explanation to be disbelieved. But I am convinced that she is no deliberate impostor, and I am further convinced that you are quite sincere in your belief in her. I want to be of help.'

Rachmaninov even offered to pay immediately for Anna to come to New York. However they both agreed that it would be better if she were brought over by her cousin, Princess Xenia. Rachmaninov agreed to ring Xenia offering support; this, in turn, spurred Xenia into finalising plans for Anna's journey to America. When Anna's ship finally docked in the New York harbour, Rachmaninov's manager, Charles Foley, was amongst the group boarding the steamer to help deal with immigration authorities. Their cutter had initially been prevented from going out to the steamer because of fog; by the time the cutter was allowed out the following morning, there were 30 reporters anxious to meet Anna. Gleb and Foley were obliged to scuttle at speed up the rope ladder then run to her suite, locking the door behind them.

Gleb was worried that Anna would assume the delays caused by the fog had something to do with her. But when she finally emerged from her room, he was thrilled to find her relaxed, even happy. 'I hardly dared to believe my eyes. Here she was at last – "the little one" – looking much better than she had in Seeon, wearing a new and quite becoming dress and obviously very pleased to see me.' She would have been gratified by Gleb's grand greeting: 'I must ask Your Imperial

Highness's forgiveness for dashing into the room like this. But we were pursued by reporters.'

Delays continued before Anna was allowed to disembark and the reporters hung about her door all night. It was Foley who seized one reporter by the collar and sent him flying along the corridor. Another reporter shouted that he'd have Foley done for assault and battery. The reporters took photographs of every woman emerging from the ladies' bathroom until they were told that Anna had her own private bathroom.

At around this time Grand Duke Alexander, the husband of Anna's enemy, the Tsar's sister Grand Duchess Xenia, cabled the *New York Times* accusing Gleb of trying to claim money in England which was rightfully his wife's. The suggestion that there was, after all, money at stake was well received by Gleb. 'Good old Grand Duke Alexander', he wrote to a friend, 'This certainly is letting the cat out of the bag.'

Undaunted, Grand Duke Alexander proceeded to carry out lecture tours around the United States about the 'excitable pretender', as he called Anna. A confirmed spiritualist and table-rapper, Alexander claimed that Grand Duchess Anastasia's spirit had returned and incorporated itself into another body. His proclamation revealed the extent to which he was impressed by Anna's memories. 'She knows so much about the intimate life of the Tsar and his family that there is simply no other explanation for it; and of course it wouldn't be the first time that a spirit has returned to earth in a new physical form.'

Meanwhile, Princess Xenia had decided, shortly before her

purported cousin's arrival, to go on a cruise to the West Indies. She would not be back in time for Anna's arrival and suggested the 'Grand Duchess' be housed temporarily with a Miss Annie Burr Jennings in an apartment in New York. Gleb was put out by Xenia's departure, feeling that it looked bad and was damaging to Anna's cause. He asked one of Xenia's friends why she had had to leave at that particular moment; the reply was peremptory: 'She needs a rest.'

Miss Jennings, daughter of a director of the original Standard Oil Trust, had a house on Park Avenue in the so-called Upper Thirties. Neither Gleb nor Anna fought shy of finding fault with the house, though Anna was pleased to be presented with a huge orchid by her new hostess. 'She hadn't had one since she left Russia,' purred a rapturous Gleb. But he did not approve of Miss Jennings's interior decoration, describing the house as 'a perfect replica of the habitats of rich Moscow merchants buying indiscriminately valuable and worthless things, just to fill the space.' Despite finding what she breezily deemed a good copy of the *Mona Lisa*, Anna was keen to flourish equally refined sensibilities: 'There are a lot of things which are lacking in good taste.'

In the subsequent weeks Anna entertained a stream of guests with complaints about the 'stormy and disagreeable' weather throughout her crossing from Cherbourg. She declared herself unimpressed by the luxury Cunard liner: the ship was clean, she sniffed, but did not compare with the *Standart*.

Anna was nothing if not capricious; she now announced

that she wanted to go to the movies. It was settled that Gleb would be her escort. Unfortunately the evening got off to a bad start when Gleb appeared without uniform or scent. Anna made much of the slight and, in what might be interpreted as a clumsy bid at flirtation, insisted on splashing his clothes with her own scent.

At first she was adamant that Gleb must call her Mrs Tschaikovsky rather than 'Your Imperial Highness'. But eventually she settled for the name by which he had known her as a child: Anastasia Nikolaievna. Gleb eked out the romance of the evening. 'It remained difficult enough for me to grasp fully the fact that Anastasia – "the little one" – was alive, had never been dead, belonged wholly to the normal everyday world. Still, it was somehow easier to comprehend the fact as long as she remained in the fantastic surroundings of Castle Seeon or even in Miss Jennings's weird house on Park Avenue. But to be sitting at Anastasia's side in that epitome of modern New York – a Broadway movie theatre – was simply incredible... And so while she kept looking at the picture, I kept looking at her, as if unconsciously afraid that she might suddenly dissolve in thin air, like a ghost.'

These events are described in Gleb's memoir, *The Woman Who Rose Again*, to which Anna, incidentally, gave her endorsement. A label was included in early editions, signed by Anna as Anastasia; it read: 'I am very pleased with the book... It is the very first time that my case has been described with such exactitude.' The events are also described, however, in Gleb's novel, *The Baron's Fancy*, written six years earlier. Gleb clearly felt driven to give an account of his experiences, and believed, at first, it would be best presented as fiction. While it is tempting to presume that the more detailed descriptions in the *The Baron's Fancy* are closer to the truth, they may represent no more than Gleb's wishful thinking.

Anna in America

In *The Baron's Fancy*, Gleb describes a romantic reunion in 1927 in the house of an elderly millionairess, Miss Emmy Dill Jones, between childhood friends Baron Max Von Waldenscherna and a Duchess Alexandra. Miss Jones he describes as 'a very nice old pillow but (who) also has the kind of brains one would expect in a pillow stuffed with feathers'.

Alexandra has escaped from Russia and married a Jewish man called Rosenkrantz. Max, an artist like Gleb, is immediately entranced: 'What could compare in beauty with these eyes? Sorrowful and yet radiant, suffering but kindly, old in experience but childishly innocent. Eyes of a Madonna... Her forehead was also beautiful. Like her hands it seemed to have been chiselled out of marble.' The big clue, however, is in the description of Alexandra's face: 'The lower part of her face was irregular. There were unmistakable signs of degeneracy in her jaw, but even this possessed a peculiar charm of its own.' The Duchess has a pekingese dog called Jimmy – the name of the Grand Duchess Tatania's dog before the Revolution.

Max and Alexandra also enjoy an evening at the movies. She complains that he is not wearing uniform, then splashes him with scent. During the film, Max, like Gleb, cannot take his eyes off his refound childhood friend. The difference is that Max holds her hand: 'She let him hold her hand for a while and then quietly withdrew it.' A further brief romantic interlude takes place upon the couple's return to Miss Jones's flat. Having invited Max to dinner, Alexandra slips suggestively into a kimono. After dinner she makes herself comfortable on her bed. Then, perhaps unfortunately, she passes out; Max is obliged to leave after kissing her chastely on the forehead.

After their visit to the movies, Gleb and Anna walked through Times Square, gloating over the reporters they were managing to avoid. In fact the reporters were staked outside Gleb's house on Long Island. The media interest in Anna had been such that a new batch of claimants had emerged, including a nephew of Leon Trotsky in Austin, Texas, who insisted that he had personally rescued the Grand Duchess from Ekaterinburg.

Gleb now decided that Anna was in a sufficiently good mood to be introduced to Rachmaninov. But, though Anna had been impressed by Charles Foley, she remained unwilling to meet Rachmaninov. She announced grandly that she had not forgiven him for leaving Russia. She disliked him being, 'rich and happy and living in safety abroad... Where was he with all his goodness when the Revolution began? Or did he not consider himself bound by his oath to serve his Emperor faithfully and die for him if necessary?'

Rachmaninov was shy and, though eager to meet Anna, reluctant to go to a stranger's house. His reluctance seemed justified when, upon his final arrival in the Park Avenue entrance hall, Miss Jennings failed to greet him. Eyeing him suspiciously and pointing at him in 'a gesture characteristic of rich New Yorkers', she simply said: 'Who is this man?' When Gleb replied: 'Rachmaninov', emphasising the Russian vowels, Miss Jennings failed to recognise the name. Only half-convinced, she replied: 'As long as you know him it's all right'. Gleb described Rachmaninov as pressing himself to the wall, looking as if he wished it would give away and permit him to escape.

Anna's attitude to Rachmaninov, meanwhile, showed no signs of improving. By the time he entered the bedroom, she had got into her bed and pulled the blankets up to her nose. 'Mr Rachmaninov approached her bed, but she looked at him without uttering a word, her eyes full of tears. All three of us froze in utter embarrassment but I think that I felt worse than anybody else, being wholly responsible

154

for that painful scene.' After a few minutes of silence, Rachmaninov tiptoed out of the room.

In *The Baron's Fancy*, Gleb gives full descriptions of Max's fluctuating feelings towards the Duchess. 'Alexandra could sulk for hours. Her beautiful eyes would suddenly lose all expression, as if made of glass... She classified all people as either "nice" or "terrible" and it was not easy to qualify in her judgement as "nice".' The tiresome constraints Alexandra placed upon the couple's encounters must surely echo Anna's: 'One had to kiss her hand, call her Imperial Highness, and always sit straight, erect and without crossing one's legs, and one could never contradict her – at least not directly. The word "no" she considered grossly insulting. One could never ask her questions.'

He adds that personal presentation counts a great deal with Alexandra. 'People who wanted to see her had first to cut their hair, manicure their nails, put on their best clothes, and perfume themselves. It was better still if they discovered first Alexandra's favourite colours and matched their gowns and neck-ties accordingly'. Alexandra, 'with truly Byzantine maliciousness', seems to enjoy making it difficult for her visitors to adhere to the rules. She tells them that she is no stickler for time, only to be furious when they are late. When she is addressed as 'Your Imperial Highness', she demands to be called 'Mrs Rosenkrantz'. In the course of conversation, she makes absurd statements that are difficult not to contradict. Lastly, she enjoys seating her visitors on the softest sofas and watching them struggle to sit straight. Max's story of his 'little kitten' Alexandra screaming, trembling and stamping with fury when he is late for his appointment – in fact her clock is fast – sounds as though based on reality.

The fictitious couple are happiest enjoying lofty exchanges about Alexandra's glorious future as Russian leader. Luxurious hours are spent weighing up the suitability of various ministers and speculating as to where best they might procure armies. She issues threats against the surviving members of her family. 'I'm going to hang every one of them on lamp-posts. Not even that. I'm going to pave the road from Petersburg to Moscow with their skulls.'

In his memoir, Gleb gives every indication that his relationship with Anna was platonic. Indeed, though Faith Lavington insisted that Anna flirted with Gleb, most friends regarded them as enjoying nothing more than a respectful companionship. Anna was in the charge of Miss Jennings and so the nature of the pair's relations was under close scrutiny. Eyebrows were raised when Miss Jennings referred to what she called improper letters from Gleb to Anastasia. But the impropriety, it seemed, existed in nothing more than Gleb's occasional tendency to address his friend in the *tu* form.

But Max and Alexandra's relationship is, intriguingly, a full-blooded affair in which both see themselves as victims of the other's passion. At one point she says: 'I clenched my teeth and decided to bear, as best I could, your brutal kissing. I marvelled at your bestiality.' Max suffers her devotion: 'Alexandra threw her arms around his neck, pulled down his head, and pressed her lips to his... Alexandra had a peculiar tongue. It was so rough. It reminded Max of a strip of moist flannel used in Russian post offices for pasting postal stamps. He felt it his duty, however, to prolong the kiss until Alexandra was out of breath and, releasing him, sank with a happy smile back on her pillows.'

The turbulent courtship does not stop there. At one point Max kisses her boyish, diminutive body all over; he then perversely tells her that he likes a woman with curves. She makes a show of not minding the slight, but later accuses him of shabbily failing to pay tribute to her more modest physical charms. He maintains that he is obliged to keep on kissing her to stop her ranting: 'He could not permit an Imperial Highness to talk like a whole union of laundry women.'

***

Not long after her arrival in New York, Anna began to receive death threats. At one point Miss Jennings received a phone call telling her that there was a bomb on the premises. On a separate occasion, Princess Xenia's husband, Billy Leeds, rang to say he had been told that an alarming discussion had been overheard on the subway. Two men were exchanging information about the location of Anna's room and discussing the possibility of climbing along the edge of the roof. Miss Jennings immediately moved Anna to a room on a different floor. The elderly woman issued a stout reassurance to Gleb: 'You can rest assured that nothing will happen to this little lady as long as she stays with me. I am not afraid of anybody.

I am a fighter. I will defy King George himself with all his fleet, if necessary.' She summoned private detectives who, Gleb recalled, resembled nothing so much as professional thugs.

The incident is described with more detail in *The Baron's Fancy*. Max is granted a central role and is himself the proud receiver of a note with a death threat. Actually the note proved prophetic: Gleb did receive a visit from someone threatening to kill him, later on, in the 1930s. Max's note read: 'The fight you have put up for DA (Duchess Alexandra) showed you to be a real *chevalier sans peur et sans reproche*. But I know from unimpeachable sources that if you make another move you will endanger not only your own life but also that of DA.'

While she was still at Miss Jennings's house, Anna talked to Gleb about the 20 million roubles she claimed the Tsar had deposited in the Bank of England. She insisted that her old supporter Zahle had assured her that her claims were correct; she had seen a corroborative letter addressed to Zahle from the bank. Ten years after the shootings, on 17 July 1928, the Tsar's sisters would be able to claim the money. In his recollection Gleb records an impassioned and improbably lucid speech from Anna. It was with speeches like these, however real, that he justified his lifelong commitment to her cause: 'Promise me that even if I should quarrel with you, you will not let them have it! Let it disappear, vanish, but promise me that my aunts will not profit by their treason.'

In early spring Princess Xenia at last returned from her sojourn in the West Indies and took Anna to her estate at Oyster Bay, Long Island. The Princess later recalled her first sight of the woman she believed was Anastasia in Miss Jennings's crowded salon. As soon as she saw the way Anna offered her hand to Gleb, she was convinced that she was the Grand Duchess. The movement, she enthused, was 'so unforced – in no way a theatrical gesture. With it she radiated a natural grandeur and I was impressed on the spot'.

The Princess's subsequent weeks with Anna only served to confirm her initial impression. At one point, one of the Grand Duchess Anastasia's cousins, Prince Dmitri (son of Anna's dreaded 'aunt' Xenia), came with an American friend to play tennis. The pair were on a vine-covered court next to Anna's room; the players could be heard but not seen. As Xenia recalled: 'Going to the claimant's room to say good morning, I found her sitting by the open window. On my entrance she turned her head away from me and refused to answer my greeting... "You lied to me, you promised not to bring them here... I know his voice, it's one of my cousins". Her voice was filled with emotion.' Another time Xenia's four-year-old daughter was wearing a brimless sailor's cap like those worn in the Russian Navy. Anna was apparently reduced to tears by the sight. As Xenia remembered: 'Through her sobs she begged me not to allow my daughter to wear such a cap because it reminded her of her brother.' Overall, said Xenia: 'She was herself at all times and never gave the slightest impression of acting a part... I am firmly convinced that the claimant is, in fact, Grand Duchess Anastasia of Russia.'

Anna was not so impressed by Xenia. She did not like the Princess's dark eyes. As she said to Gleb cryptically:

'Dark eyes are a screen which shields a person's thoughts and feelings. People with dark eyes are much more likely to be false than those with light eyes.'

Xenia presented her new guest with two parakeets that proved invaluable, not least for their contribution to the language question. Anna's enemies continued, of course, to make much of her apparent inability to speak Russian. From now on, the claim from her supporters was that she could be overheard cooing to her pets in Russian; the birds could not, of course, testify otherwise. At the Oyster Bay estate, Anna inhabited her own suite of rooms and enjoyed a choice of unlikely activities including tennis, riding and sailing.

Years later Anna gave characteristically sparse descriptions of the appearance of her host and hostess; she appeared to recall further, with disapproval, her host's colourful misdemeanours. 'The estate was Oyster Bay at the ocean where I was living. Xenia Leeds, nicely tall, well groomed, and... William Leeds, a tiny creature – like a little dwarf with brown eyes. And William Leeds went with this dancing girl (Adele Astaire, the sister of Fred) on a boat, they went on a boat and then the boat exploded. And the dancing girl was heavy injured... and he almost lost his eyesight. He had not only one dancing girl but all the secretaries... He was travelling with these secretaries and who knows what.'

Having settled Anna at Oyster Bay, Gleb began to feel his task was complete. To a certain extent, it was. He had established Anna with rich relations who were convinced that she was the Grand Duchess. It is impossible to know, whether it was in a spirit of forbearance or relief that he informed Princess Xenia he would only visit Oyster Bay by special invitation. There's every possibility that he was unsure what he felt himself.

In any case, his feelings were barely put to the test: within weeks he had received a phone call from Xenia inviting him to visit. She met Gleb in New York and they travelled out to the estate together. In the course of their first conversation, it became clear that Xenia still relished Anna's company: 'One story she told me about roaming in a forest with hungry wolves howling on all sides really made my hair stand on end.'

But it also became clear that she regarded Gleb as a sort of spectre in Anna's life, as ever-present as he was unwelcome. She had evidently agreed to the couple's meeting only under duress. As she said rather sourly: 'When it comes to such technical problems, about the only answer I can obtain from her is "Ask Botkin. He knows what to do". From the way Anastasia talks of you one would think that there is nothing in the world you do not know or could not do. You see it appears that you are still quite indispensable to us.'

Over the following months, however, Xenia succeeded in dissuading Anna of Gleb's indispensability. Gleb was informed that Anna was angry with him and was refusing to see him. The reason, he was told, was that she was upset because he had been writing about her in the newspapers. Gleb was not convinced by the reason; according to him, she had always known that he wrote for papers. The news that upset him more was that Xenia was not planning to take Anna to see the Grand

Duchess Anastasia's grandmother, the Dowager Empress. While believing that Anna was the Grand Duchess, Xenia preferred to keep her recognition unofficial. With official recognition would come endless complications, not least Anna's status as head of the family.

Gleb was unable to view the situation in any sort of calculated way. While it probably would have occurred to him that he would benefit from Anna being officially recognised, his primary motivation was a sense of justice. With his strong feeling for righting wrongs, he proved unable to resist demonising the Grand Duchess Anastasia's aunts, Olga and Xenia. In about a month's time they would be able, theoretically, to claim the Tsar's money from the Bank of England. Gleb's thought was that, once the aunts had claimed the money, they could never acknowledge Anna as Anastasia, even if they wanted to. He felt he had to act swiftly; he consulted a lawyer called Edward H. Fallows, the son, as he reported, of the late Bishop Samuel Fallows of the Reformed Episcopal Church.

Fallows wrote to the Bank of England and promptly received a reply which was seized upon by Gleb as an admission that the legacy existed: the bank advised that a court order be obtained to prevent the money being turned over to the aunts. At this point Gleb began to wonder how he could communicate with Anna and keep her abreast of the news. One of his friends volunteered to secure a yacht and approach the Leedses' estate from the sound. The idea would be to wait until Anna came out for a walk on the beach. It was agreed, however, that Anna might not respond well to being accosted by a stranger.

Gleb subsequently reported a weighty telephone conversation in which he declared his intention of pursuing Anna's case in court. One of Princess Xenia's friends had rung to tell him that the Princess was choosing not to pursue Anna's cause in order to save the reputations of various members of the Romanov family. The friend was full of what Gleb would have regarded as gratifying warnings: 'Do not forget two sons of Grand Duchess Xenia, Dmitri and Rostislav are in this country... I am utterly certain that, should you make one more move in defence of Anastasia, an attempt on your life will be made.' Gleb's reply was resonant: 'But my answer to all such princes and monarchists is to betake themselves to the devil. They shall not frighten me.' Unfortunately, shortly after the conversation, Gleb lost his intermediary; she was obliged to devote her time to her family after her daughter was knocked on the head by an aeroplane propeller.

Billy Leeds now issued a formal statement saying that he and his wife, Princess Xenia, were not willing to pursue the formal identification of Anna as Anastasia; he also said they were not interested in claiming her fortune. Gleb retorted with another statement saying Leeds had no right to waive Anna's rights. Gleb then wrote letters of protest to Princess Xenia and Anna; the letter to Anna was intercepted and returned to Gleb by the Princess. 'I received your letter,' it said, 'and having read the enclosed copy of the letter you wrote to the Grand Duchess, I feel that in her present weak and extremely nervous condition, I could not give your letter to Anastasia Nikolaievna'. Gleb's account of the exchange in his memoir includes a thunderous footnote: 'The original letter with seal unbroken and with proper cancellation by the Oyster Bay post office, intercepted by Princess Xenia, is in the possession of the author.'

However Princess Xenia did add that she would like to meet Gleb at Oyster Bay. On 22 July Gleb was duly conducted to the estate boat house. Presumably the curious venue was chosen in order to keep the meeting secret from Anna. The following stormy discussion between Gleb and the Leedses is recorded in Gleb's memoir, but appears, once again almost exactly, in *The Baron's Fancy*.

As before, the fictional version is more extreme; once again, it is hard to know whether the novel is closer to the truth. In the fiction, Gleb presents an unflattering description of Billy Leeds – or Jimmy Brooks – a 'chubby little fellow with broad hips, short legs, yellow hair parted in the middle and polished like a shoe and a round face with a perennial, somewhat foolish smile... he tried to add to his age by carrying always in the corner of his mouth an enormous pipe. He wore a khaki coat with a girdle, white trousers with black stripes, green socks and white shoes with brown leather bands. Gleb adds in distaste, 'He looked like the son of a wealthy Moscow merchant.'

In his memoir he reported that both the Leedses were initially friendly, though Princess Xenia was ill at ease. But Billy Leeds shortly began hostilities. Denouncing Gleb's reply in the press as 'not so hot', Leeds insisted that he had never meant to waive Anna's rights to her legacy. Xenia then accused Gleb of preventing Anna's aunts from claiming the Tsar's legacy. Gleb received the accusation with glee. He had not known, until that moment, that his intervention with the Bank of England had had any effect.

Xenia now raised the spectre – as terrible as it was unexpected – of Anna as Tsarina. While Anna and Gleb had certainly weighed up the pros and cons of sovereignty, there is no evidence that either of them saw her coronation as a serious possibility. Xenia was jumping several guns as she lambasted Gleb for failing to consider whether Anna would make a suitable Tsarina. She confounded him by claiming that it was not Anna's identity that worried the Romanovs, but her obvious unsuitability. '...Do you care nothing about the welfare of the Russian people?' Xenia raged. 'Do you know that she threatens to hang all her relatives on lamp-posts for what she calls their treason the moment she becomes Empress?... Anastasia's regime would be worse that anything they've had in Russia since the Revolution... She says herself that Ivan the Terrible and Peter the Great are her ideal rulers.' She accused Gleb of harbouring plans to put Anna on the throne simply in order to gain power himself.

The fictional Princess Irina, during a similar tirade in *The Baron's Fancy*, goes a step further with her accusations: 'You'll make Alexandra murder all of us, and then you'll murder her!'

Meanwhile Billy Leeds, accustomed to his wife's temper,

carried on sipping what Gleb referred to as 'liquid refreshment', finally rousing himself to remind Xenia that the purpose of their meeting was to discuss an offer made by Anna's purported aunts. Wresting herself from her visions, 'like a woman emerging from a trance', Xenia now revealed that the aunts wanted to come to an arrangement regarding Anna's money. If Gleb lifted the block preventing them inheriting the money, they were willing to install Anna in some quiet retreat in Europe. Gleb, they added, would also be taken care of. The *chevalier sans reproche* was insulted. 'How generous! They will inherit Anastasia's money and give her "something"... As for the offer made to me personally, I refuse even to discuss it. And I repeat that, even if I were the kind of crook capable of accepting such an offer, it would not change the situation in any way. The money is securely tied up and will remain tied up until released through a litigation.'

Billy Leeds and the fictitious Jimmy Brooks both try to persuade, respectively, Gleb and Max to back down from opposing the whole of the Imperial Family. In both accounts, King George V is presented as supporting the aunts' claims for the Tsar's legacy. As Jimmy Brooks puts it in *The Baron's Fancy*, the King is 'sick and tired of feeding all those Russian bums'.

After delivering coarser insults than they intended, Leeds and his fictitious counterpart slink out of the room. Xenia and her *alter ego*, Irina, both start crying and also walk out. Leeds eventually returns, contrite and ready to engage his bemused guest in sympathetic conversation. Jimmy Brooks also returns but he is, as ever, less chary about bemoaning his lot: 'I have to stay with this crazy woman.' Gleb reported that, just months later, Xenia denied that the aunts had ever told her that they believed Anna was the real Grand Duchess. Furthermore, she denied that she had ever believed in the existence of any fortune in the Bank of England.

There followed a short hiatus. Gleb felt that Anna's legacy was secure and that she was safe with Princess Xenia. Her supporters could be relied upon to provide funds for a court case sometime in the future. It was simply a case of awaiting the return from abroad of the unlikely principal pair – Miss Jennings and Rachmaninov.

But the respite was brought to a sudden end with a phone call from Xenia. Anna, she said, was demanding to see Gleb. At her wits' end, she had reluctantly agreed to a meeting. As soon as the pair were reunited, they convinced themselves that Xenia had misled each into regarding the other as an enemy. Now gleefully united against Xenia, they forged a more intense bond then ever. Gleb had no difficulty convincing Anna that a court case would be a good idea; he had more difficulty convincing her that the case could not be pursued immediately.

It is not known exactly what Gleb's intentions were with the airing of these plans for a court case but, within days, Anna announced that she could no longer live with Xenia. Xenia, now equally ruffled, turned on Gleb, insisting he ask Anna to give up her plans. Gleb, cornered into a false position, agreed to put Xenia's request to Anna. Perhaps in an effort to establish control, he promised Xenia that, if Anna refused to give up the plans, he would come and take her away within 48 hours.

Gleb's panic when he heard that she had, predictably, refused, can easily be imagined. He now found himself in sole charge of the woman he believed to be the Grand Duchess Anastasia and faced with the gargantuan task of finding her a suitable new home. His heart must have sunk as options dwindled to a tiny New York attic baking in the August heat.

***

Anna's sojourn at Oyster Bay, which had begun with so much hope, came to an unsettling end. As Gleb carried the parakeets to the car, Billy Leeds scuttled away across the lawn, the servants disappeared and Xenia retired, crying, to her bedroom. Eighteen months after Anna left Oyster Bay, Billy and Princess Xenia divorced; the local newspaper laid the blame for the break-up of 'the tin-plate Croesus' and his 'Russian princess bride' firmly at Anna's door.

Fallows, who had agreed to pick Anna up in his car, was shaken and Gleb close to tears. However Anna was never a martyr to atmosphere; it was soon apparent that her only concern was that Fallows should drive faster. Probably relieved to find some outlet for his tension, Fallows readily agreed. Gleb, in his turn, was immediately cheered; as far as he was concerned, Anna had betrayed her identity as

Anastasia once again. She was, 'like her father, the late Emperor, particularly fond of speeding'.

Gleb recalled that his father had always been mortified by the Tsar's inclination to abuse his power by speeding through the streets of St Petersburg. As the Tsar's car sped towards them, the police would apparently reach for their notebooks. But, upon spotting the crown emblem, they would hide them away and salute.

Happily for Fallows, the American police motor-cyclist who now flagged his car down was equally obliging. Gleb did not know what Fallows said by way of excuse, but the policeman was polite and swiftly waved the car on.

Such were the straits of the trio that, upon arrival at the dusty apartment, they found they had no money for food. But Gleb's account of the night was characteristically buoyant: 'Luckily she was satisfied with a vegetarian diet... I had just enough money... to buy her some lettuce and a tomato for supper.'

In the end Anna was obliged to spend only two days in the apartment. But it was during this short period that she decided to appoint Fallows her lawyer; a contract was duly drawn up. If Anna was proven to be the Grand Duchess, Fallows stood to gain a quarter of all monies received under 400,000 dollars, then ten per cent of all the rest. At the time it was not known exactly how much Romanov money still existed outside Russia. But in 1929 the *New York Times* reckoned it amounted to 1000 million dollars.

Fallows later claimed that the Provisional Leader, Alexander

Kerensky, had told the White investigator, Sokolov, that there was a fourteen million-dollar fortune in the Bank of England. He also wrote lyrically of a 'valuable hunting lodge' in England to which Anna was entitled. However the lawyer never seemed overly interested in his own financial gain. The passionate statement he issued concerning his motivation rings true: 'Speaking now not as a lawyer but as a man, I regard the claim of Grand Duchess Anastasia not as a case but as a cause. I appeal to all who love truth and justice and mercy not to prejudge this young woman, broken in body by the frightful suffering she has endured, but clear in mind, courageous in spirit and resolute in purpose to win her heroic fight for recognition as the youngest daughter of the late Emperor Nicholas II of Russia.'

Fallows drew up an agreement which Gleb passed on to Billy Leeds; Leeds, in turn, passed it on to his own lawyer. Why Gleb chose to show the agreement to Leeds is unclear; perhaps he felt it was a way of showing Leeds that he still trusted him and wished to keep him on side. At the signing of the agreement, Anna alarmed Gleb by refusing to put an 'a' on the end of her name. The lawyers exchanged glances: it seemed that the 'Grand Duchess' had forgotten how to write her own name. The slip turned out to be grist to Gleb's mill; he later reported triumphantly that, at the Russian Court, all the Grand Duchesses had signed their names in French. This, in Anastasia's case, was 'Anastasie'.

Anna also asked Fallows to draw up a will. She clearly relished dividing up what was referred to as her potential estate. She stipulated that her patron, Prince Waldemar, be reimbursed for outgoings incurred on her account. Most of the estate, however, she wished to bequeath to the Botkin children in memory of Gleb. Rising to the occasion, Gleb directed that any money he might receive from her be given to the Red Cross in her memory.

Fallows advised Anna, instead of making a will, to assign her property rights to a company to be called Grandanor: Grand Duchess Anastasia of Russia. Fallows would be president of the corporate board and Gleb a director. At this stage she seems to have switched loyalties, now leaving any Grandanor spoils to her enigmatic brother-in-law, Serge Tschaikovsky, and her still more mysterious son. Miss Jennings was among several rich people subsequently invited to invest in Grandanor. She declined, preferring to put her money towards a mercenary force which she hoped would invade Russia and overthrow the Bolsheviks.

Two of Gleb's friends now offered to rent two rooms for Anna in the Garden City Hotel, in Garden City, on Long Island. She would remain for six months in the town of Garden City, latterly in a cottage rented for her by Rachmaninov. She registered as Gleb's sister under the name of Mrs Eugene Anderson; the name Eugene was chosen in memory of Gleb's father. From now on she would be known as Anna Anderson.

During this period Anna was reported in the *New York Evening Post* as having disappeared. Whether Gleb maintained the secrecy to protect Anna or himself is hard to know. Did he find it a burden, or did it lend his project charm? What is known is that he relished her proximity. His house at Hempstead was nearby and he was able to visit her on an almost daily basis. They both derived enjoyment from the idea that, posing as brother and sister, they had no choice but to *tutoyer* each other when they spoke in German.

In October 1928 the Tsar's mother, the Empress Dowager, died. In her lifetime, the Dowager had forbidden the release of any public statement regarding Anna. Now Anna's old adversary and 'aunt', Grand Duchess Xenia, issued a statement signed by eleven Romanovs declaring that she was 'firmly convinced that the woman bearing the name of Mme Tschaikovsky, living at the present time in the United States, is certainly not the Grand Duchess Anastasia Nikolaievna'.

Gleb wanted to ignore the statement, but changed his mind after being told that his failure to act would result in Anna's deportation. This, he insisted, he heard from a friend, 'very close to some of the highest officials in Washington'.

He decided to write a letter to Grand Duchess Xenia and send a copy to *Associated Press*. The letter pulled no punches: 'It makes a gruesome impression that even at your mother's deathbed your foremost worry must have been the desire to defraud your niece... You know very well that Grand Duchess Anastasia Nikolaievna (Anna) remembers the slightest details of her childhood, that she possesses all her physical signs including birthmarks, that her handwriting is at present the same as it had been in her youth, that in appearance she has changed so little that it is difficult to tell some of her pre-Revolutionary photographs from new ones... Before the wrong which Your Imperial Highness is committing pales even the gruesome murder of the Emperor, his family and my father by the Bolsheviks. It is easier to understand a crime committed by a gang of crazed and drunken savages than the calm, systematic, endless persecution of one of your own family... whose only fault is that, being the rightful heir of the late Emperor, she stands in the way of her greedy and unscrupulous relatives.' The letter ended with Gleb's stylish signature, a full two inches high.

The letter served its purpose. The authorities granted several extensions to Anna's permit to remain in the United States. But Gleb found himself ostracised by almost all his friends in America and Europe; Rachmaninov was one of the few who stood by him. Indeed the composer made a point, shortly afterwards, of confronting the Grand Duchess Xenia in England; he wanted to quiz her directly about Anna. Gleb later reported the conversation verbatim, as he heard it from Rachmaninov. 'I told Xenia that the friends of Mrs Tschaikovsky (Anna) are basing their belief in her identity as Anastasia on a tremendous quantity of very weighty evidence. Having heard only one side, I now wanted to learn what the other side had to say about the matter. But the only comment I was able to obtain from Xenia was: "I simply know that she cannot be Anastasia."' Rachmaninov apparently persisted: '"Can't you give me at least one single concrete reason for your assertion that she is not Anastasia?" I said. But Xenia kept staring past me at the wall and repeating like a wound-up mechanism: "I simply know that she is not Anastasia."' The only explanation Rachmaninov could give for this denial was that she was convinced that Anna was Anastasia. 'I left Xenia with the impression that she is just as convinced of the fact as you yourself are'.

Rachmaninov instructed his secretary to pay all of Anna's immediate expenses; Gleb also managed to secure a large advance from a publishing company. The idea he proposed was that Anna would dictate her memoirs to him. He expressed his amazement at discovering that she was incapable of imbuing anything she said with wit or even interest. Whether he really was amazed or was simply being gallant is hard to gauge. 'Anastasia, who was one of the wittiest and most brilliant conversationalists I had every met, proved also the dullest and most injudicious of authors. Not only the so-called "undressing in public", but any kind of informality in print, appeared abhorrent to her. In consequence her dictations were void of any sentiment, indeed, of any life.' Anna apparently dictated, at a slow pace, some 30,000 words of her memories. She insisted that these be written verbatim. Alas, they were unpublishable and read, according to Gleb, like so many dry paragraphs from a court calendar.

Fortunately, the publishers took a charitable view, waiving the return of their advance. Meanwhile Miss Jennings returned from abroad in late fall and undertook to pay Anna's expenses. Though Miss Jennings's offer brought immediate relief, Gleb still faced the task of raising a lump sum for litigation. His current plan was to bring suits not only against the Bank of

England but also the Mendelssohn Bank in Berlin, where the Tsar had deposited money. In the case of the Mendelssohn Bank, there was no doubt about the money's existence.

During these days in Garden City, Gleb got to know Anna better. His children could hardly avoid being aware of his preoccupation. His daughter, Marina Schweitzer, later recalled hearing him discussing Anna's story for the first time. 'He had lost his father because of the Revolution, and all he was ever interested in was seeing Anastasia returned to her family, recognised by them. The actions of the surviving Romanovs were deplorable to Father, and he had already become thoroughly disgusted with Royal and Imperial persons.'

Any time Gleb was inclined to be exasperated by Anna, she would remind him, apparently inadvertently, of her terrible past. In her room at the hotel she had two beds. During the day she always lay in one by the wall. But when Gleb suggested the second bed be removed, she revealed that she always spent the night on the one in the centre. 'I prefer to lie by the wall, and when you or somebody else is with me, am not afraid to do so. But when alone I am afraid, for should somebody come to kill me I should be trapped.'

Gleb described one dramatic evening which began with the pair enjoying a gentle discussion about embroidery. Anna's face suddenly crumpled into an expression of misery as she revealed that she had started a piece of embroidery on the fateful night in Ekaterinburg. She then gasped in disbelief when Gleb said that he already knew about the embroidery: he had read about it in the White investigator Sokolov's report. She insisted she had no idea that any such report existed; up until then she had thought no-one except her knew what had happened.

Exhausted by her discoveries, she lay down in bed and covered herself up to her chin, as was her wont, in blankets. Gleb describes himself picturesquely, smoking a cigarette in silence. She then began a rare account of the events of that night, the story her supporters were aching to hear: 'We were awakened in the night... They told us that there were disturbances in town, that we had to go down to the basement... We believed them. We never suspected what was to happen... We dressed in haste and went downstairs. Suddenly Yurovsky and several of his men ran into the room. Yurovsky shouted something and began to shoot... He shot at my father... shot him through the head... I saw Father fall dead... I was hiding behind Olga. Then I heard Olga scream... I can still hear that scream... And then I remember nothing more...'

In less charged moments, the pair enjoyed theological discussions during which Gleb discussed his studies and subsequent disappointment in the tenets and practices of the Orthodox Church. She insisted, intriguingly, that the worst day of her life was the day she lost her faith. 'And the sudden void which opened before me was more dreadful than anything I had experienced before or since. Nothing can be worse than to lose the faith of one's childhood.' Gleb was impressed. 'Sincerely religious people... will perceive the touch of true greatness in that woman to whom the worst earthly trials and tragedies appear less important than the spiritual suffering of discarding beliefs dear and comforting but untenable to her as abstract truth.'

However, most importantly, they discovered the shared passion that would divert them so pleasurably into old age: obscure facts connected with royalty. The pieces of information they now bandied between them included the regulations pertaining to the Duke of Hanover's porcelain collection and the definitive explanation of the death of the Tsarevich Alexis in 1718. She insisted she had read in secret archives that Alexis had been decapitated on the orders of Peter the Great. Apparently Gleb later found confirmation of the story in a memoir of one of Peter the Great's nearest lieutenants.

Anna also claimed that Catherine the Great was the daughter not of an obscure Prince of Anhalt-Zerbst but of Frederick the Great. Frederick, she claimed, had impregnated Catherine's mother when she was aged just sixteen. This Gleb also confirmed. Emperor Paul, she insisted, was the son of a Saltykov. 'The present Romanovs, yourself included, being the descendants of Catherine of Anhalt-Zerbst and Saltykov, have not a drop of the Romanov blood in your veins,' Gleb observed at the time. He recalled Anna's delighted response. '"That's right", she said. And she began to laugh like a naughty child, apparently vastly amused by the consideration that she was a Romanov without having a drop of Romanov blood in her veins.'

When pompous visitors arrived, Anna would make grimaces behind them, or issue insults in German. Gleb was, as usual, indulgent. 'It was however a form of cruelty I forgave her only too gladly which, in fact, I enjoyed immensely. For it was when in such a mood that Grand Duchess Anastasia would become wholly the adorable naughty princess, the beloved 'little one' of the happy days of our childhood.' She particularly enjoyed shuffling up and down the carpet then pressing her fingers on the back of Gleb's neck, giving him an electric shock.

Gleb would leave Russian books with her; these he believed she read on her own. When he heard her speak, he was convinced she retained the unusual accent she had as a child. Anna's accent was actually, of course, predominantly German.

But while Gleb was relishing the increasing security of his conviction, Anna preferred to harp on about the hopelessness of her situation. Her complaints had a sour edge. On one occasion, the couple were guessing the origins of pieces of music on the radio. Gleb mistakenly identified a Finnish song as Spanish. Anna immediately insisted that, if he could not tell Finnish from Spanish, he would never convince Gilliard he had been born in Finland: Finland was indeed Gleb's birthplace.

On another occasion he failed to recognise a knife which had belonged to his father. Anna had been given it by Gleb's sister, Tatiana. She was delighted: 'I do hope, for your sake, that you will never have to establish your identity on the basis of your childhood recollections.'

Miss Jennings now began making strong overtures towards her protégée. She told Gleb that she loved Anna as if she were her own daughter. She was prepared to offer both of her sumptuous homes – her New York apartment and her estate in Connecticut – as lifelong refuges. Gleb had misgivings about Miss Jennings and her offers. Whether he really viewed the millionairess with suspicion or simply dreaded forgoing his central role, cannot be known. What is clear is that, with few prospects of his own, he felt obliged to press Miss Jennings's suit with Anna. She greeted the proposals with fury, accusing Gleb of simply wanting to be rid of her. Convinced his interest in her was waning, she became increasingly paranoid and jealous, begrudging any time he spent away from her.

In his memoir he recalled Anna launching a curious offensive, declaring grandly that she mistrusted him because of his devotion to her. 'Had I suddenly become the Empress of Russia I could not find a better prime minister than you. And yet people of your type have always been regarded by autocrats as most dangerous... A man who serves you, not in order to acquire either wealth or glory or any other personal advantage, but purely out of personal devotion to you is never completely in your power. He can neither be scared nor bribed into doing things he does not feel like doing. Besides, devotion is a matter of moods.' Gleb was so worn out after the ensuing exchange that he succumbed to a serious bout of influenza.

In *The Baron's Fancy* Gleb depicts Alexandra berating Max with the same dispiriting diatribe. Max also succumbs to influenza and Gleb gives a gothic description of the delusions his hero suffers during the fever that follows. Max dreams that Alexandra is the Empress besieged by angry mobs; he beseeches her to get rid of Rasputin. Meanwhile Alexandra can only repeat that Max has been five minutes late for his appointment. Max finds he dislikes the Romanovs more than the mob: 'What he began to hate were these cold, obstinate faces, the eyes of glass, the Emperor, the Empress, the Grand Dukes and Grand Duchesses... they all had her stern eyes, her red spots, her sulking brow.'

In his memoir Gleb reported baldly that he was laid low with a fever just before Christmas 1928. Anna refused to believe Gleb was ill, denouncing his illness as what she called a 'purely diplomatic' ruse. She never saw why anyone else should indulge in the prolonged periods in bed she herself so enjoyed. In January, Gleb saw Anna for the last time before she left Garden City for New York. She had decided to take his advice and live with Miss Jennings; he offered no further detail. The pair would not meet again for nine years.

In *The Baron's Fancy* Gleb describes in grim detail a final, bitter farewell between Max and Alexandra. Max is seeing Alexandra for the first time since he became ill; he has not been forgiven for his absence. He combats Alexandra's coldness towards him with a wry inquiry: 'I hope my illness hasn't affected your affairs...'.

'Oh no,' she replies, '...my affairs can wait when the Baron chooses to get sick.' Alexandra now insists that Max has compromised her by visiting her every day and yet not marrying her. She threatens to ruin Max, telling everybody he has made her his mistress. Again, it seems likely that this thorny conversation was based on reality.

There follows a tussle, with Alexandra trying to prevent Max from leaving without her permission. At this point Max manages, rather improbably, to stall the argument with a manly gesture: 'Taking her by the shoulders (he) kissed her gently on the mouth. She threw her arms around his neck and began to to kiss him passionately. Then Max kissed her hand, stroked tenderly her hair, and said, "Goodbye".' There follows an altercation as Max finally insists on leaving without permission. She follows him shouting: 'It will have the gravest consequences for you!'

If these were indeed Anna's parting words to Gleb, the gravest consequences were long appearing. Gleb's first duty for Anna, following their parting, was simply to carry on a correspondence with a woman claiming to be a friend of Harriet, a Mrs Asta Noeggerath. The recurring theme of Mrs Noeggerath's letters was Fallows's professional shortcomings. In March 1930, Gleb wrote to reassure the lawyer that he was entirely indifferent to Mrs Noeggerath's views; he disapproved of the way in which she had tried to undermine the lawyer: 'This she tried to achieve in a very subtle manner, under the disguise of friendly and witty jokes, all of which, however, if believed, could cause one impression only, namely that you were not seriously attending to the affairs of the Grand Duchess.' Gleb set little store by his correspondent's boast that she had access to the Grand Duke of Hesse, even less by her assurance that she could produce Anna's long-dead husband, Alexander Tschaikovsky.

Gleb now wrote a convincingly sober piece for the *North American Review* in which he evoked Anna's difficult temperament. 'Her personality hasn't changed in the least. She can still be witty and humorous, kind and adorable but she can also be an *enfant terrible*, and what seemed just naughtiness in childhood can be very trying in a grown-up person.'

But his claim that he was no longer involved in her cause was premature and may have betrayed a lack of self-knowledge. 'I can speak with freedom now, because I have officially and actually withdrawn from the case. I have not seen the Grand Duchess for about a year and do not propose to see her. I feel no particular interest in the eventual outcome of her case,' he wrote.

***

Following the couple's farewell in January, Anna probably spared little thought for Gleb. She was soon busy enjoying the luxuries, once again, of Miss Jennings's apartment and the Jenningses' family estate in Connecticut: 'Sunnie Holme'. Miss Jennings showered her guest with gifts and improbably stylish clothes. Anna was expected to appear at an unending series of parties and impart, as the *Evening Journal* put it, 'a highly spiced flavour to the fashionable chatter'. Not everybody was impressed. A woman in Connecticut reported: 'She had thick ankles and wrists and looked anything but patrician.'

Rumours abounded that Miss Jennings would adopt Anna and leave her the family fortune. Subsequent rumours spread that Anna was engaged to various businessmen or, as one supporter described them, 'upper-crust party-goers'. Her rising status generated mildly critical articles in which it was claimed that she was giving herself airs; her denials were undermined by the lofty tone in which they were delivered. She declared herself outraged by reports that everyone had to kneel and kiss her hand, and further that she would not dance with anyone but the Prince of Woho.

Her public profile had been further raised by the appearance of a silent film based on her story called, obscurely, *Clothes Make the Woman*. Starring Eve Southern and Walter Pidgeon, it was produced in Hollywood in 1928 without Anna's consent and without any payment.

During the summer of 1929, Anna agreed, once again, to dictate her memoirs. Miss Jennings's brother, Oliver, assured her she would make millions. Sadly her second foray into the world of letters proved no more successful than the first. After two months of daily interviews in Fallows's office, her recollections were denounced by the lawyers as useless ramblings. Her delivery had deteriorated; such detail as she was prepared to give was now disorderly as well as dry.

However Anna had no difficulty expressing her rage about the subsequent failure of the project. 'Now no report has come to me in regard to this book,' she ranted. 'This was taken in shorthand and not a single word has come back to me for me to look over and read. I wanted this book to be finished and sold and the money coming from it used in these various expenses... I am very tired of this treatment.'

In the general malaise, Fallows began to come under fire. In his capacity as her lawyer, he was obliged to spend long periods of time abroad and incommunicado. Anna, who used lawyers as others use therapists, found his unavailability irksome and even offensive. She refused to accept that he was working on her case, preferring to believe he was squandering Miss Jennings's money on a mistress.

Eventually, exhausted by the complaints, Miss Jennings found her another lawyer, Wilton Lloyd-Smith. He unfortunately antagonised Anna at their first introduction by greeting her sitting cross-legged on the floor of the Jenningses' salon. '...In every country a man with the pretensions of Mr Lloyd-Smith rises when a woman enters the room,' she commented crisply. 'If he does not, there may be several reasons for it. He may be drunk, he may wish to be rude.'

Fallows returned to New York at the beginning of March 1930, after a year's absence. He had worked hard on the case, not least attending what Anna described as a seance with Harriet and Dr Rudnev. Fallows set enough store by seances to keep some fifteen pages of transcript from an earlier session, at the top of which was written: 'Berlin, July 13 1927... I beg to forward a copy of protocol number 3 of the "Clairvoyante" from B. Osten-Sacken,' (presumably the same Osten-Sacken who had accompanied Anna and Harriet on their ill-fated holiday). Throughout this seance, the medium apparently kept a parcel lying beside her containing a cross belonging to Anna. To at least two of the questions – 'Is the person to whom it belongs Anastasia Romanov?' and 'Where is the father of the child?' – the unhelpful spirit simply replied: 'You are a fool.'

The lawyer had located a Lieutenant Ivan Arapov who said he had met the Grand Duchess Anastasia in 1915. He cabled for details and Anna's response was immediate: 'Does Arapov limp one leg short?' Fallows thought she might have made a mistake. She claimed at one stage that the Grand Duchess Anastasia's former English tutor, Sydney Gibbes, also had a limp, a claim he stoutly denied. The lawyer was relieved to discover that Arapov's leg had, indeed, been injured in the war.

For a brief period Anna's confidence in the redoubtable Fallows was restored. She was delighted to hear his prediction that she could expect legal rehabilitation within the year. His further announcement, that he must now return to Europe was greeted, however, with less delight. In Fallows's renewed absence, Anna vented her frustration upon the unfortunate Lloyd-Smith, whom she fired on a regular basis. She failed to appreciate Lloyd-Smith's thrice daily visits, or his insistence that she visit the dentist. She summed up this period of her life dramatically: 'What I went though at that time in Miss Jennings's house cannot be expressed in words.'

What Miss Jennings herself went through should not be underestimated. The elderly lady found her protégée increasingly unmanageable. She discovered, with a sinking heart, that Anna had developed a passion for expensive underwear and wrote in anguish to Lloyd-Smith: 'She ordered a wrap that will cost $450... I had no sort of an idea that she would go to Altman's and buy so expensively in the lingerie department.'

Events took a further downturn with the arrival on the scene of a woman claiming to be an English Countess, Lady Huntingdon. The Countess assured Anna that she owned several estates in England and was on intimate terms with the Queen. Lady Huntingdon also went under the lesser name of Jill Cossley-Batt; as such she claimed to have published a book called *The Last of the California Rangers.* She was now working on *The Adolescent Life of Christ.* The only information Lloyd-Smith was able to obtain about Miss Cossley-Batt was that she had had some training as a chemist.

Miss Cossley-Batt insisted that she had known the Grand Duchess Anastasia before the Revolution; they had met at the opera in St Petersburg. It is not known whether Anna deliberated before responding to this claim, but in the end she plumped for the right answer: she had no recollection of ever seeing the Countess. The Countess was unruffled; when she attended operas, she said, she always wore glasses.

Anna later claimed that her encyclopaedic knowledge of genealogy set her in good stead when the Countess then declared herself the daughter of Alexander of Battenberg. Anna knew that Alexander had died young and childless.

Did Anna realise, at that point, that she was getting a taste of her own medicine? Years later, she made much of her acuity in recognising Miss Cossley-Batt as a fraud. But her conduct at the time gives every impression that, initially at least, she took the Countess at her word. The pair forged endless plans for Anna's rehabilitation in England, meeting at Miss Jennings's flat two or three times a day over a two-month period.

Miss Cossley-Batt and her 'manager', Irvine Baird, a self-proclaimed Duke's son, made themselves at home, rifling through Miss Jennings's correspondence and raiding the drinks cabinet. Miss Jennings's cables and letters begging Anna to join her at 'Sunnie Holme' were, needless to say, not looked well upon by her new friends. Indeed Miss Cossley-Batt managed to convince Anna that Miss Jennings should now be viewed as an enemy. She told Anna that if she went to 'Sunnie Holme' she would be committed for life to an asylum.

In May 1930, at the instigation of her new 'aristocratic' friends, Anna dictated a letter addressed to Fallows in which she declared roundly that he had made no progress and was being fired. She demanded the return of all her papers: 'I have made other arrangements regarding my life story with Mr Irvine Baird and Jill Cossley-Batt (Huntingdon) who have collaborated with me and who have now in their possession all photographs and material together with a contract for the publication of said life story.' She complained bitterly about an agreement she believed Fallows had forced her to sign. 'Regarding the second agreement which you cleverly arranged and hurriedly had me append my signature to without having time to analyse same, seems to me a gross injustice and apparently drawn up with selfish intent and purpose, in fact very unfair and illegal... I wish to express emphatically my indignation, after perusing its contents, and had I not been in a sick bed at the time, I never would have agreed to signing such an instrument.'

Alarmed by these new developments, Lloyd-Smith made further attempts to check up on Miss Cossley-Batt. Recalling that she had claimed to be a reporter from *The Times* in London, he contacted the newspaper's New York correspondent. The reply ran as follows: 'Dear Mr Lloyd-Smith, Miss Jill L. Cossley-Batt about whom you inquire in your letter of June 17th has no connection whatever with *The Times* (London). If she represents herself as being a member of *The Times* staff – as I have heard from several persons she has done – it is quite falsely. As for her claim to the title of Dowager Countess of Huntingdon, I know nothing of that except what you have told me, but I am informed that there has been no such person since the early 80s (1880s). When she was in California about five years ago she misrepresented herself as being a member of *The Times* staff and, at that time, I was told she called herself 'Lady Lillian Huntingdon-Mountbatten'. The title is purely fictitious.

'My attention was first called to Miss Cossley-Batt's misrepresentations in July 1925 when the editor of the newspaper called the *Progress* in Sonoma, California wrote to the Manager of *The Times* in London inquiring into her pretensions. The manager cabled to him the following message: MISS COSSLEY-BATT NO CONNEXION WHATEVER WITH LONDON TIMES. SHE ONLY CONTRIBUTED FEW ARTICLES TO TRADE SUPPLE-MENT YEARS AGO. IF ACTION POSSIBLE WILL

SUPPORT AND SHARE EXPENSES AS HAVE HAD
SEVERAL PREVIOUS COMPLAINTS.'

Perhaps it was as well for all concerned that Cossley-Batt
and Baird ended up disappearing as mysteriously as they had
appeared. But their legacy remained as Anna continued to take
up cudgels against Miss Jennings. At one point she set about
making highly slanderous speeches on the main floor of
Altman's department store. Anna later recounted: 'I said I
knew she was a gossip and that she drank but I had not known
she was a crook... I said I would not rest until I saw them all
in jail.'

Lloyd-Smith now wrote to Miss Jennings at 'Sunnie
Holme' with alarming descriptions of Anna's increasing paranoia. He said she had begun throwing heavy objects out of
windows to attract the attention of the police. 'She went into
terrific tempers, attacked people who were waiting on her, with
sticks or whatever she could find... She ran about on the roof
without anything on, attracting an enormous amount of
attention. Altogether the situation was a holy mess.'

The crisis came one evening when Anna, in another fit of
rage about Miss Cossley-Batt, stepped on and killed one of
her own parrots. 'She began screaming and shouting and
demanding another bird. She was told that no bird could be
got at that time of night. She did not believe it... She spent the
entire night screaming and did not sleep.'

Miss Jennings wrote Anna what was, for her, a severe letter
of reproof; by this time, according to Charles Foley, Anna had
spent 35,000 dollars of her hostess's money. The letter con-

cluded with her insistence that Anna move to what she referred to as a home, probably some kind of sanatorium. 'I know of your attitude toward those who have helped you in the past. You have now assumed a similar attitude toward me. I find the situation intolerable when a guest in my own house feels about me as you now feel... I am sure, therefore, that you must realise the necessity for leaving my house and, in view of your personal attitude toward me, I must insist that you go as soon as you can arrange your clothes and baggage.'

Lloyd-Smith decided to begin procedures to have Anna formally committed. He told Anna's former patron, Princess Xenia, that he was having her examined by three doctors before the commital. Princess Xenia heartily agreed with all Lloyd-Smith's proposals. Gleb would have been less agreeable, but he was now distanced from events. The tenor of his reply to one of Lloyd-Smith's earlier inquiries about Anna's sanity betrayed a characteristic combination of levity and pedantry. 'I answered that in the colloquial use of the word (crazy) one can say that the Grand Duchess is "a crazy person" and does crazy things, but that she certainly was in no way insane in the medical sense.'

In the end it was Miss Jennings's second brother, Walter, who filed the formal application with Judge Peter Schmuck of the Supreme Court of New York. '...Miss Anderson, without any near relatives in this country, has been the guest of, and supported by, my sister for eighteen months. She believes attempts are being made to poison her, refuses medical assistance, spends most of her time confined to her bedroom, talking to two birds.' He added that later, having killed one of her birds, she refused to allow it to be removed. 'She threatened to shoot the last representative whom my sister sent.'

On 24 July 1930, a nurse and two orderlies broke down Anna's door and carried her away to the 450 dollars-a-week Four Winds sanatorium in Katonah in Westchester County. Though Anna later complained about the sanatorium, she enjoyed four rooms, a personal attendant, use of the tennis court, shopping trips to town and occasional nights out at the opera – all at the expense of the unfortunate Miss Jennings.

CHAPTER FIVE

Anna returns to Germany

A year later Anna returned to Germany. Gleb, who was not kept abreast of her movements, only found out some time later. In September 1931 he wrote a bitter letter to one of Anna's few remaining American supporters, a friend of Miss Jennings called Adeline Moffatt. He revealed that, though he knew Anna was in Bavaria, he had no idea of her address. He was clearly not impressed by Lloyd-Smith's role in her departure. 'The whole thing has been organised by our charming Mr Lloyd-Smith,' he huffed, before digressing: 'Did you see in the papers that his brother has thrown himself out of a window a few days ago?'

In his letter Gleb made it clear that his anger with Lloyd-Smith was matched by his anger with 'the even more charming Xenia Leeds'. Gleb wrote that, though it had been

Lloyd-Smith's decision to send Anna back to Germany, the lawyer had received Xenia's full support. 'Mrs Leeds answered that she had no objections, for she is too poor to contribute towards Anastasia's support, and therefore has nothing to say. Naturally poor little Xenia is very poor,' Gleb raged. 'Her income is variously estimated as being between $30,000 and $60,000 a year so the poor girl is well-nigh starving.' His one consolation, he added, was that Anna would be safer in Bavaria than in Prussia or any state where she could be caught by her uncle, Grand Duke Ernest of Hesse. Meanwhile he denounced the result of Anna's stay in America as 'a sorry mess'.

Gleb in the 1930s

According to Gleb, the Jenningses had undertaken to pay for Anna to stay in a German sanatorium for several years. Actually they had agreed to pay for only six months, which would cost the same as two weeks at Four Winds. The arrangements for Anna's journey were made by Charles Foley, who visited the German consul in New York.

It seems that various cloak and dagger procedures had to be gone through in order to procure Anna's passport. Legend has it that Foley was accompanied by a dark blonde woman pretending to be Anna Anderson. In any case, Foley and the mystery woman succeeded in acquiring a German passport stating that the bearer was born in Berlin; it was signed with a large cross.

Anna was taken from the sanatorium and driven off to New York harbour where she boarded the *Deutschland*, bound for Germany. The nurse who met Anna at Cuxhaven was amazed to discover that the new patient had no medical records, letters, or documents of transferral. Anna had travelled with a Finnish nurse who disappeared from the sanatorium before dawn the following day. During the sea voyage, the nurse had kept her charge locked in the cabin and taken away the key to her trunk. Anna was livid: 'I had no toothbrush, no soap, no comb, no face-cloth – nothing whatever. I was left without any sort of toilet article.' The only information the elusive Finnish nurse would divulge was that Anna washed, without her toiletries, 50 times a day.

The mystery hanging over Anna's departure soon became public. Newspaper stories appeared in the United States claiming that Anna had fled to England to avoid arrest. Others said she had been kidnapped and was now dead. Lloyd-Smith reassured Fallows with a cable: 'Newspaper reports absurd... If Grandanor dead I'm a rhinoceros.'

By the second day, the doctors at Ilten had overturned the verdicts of the three American doctors, formally declaring Anna sane. Dr Hans Willige allowed her no more than difficulties of temperament; such were the difficulties that he did not feel she could be an effective claimant. 'Hers is however a personality of unique character, consisting to a high degree of a strong wilfulness, a highly egocentric outlook and interior haughtiness... To be able to impersonate another would require a surpassing intelligence, an extraordinary degree of self-control and an ever-alert discipline – all qualities Frau Tschaikovsky in no way possesses.'

A new problem arose: if she were sane, she would have to find somewhere other than the sanatorium to live. The Duke of Leuchtenberg was now dead – Anna was morbidly convinced that he had been poisoned – and even she hesitated to approach her old adversary, the Duchess. Tatiana Botkin remained an indefatigable supporter, but she lived in France and Anna was worried that, if she tried to go abroad, she might have problems with her irregular passport. For some unknown reason, she dismissed out of hand the idea of contacting her former champion, Herluf Zahle.

She need not have worried. Her whereabouts soon became known, and the inevitable band of admirers assembled. Her trusty lawyer Fallows was among the first to pay his respects. He had clearly decided to overlook Anna's furious dismissal of him. She now received Fallows graciously, even agreeing to reinstate him, though, true to form, she fired him a month later.

It was while his position was in a state of uncertainty

that Fallows began action against the *News of the World* in September 1932. The newspaper claimed that a grave containing the Romanov remains had been unearthed: 'One of the skeletons conforms in all respects to the known description of the Princess Anastasia.' The report claimed that Anna had admitted she was an impostor and, further, that she was a Roumanian actress who had been hypnotised into playing a part. The hypnotist was a manservant from the Russian court called Serge Borikov. The report concluded with the claim that the Romanovs had said they would only drop proceedings against her if she signed a confession and entered a convent. The case lapsed during the Second World War, when, as a German resident, Anna could not sue in England.

Fallows was reinstated as Anastasia's lawyer in 1935. He spent a long subsequent period working in London, during which time he kept a meticulous record of his movements. Each day was headed with a summary of the weather in capital letters: 'Tuesday April 25, 1939 LONDON WARM WITH SUNNY INTERVALS... Wednesday April 26, 1939 LONDON COOL BUT CLEAR MUCH SUN... Friday April 28, LONDON COOL SUNNY INTERVALS.' He referred repeatedly to the confidential nature of his entries: 'Most confidential – carrying forward my confidential entry of April 21st.' On 28 April he referred over-optimistically to one of Hitler's speeches: '4pm, I have just heard English digest of Hitler's speech. I interpret it to mean no war for some time to come.'

Among recurring annoyances were articles such as the one

appearing in the *Sunday Express* in January 1939 in which Anna appeared in a list of 'Famous Hoaxes'. The article, which Fallows carefully preserved, featured a photograph of Anna on which appears to have been drawn eyes, eyebrows and mouth. She is pictured beside a second famous hoax: the Native American 'Grey Owl'.

Fallows worked for Anna until his death in 1940. His family later put his death, at just 65, down to his punishing commitment to Anna. As he once wrote: 'I am nearly broken in spirit as I am entirely in purse.' In the course of the twelve years he spent on the case, Fallows sold all his assets including a New York apartment and his country house. He spent 40,000 dollars of his own money in her cause. A poignant collection of Fallows's papers, comprising thirteen densely packed boxes, is still stored at the Houghton Library, Harvard University.

Among Anna's new band of admirers at Ilten was Gleb's keen correspondent, the stout-hearted Adeline Moffatt, who had travelled from New York to embark on a third attempt at Anna's memoirs. She reported bitterly afterwards that Anna had said all she wanted to say about the 'horrible persons' in her life then sent her friend packing without even a goodbye.

The more successful champions included Empress Hermine, second wife of the deposed Kaiser Wilhelm II. Born Princess Hermine of Reuss, she was attached to one of Germany's most illustrious families. Anna described her as 'swimming in gold'. But this did not stop her pulling rank as the two ladies sat down on a sofa; Anna, as senior lady, seized the left-hand spot: 'Who is the Princess of Reuss?' she snapped ungraciously. The band gained an invaluable publicity outlet with the support of the unhappily-named owners of the newspaper *Hannoversche Anzeiger*: Paul and Gertrude Madsack.

However Anna's most important conquest was Prince Frederick Ernest of Saxe-Altenburg. He had long been interested in Anna and had been at the seance that Fallows attended with Harriet and Dr Rudnev. Prince Frederick came to Ilten in October 1931 on behalf of his brother-in-law, Prince Sigismund of Prussia, who had known the Grand Duchess Anastasia. Prince Sigismund had compiled eighteen questions for Anna, all of which she answered correctly, though it took her five days. Sigismund later puzzled for some time over whether he would be able to recognise his childhood friend. Dr Bonhoeffer's advice to Sigismund was: 'Look for the smile.'

Prince Frederick's brother-in-law, Sigismund

Prince Frederick never divulged the nature of all Sigismund's questions or of Anna's answers, though some definitely related to his brother-in-law's last meeting with Anastasia in Spala in 1912. But Prince Frederick declared himself convinced she was the Grand Duchess and she, in her turn, formed a favourable impression of him. She had initially been reluctant to see the Prince; her excuse had been unexpectedly sharp: how did she know he was not a Polish factory worker?

Prince Frederick

The Prince was fondly regarded by friends as a mercurial figure. When asked where he was, they would reply, with heavy German humour: 'He could be upstairs or he could be in Istanbul.' He could match Anna's moods and when she raised objections to his plans, he would sit out the storms, declaring grimly: 'Wind velocity up'.

Lord Louis Mountbatten (later Earl Mountbatten of Burma), who was also to take a fervent interest in Anna, never shared the Prince's friends' favourable view; in one letter he wrote that he deemed the Prince: 'One of those people who believe in all claimants, however incredible. Indeed he used to infuriate Berthold by supporting the claim of Kaspar Hauser!'

In early 1932, Anna left the sanatorium and lived at a spa, then with a family called Heyden-Rynsch in Eisenach. One day, following a row about a new German lawyer, she simply walked out and phoned her old friend Harriet in Berlin from a public call box. The pair were reunited and Anna decided to settle in Berlin, staying in a small hotel close to Harriet's apartment. They enjoyed an irregular but rich social life, featuring Anna's old supporter Herluf Zahle. While Zahle retained doubts about Anna's identity, he never relinquished his attachment, even issuing an invitation to her to stay at the Danish embassy.

Generally, however, their social life was governed by Harriet's commitment to a Rudolf Steiner movement called Anthroposophism. The Anthroposophists believed that the Russian Revolution was the manifestation of a major psychic upheaval. They viewed Anna sympathetically, as a helpless victim of the resulting karma; she made the most of their indulgence. Indeed she now took the jaunty step of adopting two new names: 'Frau Lange' and 'Miss Brown'.

In 1933, Anna had a meeting with lawyers who told her

that, once again, the Romanov family was willing to offer her what she viewed as hush money. This time the conspirators were two of Anna's *bêtes noires*: the self-proclaimed head of the family, Grand Duke Kyril, and Prince Felix Yussoupov. The meeting came to a predictably abrupt end when Anna stormed out of the room issuing an unlikely threat: 'If I had a horsewhip I would strike him (Kyril) in the face with it.'

In the same year, the Central District Court in Berlin ruled that the Tsar and his family had all died. The ruling was the result of legal action taken by the widow of the Tsar's younger brother, Grand Duke Michael. In the course of her life, Grand Duke Michael's widow, Natasha Brassov, had become increasingly desperate for money; she ended up dying penniless in a charity hospital.

***

Anna now decided to settle in Hanover in an apartment paid for by the Madsacks; there followed one of her rare happy periods. She recaptured the delight she derived from fast cars by taking rides on a nearby rollercoaster; she would laugh uproariously as she soared upside down. Fallows, who visited her at this time, was effusive: 'It is hard for me to adequately express the unbelievable change in her appearance, her interest in everything, her outgoing responsiveness to each one, her wit, her rippling conversation, her laughter, when stars literally shone in her eyes.' Fallows himself shook off most of his 63 years in order to enjoy fairground rides with Anna. As he recorded in his diary on 6 July 1938: 'Two rides on one rollercoaster, one on another.'

Gertrude Madsack, meanwhile, took Anna for more stately car rides. Anna's current mood was such that she showed herself willing to fall in with Mrs Madsack's strictures on outings, the first of which was that she should put her teeth in. If Anna forgot her teeth, Mrs Madsack would bring the car to a juddering halt and order her up to her apartment to get them. Mrs Madsack tried to shame Anna out of covering her mouth with a paper tissue by giving her nicknames. But Anna was not inclined to take offence, cheerily addressing herself as 'Miss Paper'.

In 1934, Harriet died, aged 44, of a burst appendix. Anna suspected she had shared the fate of her other friend, the Duke of Leuchtenberg: poisoned by the Grand Duke of Hesse. The bereavement had no effect on Anna's burgeoning social life. Indeed, by this time Anna had succeeded in establishing herself as 'at home' in grand houses and castles in every province of the Reich. Such was her confidence of a welcome that she gave no warning of her arrival and no indication of when she planned to depart. Among her sympathetic hosts and hostesses were Prince William of Hesse-Philippsthal, Feodora, Princess Reuss and Carl August, the Hereditary Grand Duke of Saxe-Weimar-Eisenach. The Grand Duke made Anna godmother to his son Prince Michael Benedict; her godson called her 'Aunt Andy'.

One of her most stalwart champions was an anthroposophist called Baroness Monica von Miltitz, who resided at Sieben Eichen castle near Meissen. But the Baroness's first impression was not favourable; Anna was clearly in the throes of an off-day: 'She looked poor and shabby... and seemed constrained.' Fortunately, she subsequently changed her mind and pronounced Anna's attitude and demeanour 'decidedly aristocratic'.

Baroness von Miltitz

Even so, the Baroness's generous appraisal was frequently belied by her protégée's behaviour: Anna was particularly slow to grasp the niceties involved in being a house guest. On one occasion, while staying with a noble lady, she shut herself up in a room for three days refusing food. She disappeared and was found more than one month later on the edge of a forest, her feet bleeding and her dress in tatters. She claimed to have survived on berries and mushrooms.

Perhaps Anna's luckier supporters were the ones who managed to maintain relations on a superficial footing. It seems that the more entrenched her supporters became, the less happy they were likely to be. One cause of unease would have been their inability to get along with each other. Gleb and Fallows, both well intentioned and intelligent, exchanged bitter letters when *The Woman Who Rose Again* was published. Gleb had been angered when Fallows suggested alterations to the book. The lawyer had further blotted his copy-book by mentioning motion picture rights; Gleb saw this as vulgar opportunism: 'Dear E.H.,' he wrote in July 1937, 'I am afraid this letter shall contain a number of unpleasant things... You are doing your best to paralyse my work and create a situation which will make further co-operation between us impossible...

'The only thing which interests me is to win Anastasia's case and I want to win her case not because of any advantages that you or the man in the moon may derive from it, but because Anastasia has suffered more than any human being should ever be allowed to suffer and because she is the victim of an injustice that cries to heaven... Like anger, the desire for money no matter how legitimate is a bad counsellor. If our poverty prevents us from fighting for Anastasia and the idea of abstract justice inseparably linked to her case with complete unselfishness, then the best and only decent thing we can do is to withdraw.'

Gleb, perhaps ungallantly, questioned the sacrifices the lawyer claimed to have made, pointing out that Fallows was not in his first youth when he took on the case. 'Your statements that you have sacrificed your fortune and the best years of your life for Anastasia do not, therefore, appear wholly justified.'

In 1937, Ernest Louis, the Grand Duke Hesse and by Rhine died. Within a few months, the Nazi government, apparently at the behest of Hitler, contacted Anna, insisting she confront members of the Schanzkowski family again; the authorities wanted finally to establish that Anna really was Franziska Schanzkowska. According to one report the Nazis were acting on behalf of monarchist groups to whom they were indebted for past services.

Lord Louis Mountbatten, presuming to represent the Hesse family, was also keen to discredit Anna. It has been suggested that his motive was to protect the British Royal Family. If Anna's identity were confirmed, the British Royal Family could be open to accusations of colluding with the Bank of England in keeping the Tsar's deposits hidden. Certainly Mountbatten seemed to maintain a visceral dislike of Anna. At one point, in later years, he strongly advised the BBC against interviewing her: 'I can assure you that there is not the remotest doubt that this woman is not my cousin. She was seen by all our closest mutual relations, all of whom declared there was no resemblance.' He exhorted the BBC not to abet her backers who 'simply get rich on the royalties of further books, magazines articles, plays etc'.

When Anna heard of the Nazis' interest, she shut herself away, refusing to talk to Fallows or the Madsacks. The lawyer kept a rather bleak record of his client's increasing isolation. He described an abortive meeting with her old supporter Dr Rudnev; the doctor had travelled from Berlin to meet her for lunch at the Madsacks. 'They held lunch at 1.40 when

Anastasia arrived; (but) instead of going into the reception room to greet Mrs Madsack and the doctor, she went into the little coat-room... Mrs Madsack said they were ready for lunch; Anastasia answered that she was not eating lunch but only getting some papers from her trunk upstairs... When Anastasia came down she headed straight for the front door. Doctor Rudnev followed her and tried to talk with her; she shut the door in his face. He then told Mrs Madsack he was through with her, to be treated in that manner after all he had done for her through the years.'

Fallows's own attempts to meet his elusive client were no more successful. 'Good Friday HANOVER WARM SLIGHT RAINS... wrote to A as follows... Dear Mrs Anderson, Upon my arrival in Hanover I phoned to the home of Mrs Madsack but found that you had left no message.' On one visit to her apartment, he was reduced to photographing the outside of the building; sympathetic neighbours invited him in for a glass of sherry.

It was during this period of particular frustration that Fallows's health began to suffer. On 25 March 1938 he wrote a passionate letter to an American lawyer and fellow supporter, begging for assurances regarding money. 'Never in my life have I worked so unceasingly and so unsparingly of health and strength and in such a frugal manner of living as since I left New York on January 15th – third class on trains, in the cheapest accommodation – cooking at least two of my meals daily... My family too for years have made every sacrifice – no chauffeur, no servants, letting out rooms in the Norfolk home, daughter working to keep bodies and souls together.'

Dr Rudnev was worried about the health of the lawyer. As Fallows noted stoically in his diary: 'As we talked, Dr Rudnev was observing me; he took out his watch and took my pulse. He said that he saw by the change of colour in my face that my heart was irregular... he said he thought that worry was at the root of the trouble.' Rudnev announced his decison to appeal to what he hoped would prove Anna's good nature. 'He said that he was going to write to Mrs Anderson, telling her that she was responsible for my being ill and that, like Jesus Christ, she should be merciful and make me well by writing to me that she would again co-operate.'

Unfortunately the doctor's appeals to Anna's 'good nature' proved no more effective than his health warnings to Fallows. The lawyer now came up with the exhausting idea of luring Anna from her seclusion with a lavish birthday party at the Hotel Kastens in Hanover. He sent invitations to a motley collection of people loosely described as Anna's friends. Those unlikely to attend received painstaking letters requesting birthday messages. As he wrote to Miss Jennings: 'I also am requesting a few of her friends to send me a congratulatory letter or telegram to transmit to her... I am sure she would especially appreciate one from yourself. If you feel moved to send a message and there is not time for a letter would you please cable in my care to: "Fallows Anexco Berlin".'

Fallows's first major difficulty regarding Anna's birthday party was with her old friend Gleb. Gleb and Anna had been fully reconciled after their brusque farewell in America; she had broken the ice with a conciliatory note and the pair had enjoyed a regular correspondence. But now Gleb announced his refusal to travel to Germany without several assurances from Anna. Fallows wrote a huffy letter to one of his English colleagues: 'We all hoped here that Botkin would at once respond to her request to come over and help her – without making any conditions or ultimatums – to which she has never responded favourably.'

However, birthday greetings poured in from doctors, nurses, lawyers and secretaries. Still Anna would see no one but the Madsacks' chauffeur, 'Garba', who dutifully delivered letters and clean linen. 'She is always kind to him,' Fallows recorded.

It was a joke by Fallows that finally prized her out; he wrote a letter addressed to Mrs Anderson, asking her if she could persuade the Grand Duchess Anastasia to come to the party. The joke appealed to Anna and she decided to accept the invitation, but sadly she never thought to communicate her acceptance to poor Fallows. Her party guests were left to assume she was not coming and Fallows was deliberating over what to do with the birthday cake when Anna made her dramatic last-minute entrance in a floor-length robe.

After the party, Fallows wrote to all the people who had sent Anna cards. The well-wishers would have relished the news that Anna and Dr Rudnev were again on good terms but were, doubtless, less thrilled to hear that Gleb persisted in letting the side down. On 20 June, Fallows wrote: 'Dear Friends, You will be pleased to learn that Mrs Anderson was well enough to receive Dr Rudnev and myself on her birthday, Saturday. She, however, was greatly disappointed that Mr Botkin did not appear; she fully counted on his presence in response to her request relayed by cable by myself to him in New York. Again yesterday I cabled him to come by first steamer... May I add my very deep appreciation of your response to my request, your congratulations largely contributed in making this the happiest birthday she has had since she was a child, Very sincerely yours Edward H. Fallows.'

Meanwhile the lawyer tried but failed to spare Anna a second encounter with the Schanzkowskis. She had already declared, as she so often did, that she would do 'nothing without Botkin'. Gleb, having hesitated so long, now finally agreed to come.

The meeting with the Schanzkowskis was conducted at the police headquarters in Hanover, in the presence of Gleb, Fallows and Mrs Madsack. Valerian, Gertrude and Maria Juliana Schanzkowski were joined by Felix, the brother who had previously met Anna at the bar near Castle Seeon.

The Schanzkowski siblings gained a reputation for being in a muddle: on one occasion in court they argued over the colour of their sister's eyes. But their confusion during this particular meeting might be explained by photographs which show Anna making a point, throughout, of pulling faces. They peered at her doubtfully. Valerian appeared to sum up their thoughts: 'No, this lady looks too different.' Felix added unhelpfully that she looked nothing like the woman he had met eleven years before. They seemed to be in agreement that Anna resembled no one any of them had ever seen.

Then suddenly Gertrude underwent a dramatic *volte-face*.

She turned red in the face, banged her fist on the table, then ran to Anna, grabbed her shoulders and shook her. 'You *are* my sister', she shouted. 'I know it! You must recognise me!' The police looked at Anna expectantly. There followed a curious discussion where Valerian, Felix and Maria Juliana seemed to change their minds continuously. When Anna said she had four siblings, Valerian replied as though her answer had swayed him: 'Here we are... four'. But when she said she was born in Russia, the three shook their heads in bemusement.

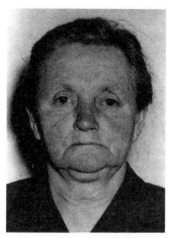

Franziska's sister Gertrude

In the end Anna stalked out of the room with Gertrude's repeated cry ringing in her ears: 'Admit it!' Gleb later grudgingly admitted that he had seen a resemblance between Anna and Gertrude: 'It was however the kind of resemblance which a horse or a bird can have to a human being.' Ian Lilburn is still puzzled by the suggestion of a link between

Anna and the Schanzkowskis. Claiming that Anna has 'natural dignity in her stance', he gazes disapprovingly at a picture of Franziska's niece: 'She could be a belly-dancer.'

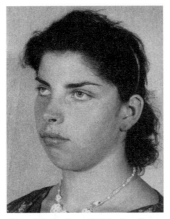

Franziska's niece, Felix's daughter

Anna now locked herself in her apartment and disconnected the phone. When Gleb called, she told him he'd better go or she would call the police. He viewed the threat with stout benevolence, as another example of Anna's irrepressible high spirit. 'I thought she was about to burst out laughing but she suppressed it,' he commented, before returning, unruffled, to New York.

Anna was left casting about for somebody on whom to blame her latest indignities. She settled on the unfortunate Madsacks, sending them a series of unpleasant notes. The venomous tone of the notes was such that Paul Madsack barred her from their house. Fallows, distraught, attempted to plead her cause with the Madsacks: 'Would you ever forgive yourself... if you now abandon her and leave her in a flat you have rented for her, mentally and physically sick and perhaps dying?' It turned out that Anna was far from spending her days alone in her flat. Indeed, tiring of her own company, she had joined a party of tourists on a bus tour of castles along the Rhine.

***

The outbreak of the Second World War had little immediate affect on Anna's life. It has been said that an upbringing at the Russian Court would have stood her in good stead for life under the Nazis. Jews, gypsies and freemasons were also regarded with suspicion in pre-Revolutionary Russia.

Anna claimed to have been paid special attention by the Führer, insisting that he once summoned her to Berlin for a private audience. She said that on some unspecified date – estimated to be 1940 or early 1941 – she had been driven in a black limousine to the Reichstag building and led through a large hallway by two handsome guards. Hitler received her in a large office, greeting her with a bow and addressing her throughout the meeting as 'Your Imperial Highness'. He said he had investigated her case and was convinced of her identity; he intended to oust the Bolsheviks and put the Romanovs back in power. Anna professed herself pleased with his plans and greatly impressed by his courtly manners.

Nevertheless, in 1943, the Nazis took the unfriendly step of stipulating that Anna must give up any idea of resuming her life as a wandering house guest; she must remain at her home in Hanover. This restriction became particularly harsh when the Allies began bombing the city, though Anna faced her changing circumstances philosophically: 'At the moment when there is danger I do not get frightened. It makes me nervous but not afraid. If I should be afraid in danger I should be now dead.'

Unfortunately Anna's fortitude was never matched by any aptitude for the more mundane aspects of self-preservation. At one point she managed to leave Hanover briefly, turning up at the castle of her patron, Baroness von Miltitz. She was seen standing, dressed in white, at the gates. The Baroness ran out to greet her but it seemed that Anna had already scuttled off to the station and returned to Hanover. Two days later the Baroness had a card from her saying she was ill. 'I went to Hanover at once and found her positively famished. For eight days she had been living only on what little food there already was in the house.' She had been prevented from applying for a ration card by her fear of what she referred to as 'brass buttons'.

When Hanover was finally reduced to rubble, Anna fled eastwards and made herself at home at another castle, Schloss Winterstein, where she stayed until the autumn of 1946. Here she claimed she had an unpleasant encounter in the kitchen with a Red soldier who tried to rape her. She claimed she pretended to be a maid and threatened her assailant with a bread knife. She later added grandly that she would have slit his throat rather than surrender.

It was Prince Frederick who finally negotiated with the Swedish Red Cross to get Anna across the border of what was to become East Germany. She crossed the Weser River on 18 December 1946 and turned up at Aalen, where the Allies issued her a pass number. The pass specified that she had no profession and that her nationality was 'not cleared up'.

She joined Prince Frederick at Bad Liebenzell in what was then the French Occupational Zone, but was almost immediately obliged to go into a clinic with a breast infection. She was ungracious about Prince Frederick's rescue efforts: 'He arranged this to get his prey back in his hands.' She also gave a grim description of a long-awaited hot meal: 'My first warm eating was grease soup with milk and sugar... sweet milk soup.'

At this point Anna wrote to Gleb asking for help. 'At Hanover I am not, for Hanover does not exist any more, and the beautiful house of Dr Madsack does not exist any more, and so many a dear friends is killed.

'I am now in the Black Forest in a Sanatory (sic) and am facing just now an operation. It is very difficult everything here, no place, no home, Prince Frederick and all friends have lost everything, we are all without a home.

'Life here is altogether very very difficult, very cold, nothing to heat, no food, no clothing. Prince Frederick has only what he has on his body. I as well have nothing whatever. And it would be very kind of you if you could manage that we could get out of this frightful mess.'

Gleb's own straitened circumstances meant that he could not help. His daughter Marina and her husband, Richard

Schweitzer, were sufficiently moved by Gleb's tales of her plight to send money. But Gleb told Anna he could only pray for her: this he did assiduously, closing his letters with: 'May the Goddess bestow Her tender caress on Your Imperial Highness's head.'

In May 1949, Prince Frederick was adding his own plea, perhaps surprising Gleb with the news that Anna was 'longing very very much indeed to come to your part of the world'. It would be nearly 20 years before Anna finally made it back to America.

That same year, Prince Frederick spent the last of his Deutschmarks on the lopsided army barrack at Unterlengenhardt that was to become Anna Anderson's first permanent home. Rudolf Steiner had once lived at Unterlengenhardt; it was there that he had founded his Anthroposophist movement. Ian Lilburn visited Anna at Unterlengenhardt. He now comments that the anthroposophists were friendly but overly analytical: 'If you were to say "good morning", they'd be wondering what you meant.'

Though the villagers knew nothing, initially, of Anna's Romanov claims, she seemed to establish herself swiftly as a sort of resident of honour, referred to as '*Hohe Frau*'. She was no doubt bemused to find herself treated to a reverential moving-in ceremony, with children lining the road carrying bouquets. One of the anthroposophists, Adele von Heydebrandt, became Anna's carer and the pair lived more or less harmoniously together in the fourteen by eighteen-foot barrack for some ten years. Mrs von Heydebrandt prepared

Anna's vegetarian meals while Anna went to the forest to collect timber for the fire and pick berries and mushrooms.

It is hard to know how frequently Gleb and Anna exchanged letters. Anna's abilities as a correspondent would have been blighted by an impossible combination of mood swings and inefficiency. In December 1949, Gleb wrote a letter in which he appeared to be getting back in touch with 'Mrs Anderson', as he called her, after a prolonged period. He gave her news of mutual acquaintances; her stalwart supporter Adeline Moffatt, for instance, had now died. He talked of a lawyer called Edward D. Pearce who was young, good-looking and rich – all of which would have appealed to Anna – and might be willing to help the cause. He was also pursuing the idea of publishing yet another book about Anna, suggesting a writer called Isaac Don Levine. Gleb was invariably conscientious: 'Christmas is approaching again and I feel so terribly guilty that I cannot even send you a present... I do so wish to see you.'

Five months later, Gleb wrote dismissing 'Mr Pearce' as a society playboy. He had heard that 'Mr Levine' had visited Anna and was worried that it had not been a success. 'Your prolonged silence worries me a great deal. In particular I am afraid that you might have been displeased by Mr Levine's visit.' Levine appeared to have committed two cardinal sins: one was to presume to send her a disparaging book about her sainted Rasputin and the other, more importantly, was to speak to her in Russian. She had not lost her distaste for the language she claimed she had been ordered to speak in front of the guards at Ekaterinburg. Gleb attempted to be soothing: 'The latter was certainly tactless of him but I am sure he meant well.'

Gleb was by now leading a sort of pioneer life in a forest in New Jersey; he had bought an acre and a half of land, dug a well and built a small cabin. He and Anna shared news of their respective pastoral idylls. As Gleb wrote: 'With time we shall of course acquire close neighbours but just now we neither see nor hear anybody except birds. Of the latter there is here a great number and an astonishing variety including wild canaries... A chipmunk is stealing paper from our toilet, but always leaving nuts in payment. So he isn't really stealing – just buying.' Anna would respond less poetically: 'Here has been a very hard and sudden winter again... Many trees are hurt.'

With her precarious finances, Anna may well have had mixed feelings when one of her grandest former hostesses, Baroness von Miltitz, arrived at Unterlengenhardt with nothing to offer but good wishes. The Sieben Eichen castle, which had belonged to the Miltitzes, now fell into the Eastern Zone and the Baroness found herself obliged to settle for an altogether humbler life in Unterlengenhardt. She, however, swiftly established a *raison d'être*, being elected chief of five elderly women in charge of Anna. Her seniority was acknowledged in the name by which she became known: 'The High Priestess of the Anastasia cult'.

Central to these women's duties was keeping unwanted people at bay. The classification of visitors as wanted or unwanted, however, seems to have been random. Prince

Frederick's brother-in-law, Prince Sigismund, whose questions she had answered so successfully upon her return to Germany in 1931, knocked at her door for three days before he was finally let in. He was never offered an explanation for her hesitation, but it might have been connected with some controversy surrounding another claimant. Sigismund had recently agreed to meet a woman claiming to be the Grand Duchess Anastasia's eldest sister, the Grand Duchess Olga; he had been in love with Olga before the Revolution. He visited the claimant at her home on Lake Como and emerged convinced that Olga had been restored to him in the exotic guise of Magda Boots.

Anna Anderson at Unterlengenhardt

Mountbatten, incidentally, made the most of Sigismund's new declaration, scoffing: 'So much for the value of (Sigismund's) testimony.' Many years later, in 1983, it was reported that a grave stood in the cemetery at Menaggio with the inscription: 'In memory of Olga Nikolaievna, 1895-1976, eldest daughter of Tsar Nicholas II of Russia.'

No such baggage attached itself to Tatiana Botkin, who came all the way from Paris in the dead of winter to visit Anna. But she too was barred from the house and, after a full eight days of being turned away, went home in defeat. Anna felt her lack of hospitality was more than justified: 'I am old and sick. Let them come again in the spring, when it will be nice. We will have tea in the garden – if I am not dead.'

Meanwhile several unlikely – and presumably unwelcome – fellow claimants were passing through the vetting system. There was one Dutch housewife who claimed to be a fifth daughter of the Tsar; she insisted she had been kidnapped from Tsarskoye Selo as a child. Another woman confronted Anna claiming to be the illegitimate daughter of Anastasia's sister Olga, and a Bolshevik soldier. She threatened to shoot her way into the barracks if 'Aunt Anastasia' did not open the door.

Occasionally, however, there were happy interludes. In 1954 she had a triumphant meeting with one of the Tsarina's closest friends, Lili Dehn. The pair apparently discussed rugs, carpets and the colour of one of the Tsarina's dresses. They appeared to remember playing cards the night the Tsarina and Marie went to plead with troops for support, shortly after the Tsar's abdication. They also claimed to remember Anastasia breaking a vase in the drawing room and saying: 'Don't worry about it. It isn't ours. It belongs to the government.'

After the meeting, Lili was adamant: 'Do not bother to tell me that she had read these things in books. I have recognised her, physically and intuitively through signs which do not deceive... As I was going away and turned round once more to look at her, she said, "Goodbye, goodbye," and the way she said it went straight to my heart, for it was exactly the way my Empress used to do it...'

That same year, however, Anna had an unsuccessful meeting with the Imperial children's English tutor. Now 78, Sydney Gibbes had become a Russian Orthodox priest, Father Nicholas. He spent three days with Anna in Paris. At first Anna had insisted everybody wore surgical masks; when that proved impossible, she elected to hide her face behind a newspaper. When Father Nicholas at last caught sight of her face, he declared that she bore no resemblance to Anastasia. He said she also failed to recognise photographs he had brought of her childhood rooms. He later famously announced: 'If that woman is Anastasia, I'm a Chinaman.'

Anna later countered by claiming that the man she saw had not been Mr Gibbes. 'A monk came... strange-looking monk with a big beard. Mr Gibbes never had a beard. He had a limping leg. He looked very pleasant in one way. This man was not limping. I never believe that that was Mr Gibbes... NEVER.'

Gibbes's limp became a bone of contention. In answer to one of Anna's earlier references, Father Nicholas wrote a florid defence of his gait, insisting, perhaps irrelevantly, that he was in possession of both legs. Meanwhile Gleb, never one to back down, issued a ruthless counter-claim that the tutor either limped or, at the very least, dragged one leg. 'He had defects in his physical build... he always held his head to one side... In general (he) makes the impression of a physically defective person.' Incidentally Anna's doubts about Father Nicholas's identity did not stop her, in later life, pestering members of the Gibbes family for the return of Romanov treasures she claimed the former tutor had stolen.

Throughout the 1950s, public interest in Anna grew more intense with every year. She was inundated with letters, ranging from death threats to invitations to invest in diamond mines, make movies, or go on safaris; she received enough marriage proposals, improbably, to fill a trunk. While the proposals may have appealed to her vanity, she responded less enthusiastically to several pornographic notes.

There were now coach tours of the Black Forest featuring her home. If keener tourists failed to catch sight of her, they would throw stones at her windows or whistle. Some particularly desperate types sent their children through the bushes with cameras. Anna found herself reduced to showering sightseers under her windows with jugs of cold water.

Anna had four massive dogs, part wolfhound and part St Bernard which seem to have been peculiarly ineffective guard-dogs. Baby, Polly, Tilly and Naughty occasionally broke loose and lolloped, snapping, through Unterlengenhardt; they once even caught and bit a reporter from *Paris Match*. Otherwise they restricted themselves to terrorising house guests. Michael Thornton, the English writer who at one point had Anna's power of attorney, recalls a party thrown for him at Unterlengenhardt during which guests sat 'frozen' in their seats as the dogs circled the table. 'You felt if you moved too quickly the dogs would have your leg off.'

One of Anna's dogs at Unterlengenhardt

Thornton put his own successful penetration of the army barrack down to his happy choice of gift: 'Twinings Russian Caravan Tea' in a green tin. He recalls the grandiose words Anna employed in what was, for her, a rare expression of thanks: 'Mr Thornton, your tea has been my consolation.'

She seemed to enjoy Thornton addressing her as 'Madame' and even responded well when he tried to suggest she had never been to England. 'Her face lit up and she proceeded to give me a detailed account of her trip to Cowes in 1909.' Though fascinated by her story, Thornton was never convinced of her claim. As he says: 'She had 64 years to learn her part – longer than Victoria's reign.'

Enough newspaper reporters made their presence felt for Anna to declare grandly: 'I am the milch cow for the journalists.' She wrote a letter of protest to Gleb, in which she referred to herself, confusingly, in the third person; her word order is resolutely German: 'You are not able to imagine what here goes on about the poor barrack. The reporters are simply coming from all over the world... Of course you will imagine that her health is in a very poor condition. Without any fresh air at all, because she cannot even look out, everywhere stands somebody. She is a real prisoner in her own little home.'

The siege-like atmosphere cannot have been helped by Anna's decision to erect a high palisade of wire and straw matting around the property. She allowed the shrubbery to become impenetrable and, in order to prevent reporters climbing trees, coated the tree trunks with lard.

But in 1955 she decided she would receive a reporter from *Life* magazine. He described her languishing on a camp-bed, switching randomly between two topics: her worries about her peach trees and her conviction that she would not survive the year. 'People want me to die, certain people. I shall soon oblige them,' she gasped. She was to live another 30 years.

Her efforts to thwart public interest were not accompanied by any attempt to make herself less conspicuous. In 1960 another resourceful reporter succeeded in gaining an interview. He gave a vivid description of her appearance: 'Suddenly, accompanied by an infernal uproar of barking, we saw the door open and there entered the strangest creature I have ever seen in my life. It was a little Madam Butterfly disguised as a

Tyrolean. She was wearing a Japanese kimono, over which she had slipped a loden coat, and over the coat a black, hooded cape. The cowl was drawn up over the Tyrolean hat, which crowned a head of chestnut hair, streaked with white. The face had a great delicacy about it, but her mouth was sheltered behind a napkin, folded like a fan, which she held in one black-gloved hand. Her feet were buried in enormous fur boots, and the indecision of her step, the hesitation you could sense, conferred an unreal quality on her presence.'

In her book, *Anastasia Retrouvée*, Tatiana Botkin describes her second, more successful, visit to Unterlengenhardt. She had not seen Anna for 30 years. 'Through a small window nearly blocked by vegetation, the dull day barely illuminated a veritable Aladdin's Cave. Picture frames, knick-knacks, postcards, photographs were piled up everywhere, a bizarre quantity of objects among which I recognised official portraits of the Emperor and Empress, old epaulettes, a Cossack officer's belt decorated with tarnished silver ornaments and everywhere unopened letters. Envelopes invaded everything and stamps in all colours bore witness to the most exotic parts of the world... And then, when my eyes had finished taking in this baffling spectacle, I perceived at the end of the room a large wooden bed, with covers, piled one on top of the other, concealing a human form. I approach. Anastasia is there. She is hiding the lower part of her face with a handkerchief. An expression of terror fills her eyes.'

The growth of Anna's popularity during the 1950s was due largely to the production of a Broadway play and two films based on her story. In the better known of the films, *Anastasia*, produced by Twentieth-Century Fox, Ingrid Bergman plays a romantic heroine who ends up running off with a Russian Prince played by Yul Brynner. The film is set in Paris, while the play had been set in Berlin, and it was advertised as 'the most amazing conspiracy the world has ever known... And love as it never happened to a man and woman before!' Twentieth-Century Fox released a love song featuring the words: '*Anastasia, tell me who you are./Are you someone from another star?/ Anastasia, are you what you seem?/Do your sad eyes remember a dream?... Anastasia, smile away the past!/Anastasia, spring is here at last!/Beautiful stranger, step down from your star./I only know I love you so,/Whoever you are.*' Fans of the film's romantic heroine were invariably disappointed to find that Anna bore little resemblance to Ingrid Bergman.

The climax of the film is a dramatic reunion between the Grand Duchess and her grandmother, the Dowager Empress. The Dowager recognises her granddaughter after she coughs; she remembers that, as a child, Anastasia had coughed when she was nervous. Anna never saw the film, *Anastasia*, and, curiously, never showed any interest in seeing it. But she did sign a contract saying that she agreed that Twentieth-Century Fox might: 'produce, distribute everywhere, exhibit and transmit (*Anastasia*) by all means now and hereafter known... To the extent that the character of Anastasia depicts me and/or points to me you may depict such character... It is understood that changes must under no circumstances be defamatory to my personal dignity and reputation or to the dignity and reputation of any member of my family.' Anna was paid 30,000 dollars. Her lawyers took what they needed to cover costs for negotiating the contract. The rest was invested, giving Anna a weekly income of about 20 dollars.

In 1957, there was a less welcome foray into the public eye with the publication of *I, Anastasia*. Subtitled *An Autobiography, with Notes by Roland Krug von Nidda*, the book claimed to tell her story in her own words. Much of it comprised accurate accounts, based on information from Prince Frederick. Nevertheless Anna claimed to have no idea of its existence until an editor turned up at Unterlengenhardt with a hundred copies for her to distribute.

CHAPTER SIX

Anna goes to court, 1933-1968

Anna's legal battle for recognition as the Grand Duchess Anastasia was the longest-running German court case of the 20th century. The foundations of the case were laid in 1933 when the Central District Court in Berlin issued a declaration that all the Tsar's children were dead. The issue of such a declaration would mean that the property of the Tsar could eventually be distributed amongst Princess Brassova (widow of the Tsar's younger brother, Grand Duke Michael); the Tsar's sisters, the Grand Duchesses Xenia and Olga; Ernest Louis, the Grand Duke of Hesse and by Rhine; and the Tsarina's sisters, Victoria and Irene.

Five years later, in 1938, the Berlin court issued a certificate of inheritance and the Tsar's deposits at the Mendelssohn Bank were paid to the next of kin. Revolution and inflation had reduced the money to a mere 157,000 Deutschmarks. It was at this point that Anna launched her 'Petition for the Revocation of the Certificate of Inheritance'. In the German press the ensuing court case was referred to as 'Anastasia's Monster Trial'.

Shortly before his death in 1940, Fallows had secured the services of a successful and well-connected young lawyer called Paul Leverkuehn to fight the case in Germany. Among Leverkuehn's partners was Helmuth von Moltke, one of the best known of Hitler's German opponents, who was to be condemned to death in 1945.

Leverkuehn and a second lawyer, Kurt Vermehren, would represent Anna for the next 20 years. Anna never expressed an opinion on the lawyers' contrasting approaches: Leverkuehn was sombre whereas Vermehren had a taste for drama. She certainly preferred Leverkuehn as a man, but, according to Ian Lilburn, this was probably based upon no more than Vermehren's advanced age. She derived much enjoyment from her nickname for Vermehren 'Vermin'.

The case was badly affected by the war. Papers were destroyed when Leverkuehn's offices were bombed. Both lawyers were obliged to abandon their professional commitments: Leverkuehn was ordered to go and fight in Turkey while Vermehren ended up interned in a concentration camp at Oranienbaum. Vermehren had been arrested following the defection of his son to England; he spent a year locked in one room with his ex-wife.

The appeal against the first negative ruling, in 1941, was

finally brought to the High Court of West Berlin in 1956. It was lost largely because a new witness appeared claiming to have been a guard at the Ipatiev house. He insisted he had new documents, including an official Bolshevik announcement of the Imperial Family's execution. He was later proven a fraud. Gleb wrote with feeling of the judgement: 'The decision of the Berlin court is so absurd and baseless that one can only wonder how any jurists could have the effrontery of writing it.'

Anna's lawyers were now persuaded to sue directly for her formal recognition. They decided to sue Prince Sigismund's daughter, Duchess Barbara of Mecklenburg, for denying Anna's identity and spending her money. The Duchess was the granddaughter of the Tsarina's sister Irene. Any relation could have been chosen, but it seemed they settled on Barbara simply because she lived in Germany.

The case opened in the High Court of Hamburg on 9 January 1958. In March, Gilliard gave testimony for the defence at the Hall of Justice in Wiesbaden. The correspondent for *Der Zeit* found him unconvincing: 'One gets the impression that this rather pedantic man had been trapped by a decision he reached too hastily. How could such a fastidious teacher and amateur detective admit that he had made a mistake?'

The judge asked to see the photographs and handwriting specimens Gilliard had reproduced in his book, *The False Anastasia*. Gilliard's selection of photographs comparing Franziska and Anna had continued to create controversy. Gleb had been particularly incensed by the suggestion that the women had similar eyes: 'Mrs Tschaikovsky's eyes are long and straight... Franziska Schanzkowska's eyes are those of a Chinaman, and besides obviously insane'. But Gilliard replied that he had burned his Anastasia dossier after the earlier negative ruling. There was apparently silence in court when he cried: 'I don't have them any more. They're burned. I destroyed them. I have nothing any more'. The tribunal told him to check and see whether he had any papers in a safe deposit box. As it turned out, he had a car crash on his return journey to Lausanne. He never recovered from his injuries and died in 1962.

Testimony was then heard from Tatiana Botkin and a soldier who had met the Grand Duchess Anastasia during the First World War at a hospital in St Petersburg. Anna and the soldier had appeared to enjoy a moving reunion at Castle Seeon. But later, Baron von Kleist's daughter, Gerda, swore that the couple had already been reunited at the Kleists' flat in Berlin. The soldier gave dramatic testimony from his deathbed. 'I swear by God to have the certitude that Mrs Anderson is Anastasia Nikolaievna, Grand Duchess of Russia.'

The judge declared that Anna would have to testify in person. For some time Anna managed to resist the demand. She made no secret of her suspicions concerning the whole proceedings; Vermehren was singled out for particular opprobrium: 'That man uses me for a golden calf', she wrote in a letter. Her assessment of his mental state had a ring of the pot and kettle: 'Mrs Anderson now thinks him not quite normal.'

Amongst further witnesses were the Wingender sisters, who

had claimed Anna had been living in their flat, as Franziska Schanzkowska, in 1920 when she threw herself in the canal. Years later Doris Wingender had been one of Anna's least welcome visitors at Castle Seeon. Now the sisters gave identical details which were deemed, by Anna's supporters, suspiciously precise. Doris produced a photograph of herself in a blue suit; she swore she had lent the suit to the woman she knew as Franziska. She then produced a photograph of Anna wearing the same suit. Police experts later said that one of the photographs had been altered: someone had drawn on buttons and a belt.

Baron von Kleist's daughter, Gerda, in whose house Anna had lived in the first months of her so-called recognition, testified that their guest had known no English or Russian and had cried out in her sleep in Polish. According to Gerda, Anna had once mistaken a German doctor for a member of the Imperial Family. Prince Frederick finally leapt to his feet to protest when Gerda added that 'Fraulein Anny' had ducked under a table to wipe her nose.

A Polish friend of Franziska's called Martha Borkowska proved a liability for Anna's opponents. She was presented with a series of photographs, several of the real Grand Duchess Anastasia and one of Franziska. She identifed all those of Grand Duchess Anastasia as Franziska while the only one she identified as the Grand Duchess was actually Franziska. When asked to be more specific about her friend's 'pretentious airs', the bulky Martha capered about performing grotesque imitations of a movie queen.

The tribunal's rogatory commission then went to Paris, London, Toronto and New York to interview Prince Felix Yussoupov, Faith Lavington, Princess Xenia, Grand Duchess Olga and Gleb. Olga had been one of the first to appear convinced by Anna's identity as Anastasia. She had subsequently denied the recognition but then been plagued by doubt. Now settled in Toronto, she reluctantly agreed to meet two lawyers at the German consulate. After several hours of questioning, she declared the meeting over and stalked out of the room. In the corridor she was assailed by yet another false Anastasia who ran to her crying: 'Aunt Olga! Dear Aunt Olga! At last!'

***

Anna's attempts to avoid testifying seemed finally foiled in May 1959 when the judges of Hamburg decided to travel to Bavaria to interview her. A court was set up in the neighbouring town of Bad Liebenzell. A Russian language expert came along to test Anna's knowledge of Russian.

But just days before the hearing, Anna's loyal carer, Frau Heydebrandt, died. On the morning of 12 May 1959, Anna had been walking her dogs in the garden when she stumbled across the dead body of Frau Heydebrandt. Her faithful companion had fallen in the tangle of weeds following a heart attack. The shock of the discovery was such that Anna developed a swelling on her arms and a rash on her chest. The ladies had eaten grapefruit the night before; Anna vowed never again to eat grapefruit. She declared herself too upset to testify.

The court made further concessions, transferring to Unterlengenhardt itself. Anna, however, remained locked inside her house. Attempts were made to entice her out; she was told on the telephone that one of her old supporters, Dr Theodor Eitel, wanted to see her. She retorted that she didn't want to see him, she wished to remember him as he was at Oberstdorf. Finally a neighbour had the bright idea of sitting next to the freshly delivered bottles of milk outside her door; he was able to confront her face to face as she emerged to retrieve her milk.

She eventually agreed reluctantly to meet the judge: 'He can stare at me for ten minutes,' she huffed. During the interview she refused to speak French or Russian; when asked the Russian words for 'customs' and 'passport' she simply turned away and called to her dog, Baby. But Judge Backen was not offended by her lack of co-operation; indeed he came out of the meeting announcing to the waiting crowd: 'I don't know who she is, but she is a lady.' He was clearly impressed by her manner *de haut en bas*: she refused to shake his hand because she was worried about germs.

Around this time, a new anthropological report from the University of Mainz, based on the study of more than 300 photographs, concluded that Anna was indeed Anastasia. Two new experts were called in: an anthropologist, 'the Nester of modern anthropology', Dr Otto Reche, and an eminent graphologist, Dr Minna Becker, who had helped authenticate

Anne Frank's diary. It was generally agreed that the conclusions of these two experts would provide the last word in the case.

Both came out in Anna's favour. It was thought that the two sides would have to reach a compromise. But Leverkuehn died in March 1960, just before the last sessions and the case was lost. The judgement came through that Anna's claim was unfounded. The counter-claim, that she was Franziska, was, however, also defeated.

Vermehren seemed to forget about Gilliard's burnt evidence and Zahle's confiscated papers, not to mention Doris's altered photograph. The experts were never called and Anna's poor opinion of Vermehren seemed to be borne out.

The opposition lawyer, Günther von Berenberg-Gossler, spoke passionately for three hours. At one point he flourished Gleb's writing paper and pointed at the letterhead: 'The Most Reverend Gleb Botkin, The Priest of Aphrodite And Archbishop'. This, he said, was an illustration of the nature of Anna's supporters: 'How can you take this man seriously?' He added that he had been sent a photograph of Botkin cavorting naked in an Aphrodisian ritual. Finally, he relished revealing that, in the course of gathering evidence, he had interviewed no less than fourteen 'Anastasias'.

***

Certainly claimants continued to appear, representing all four sisters. Though Tatianas were the first, there was no shortage of Olgas: aside from the Olga writing her memoirs at Lake

Como, there were Olgas in St Petersburg, Montevideo and Brussels. A Marie also appeared in Brussels. This Marie, Countess Cecile Czapka, confessed her 'true identity' to her grandson after being told by doctors that she had just months to live. Her grandson, Alexis Dolgorouky, subsequently claimed he was the great-grandson of the Tsar and a rightful Romanov successor.

But none of the sisters could rival the Grand Duchess Anastasia in sheer numbers of claimants. Three Anastasias appeared in Britain alone. In Canada, in 1960, yet another Anastasia appeared and succeeded in visiting her 'aunt', the long-suffering Grand Duchess Olga, in a Montreal hospital. Olga was still recovering from the hospital visit when she received a letter from the Russian Bishop in Tokyo telling her of a further Anastasia creating a stir in Asia.

Following the publication of a book by J.C. Trewin's on the children's English tutor, Sydney Gibbes, another Anastasia appeared in Rhode Island. Gibbes's adopted son, George, was sufficiently impressed to take her to see the Russian collection at Luton Hoo. She apparently took a proprietorial interest in the Fabergé jewellery. The most enterprising claimant set up the Anastasia Beauty Salon in Illinois.

However the best known of Anna Anderson's rival claimants was Eugenia Smith. Mrs Smith first claimed to be a friend of Anastasia; her initial memoir detailed several encounters between Mrs Smith and Anastasia in Roumania. But at some point after the publishers read the manuscript, they became captivated by the idea that Mrs Smith was not merely Anastasia's friend: she *was* Anastasia. They issued a breathless challenge to their author to reveal her true identity. Mrs Smith, equally alert to the advantages of a more central role, triumphantly proclaimed that she was, indeed, the real Grand Duchess Anastasia.

Among several new details Mrs Smith provided were unlikely orders issued by the Bolshevik guards on the night of the shootings. According to Mrs Smith, the Bolsheviks forced members of the Imperial Family to write letters saying they were happily settled in Sweden. Mrs Smith subsequently underwent a psychiatric evaluation which persuaded the publishers that she was genuine. She also managed to pass a lie detector test. Gleb, who had been warning the publishers against becoming involved with Mrs Smith, insisted the detector must have a screw loose.

In an interview he gave in 1998, Prince Rostislav Romanov, a grandson of Grand Duchess Xenia, described an unfortunate meeting with Mrs Smith. The meeting had taken place during the 1960s at the bank in Chicago where Rostislav worked; it was organised by a colleague of the Prince who also happened to be Mrs Smith's neighbour. 'She told me stories about my father which turned out to be untrue. He was still alive then and I was able to check with him. She had vague memories about playing in trees.'

Mrs Smith had further bad luck with her subsequent reunions. She underwent a tricky meeting with a cousin, Nina Chavchavadze, whom she was meant to have known at the Russian Court. After the cousins drew an unending series of blanks, she was obliged to excuse her poor powers of recollection: 'I have a terrible memory for such things.'

On another occasion, she was subjected to a still more testing meeting with her 'brother', the Tsarevich Alexis. This Alexis was actually a Polish army officer called Michael Goleniewsky. He laid claim to several fortuitous breaks, not least the miraculous overcoming of his childhood haemophilia. Unhappily, the would-be siblings' initial, emotional embrace soon gave way to animosity; within weeks they were both denouncing each other as frauds.

***

Hours after the verdict in Anna's case was delivered, her legal team decided to appeal. The team had undergone some changes. Vermehren had been killed in a car crash in October 1962. Anna completed her relish of the news by adding her own unlikely twist: the lawyer, she insisted, had been assassinated to get at her.

A new lawyer called Carl-August Wollmann was selected to replace Vermehren. Wollmann was not in good physical shape; he was still recovering from a serious war injury to his leg. His heartfelt commitment to Anna's case, over the next three years, did his fragile health no favours. He took amphetamines to help him work into the night; eventually he developed stomach ulcers. Anna, not known for her love of lame ducks, was unexpectedly sympathetic. 'His leg is in a bad condition and he must take remedies against the terrible pains,' she wrote to Gleb. 'I fear that he is not very long alive.'

In April 1964 the court met again in Hamburg. First to be heard was the anthropologist, Dr Reche, who insisted that a close resemblance was not possible unless the faces belonged to the same person or to identical twins. The testimony from the graphologist, Dr Becker, seemed equally conclusive. In just one set of documents, she had found 137 identical characteristics in the handwriting of Anna and the Grand Duchess Anastasia.

In a chronological twist, there followed crucial arguments about whether the Grand Duchess Anastasia could have survived the Ekaterinburg massacre. Obviously if the Grand Duchess had died in Ekaterinburg, it would not matter how many facial similarities existed between Anna and Anastasia. These arguments were followed by conflicting medical and dental reports. The tireless Wollmann, meanwhile, managed to find 20 new witnesses.

By this time Anna had transferred from her old barrack to a new chalet. Though the chalet had been completed in the spring of 1960, Anna had initially refused to move from her rotting barrack. Increasingly desperate attempts by her doughty friends, Baroness von Miltitz and Prince Frederick, to lure her into the chalet had backfired. The more they argued, the more intractable she became. Her initial accusations, that they were simply interfering, developed into full-blown attacks. She accused the Baroness of stealing and spying; the Prince, she snapped, was only interested in fame and money. Though she did at one point venture into the chalet to have a cup of tea with Tatiana Botkin, she did not actually transfer her belongings until July 1961. She wrote to Gleb that her reluctance to move was due to her failure to find 'an inner connection'.

Tatiana Melnik (née Botkin) and Anna Anderson

***

Over in America, Gleb was in the process of meeting the man who was to play such a crucial role in bringing about his final reunion with Anna. Alexis Miliukov had read Gleb's books and was convinced of Anna's claim. In 1961, he contacted Gleb, offering his services to the cause. Gleb suggested Miliukov visit him at his home, a 'small hut' in Cassville, New Jersey. In a detailed letter, Gleb explained that the hut was surrounded by woods, 125 feet back from a track. There was no signpost indicating his name or the name of his house, but Miliukov would find a neighbour's signpost on a nearby tree. He added that he had no telephone but was at home at all times. Incidentally Gleb did eventually get a phone; in one of his sister Tatiana's letters she describes how moving it was to hear his voice for the first time in nearly 50 years.

Miliukov declared himself anxious to get to know Anna; Gleb was sufficiently impressed by his new recruit to provide him with full guidelines. First, Miliukov must not alienate the Baroness. Of Prince Frederick he added: 'Like the Grand Duchess, he can be very suspicious and very abrupt, but can also be most friendly and charming. You will see at once that they are cousins. There is even a bit of resemblance between them.' He advised Miliukov to send Anna gifts: he should send her coffee as well as lavender water and soap produced by Yardleys. 'She had those Yardley things in her childhood. She eats very little but she does love citrus fruit of whatever kind. You could make her very happy by supplying her with oranges.'

While Miliukov embarked upon his courtship, he began to investigate the possibility of making a deal with the Romanovs. At that point he unwittingly upset Gleb by contacting Anna's old enemy, Prince Felix Yussoupov. Perhaps because Yussoupov was the best-known White Russian connected to the Romanovs, Miliukov mistakenly assumed he was the head of the family. Gleb was furious when he heard that Yussoupov was involved, and still more furious when he was told that

Yussoupov had promised to recognise Anna, providing he could have a share of her money. Gleb ranted: 'He knows perfectly well that Anastasia is what she claims to be and his fight against her is a crime more horrible and cruel by far than even the murder of Rasputin.' It says something for the strength of Gleb's continuing regard for Miliukov that he allowed himself to overlook the gaffe.

When Miliukov finally arrived at Unterlengenhardt, he found his painstakingly selected parcels had made little impact. Anna would agree, initially, only to a short conversation through the window. Gleb suspected her friends were poisoning her mind against Miliukov. As he wrote: 'Both (the Prince and the Baronesss) can appear to be so very friendly to the rest of us, but I am not so sure that they are as friendly, in fact. They certainly do not seem to want the Grand Duchess to really trust anybody but themselves.'

It was not until 18 June 1963, on what would have been the Grand Duchess Anastasia's 62nd birthday, that Anna allowed Miliukov in, brought round, no doubt, by the promise of yet more gifts. She was immediately taken with her new visitor, even agreeing to let him interview her and record the answers. The ensuing reminiscences acquired ever more startling detail. At one point she insisted that the Tsarevich was not the natural child of their parents and that he had never suffered from haemophilia. Gleb worried that the more outlandish material might damage her cause; as Lilburn admits: 'She had sick fantasies and talked a lot of rubbish.' She, however, assured Prince Frederick at the time that she was always cautious: 'You don't think I tell him (Miliukov) anything important, do you?'

By the summer of 1965, Anna's way of life was becoming increasingly eccentric. Mourning the deaths of two of her dogs, she consoled herself with 20 new cats. Pressing their numerical advantage, the cats began to occupy the masterbed that Anna claimed had been slept in by Queen Victoria; their mistress, meanwhile, was consigned to a sofa.

While the cats made themselves at home, the lawyer Wollmann and Prince Frederick were forbidden entry. Whenever the two men called, she addressed them shouting from an upstairs window. She made it clear that she had entirely lost interest in court cases. The only news that interested her came from Gleb, the choicest snippets involving a fresh start in the New World. Gleb told her he had found an important new supporter: Jack Manahan of Charlottesville, Virginia. Manahan was the son of a real estate millionaire. He had acquired a PhD in history from Harvard then taught at small colleges in the South. Fascinated by Gleb's story, the former professor was now making fulsome offers to look after the Grand Duchess Anastasia.

It is hard to know whether Gleb's first references to Jack Manahan struck any chord with Anna. Accustomed to patrons with titles and six-syllable surnames, the name of Jack Manahan may well have struck her as rather plain. In any case her letters never gave much indication of excitement; she continued to close her replies cursorily: 'Now goodbye! For today, enough of this terrible dirt.'

242

One of Anna's last encounters with any member of the Imperial Family was with Prince Alexander Romanov. Prince Alexander was a grandson of two of Anna's bitterest enemies: her 'aunt', the Grand Duchess Xenia, and the table-rapping Grand Duke Alexander. Prince Alexander was introduced to Anna by Ian Lilburn. A German speaker, Lilburn had proved his mettle, attending every court hearing between 1964 and 1970. Over the course of the years he also drove tirelessly around Europe collecting witnesses. Today he retains his unshakeable conviction that Anna was the Grand Duchess. 'She was a lady even when she marched down the garden calling Prinz Friedrich a pig.'

Prince Alexander Romanov

Lilburn now looked forward to recruiting Prince Alexander as an invaluable ally. Such was his own commitment that he believed all he had to do was to bring the pair together. The Prince would of course be smitten; his support would be assured.

Unfortunately, upon spotting her visitors, Anna fled

from the garden and rushed indoors, bolting the door. She apparently hit the nail on the head as she cried to Prince Frederick: 'That can only be a descendant of Grand Duke Alexander. I recognise him by his oceanlike walk.'

Anna Anderson and Ian Lilburn

Anna was eventually enticed out and enjoyed tea with her visitors. But, after a full two hours, the Prince was not sufficiently smitten to contribute any more than an oblique announcement: he was no longer willing to say that Anna was not who she said she was. Gleb received news of the visit with dismay. He set no store by the mildly positive nature of Prince Alexander's prognosis: indeed the suspicion with which he now regarded the Romanovs led him to denounce the Prince as a spy.

The villagers at Unterlengenhardt were generally supportive of Anna, many of them believing her claim. They probably found the show of loyalty from such distinguished friends as Prince Frederick and Baroness von Miltitz convincing. They could not have failed to be moved by the sight of the Russian Orthodox priest praying annually at her gate on the anniversary of the shootings.

However, on a more immediate level, her inability to look after her pets was creating tension. The third of her original four dogs had died and was now buried in a shallow grave, where it began to rot and smell. The cats, meanwhile, had multiplied. There were now more than 40 of them, under-nourished and inbred, some of them blind and crippled. According to one friend, Anna spent all her money on her pets which were, he complained 'fed good hamburger meat, from the butcher no less!'

She may have been dimly aware of rising discontent; she certainly had no compunction about proclaiming that she now trusted no one but Gleb. She sniffily dismissed friends trying to help with the court case as underhand or, as she preferred, playing parts: 'Princess Marianne from Herleshausen is playing a very strange part in all this.' Even poor Ian Lilburn came under fire: 'I fear that he is playing a bleak part at the Bank of England'. The elderly women who looked after her were not above suspicion: the Baroness she now regarded as actually dangerous. Gleb had not helped the situation by, at one point, calling the Baroness a liar. Lilburn is still incensed by this: 'But the Baroness was like a second mother to Anastasia. Gleb was a menace.'

In September a new judge and language expert arrived at the town hall in Unterlengenhardt. Lilburn describes Prince

Frederick's desperation when, at the last moment, Anna was persuaded against seeing this judge by a letter from Gleb. He recalls one of the elderly carers waving the letter which assured Anna that, in a civil case, she could not be forced to see the judge. Lilburn still harbours some anger against Gleb: 'He wanted to be the hero.' Gleb had not endeared himself to Anna's European supporters by referring to them as 'moth-eaten princes'.

By the time Anna was finally coaxed into the town hall, she was in a fluster. She was further thrown by the sight of the opposition lawyer, Berenberg-Gossler, whom she had been assured would not be present. But as the handsome lawyer was duly hustled out, Anna's gratification may have been tinged with regret. Her hostility was evidently vying with a keen interest in his physical attributes. 'I mean Mr Berenberg-Gossler is a playboy... And a copy of Yussoupov when he was young... You can believe me, everybody fell in love with him.'

She was asked to read Russian poetry but she had forgotten her glasses. Fortunately she and Prince Frederick shared the same optician's prescription; he had a pair of glasses he was willing to lend. Less fortunately, they did not fit. Anna was obliged to hold the glasses with her one good arm while trying to hold the book with the other. After a desultory struggle, she eyed the judge and the female language expert with interest. 'Are you married to this nice lady?' she asked the judge. After an hour and a half of questions in Russian, English and German, she was sufficiently relaxed to ask when the interrogation would start; she had been silent for most of the session. The judge bowed to the romance of the occasion by singing Russian songs.

Back in Hamburg, endless evidence followed concerning Anna's claim that the Grand Duke of Hesse had visited Tsarskoye Selo during the First World War. Prince Dmitri Galitzine claimed he had noticed a gentleman in civilian dress at the court in 1916. The director of the Tsarina's relief services, Vladimir von Mekk, had told him that the gentleman was the Grand Duke of Hesse. The stepson of the Kaiser re-enforced Galitzin's story; he testified that the Kaiser himself had told him about Hesse's Russian peace mission. Lastly the German Crown Princess Cecilie, who had earlier denounced Anna, now made it clear that she had changed her mind on all counts: she believed that Anna was the Grand Duchess and even detected a resemblance between Anna and the Tsarina. By the same token she was ready to claim that: 'Our circles knew about it (the visit) at the time.'

Anna would have been pleased to hear the testimony of the last three witnesses and to hear of the poor impression given in court by her bitter enemy, Doris Wingender. During what turned out to be Doris's last appearance, lawyers produced the photograph she was meant to have identified as Franziska. The photograph turned out to be little more than a blur. When Judge Petersen insisted Doris should take an oath, she retorted dramatically that she could not because she was suffering from influenza: 'I can't. I can't tonight. Take my pulse.'

In the end, however, the judgement went against her. Despite the positive evidence from the graphologist and the anthropologist, Anna had failed to prove her identity to the satisfaction of the court. Within a day the Bank of England had formally denied that it held any funds for the heirs of the Tsar. As Anna's beleaguered lawyer, Wollmann, left the court by a side door, he bumped into an elderly, dumpy German *Hausfrau* dressed in a brown woollen coat. She was smiling and shouting jubilantly: 'The verdict is just! I am Anastasia!'

***

Anna's opponents might have been forgiven for assuming, at this point, that the battle was over. But a new phase was just beginning. A titled lawyer, Baron Curt von Stackelberg now took up cudgels on Anna's behalf. The Baron specialised in life's grey areas. He announced at the outset that, with regard to Anna's identity, he was aiming for no more than what he called a reasonable certainty.

Some members of the Baron's family strongly objected to his involvement. His cousin, Steno von Stackelberg, carried on a passionate correspondence with Mountbatten in which he expressed increasing exasperation. According to Steno, the lawyer accepted the case: 'Based on a completely misconceived loyalty to the Emperor. I hope I have opened his eyes – but too late... He is actually very DISLOYAL as the Empress Dowager, the Emperor's two sisters, your mother Princess Henry (actually Mountbatten's mother was the Tsarina's sister Victoria), your uncle the Grand Duke of Hesse have already declared that that woman was NOT the Grand Duchess. Did he doubt THEIR word?'

Clearly unfazed by the views of his relations, the vigorous von Stackelberg set about submitting to the Supreme Court at Karlsruhe more than 80 examples of what he called crass prejudice. The lower court, he contested, had failed to believe its own scientific experts, failed to submit new photographs of Anna's ears to experts and failed to hear more than 30 witnesses cited by Wollmann during his last plea. He completed his brief in July 1968. It was a further eighteen months before the Supreme Court found time to review the case. Lilburn describes the colourful nature of the proceedings. 'The lunatics all gravitated to our side. You almost got the feeling that the opposition had paid them. At one point a woman got up and and shouted: "She's not Anastasia, she's Tatiana; I'm Anastasia".'

The last negative judgement from Hamburg had thrown Anna into a depression. The floors of her chalet were encrusted with cat dirt and littered with papers, empty cans of pet food and milk bottles. When she was told that the ballerina Mathilde Kschessinska, the 95 year-old widow of her supporter, Grand Duke Andrew, wanted to see her in Paris, her response was oblique and ungracious: 'I will never go to Paris. Prince Frederick would do better to look after my affairs with the King of Denmark, now that he has lost my case in the court!'

However, her friends were delighted when, in a change of heart, she announced that she would go to Paris after all. She had apparently been swayed by the idea of being involved in a documentary being made about her. Though the documentary would contain fictional elements, the director's plan was to record the actual testimony of witnesses. Anna's much-vaunted shyness gave way, as it occasionally did, to monomania; she was soon installed in the car, undaunted by the prospect of a twelve-hour drive. Upon arrival in Paris, she proved a tireless tourist, rushing up the Eiffel Tower and through the cathedral of Notre-Dame, dressed in furs, veils and large sunglasses.

Anna Anderson and Prince Frederick

Meanwhile the director had arranged a screening of old newsreel clips of the Russian Imperial Family. Anna's companions were favourably struck by her reactions; she put her hand to her heart when she saw the Tsar. Indeed Lilburn says it was Anna's reaction to the footage that convinced him finally that she really was the Grand Duchess Anastasia. At one point she spotted a breach of etiquette during some interaction between

Grand Duke Nicholas and the Tsar. As the cousins spoke, the Grand Duke failed to turn to face the Tsar; the Tsar, the shorter of the two, was obliged to turn around himself. Anna was outraged: 'Impertinent', she snapped. Upon seeing footage of the storming of the Winter Palace – probably Eisenstein's film – she went and stood by the wall, crying.

Her response upon seeing the Grand Duchesses, was, however, more bizarre. The three elder girls appeared on the screen; they were later joined by their youngest sister, Anastasia. Her remark, when the first three appeared, was simply: 'There's one missing'.

Anna in Paris

The meeting with Grand Duke Andrew's widow, Mathilde, never took place. Mathilde's wish had been to meet Anna before she died. She wanted to reassure Anna that she and her husband had always believed her claim. But when Anna and her supporters arrived at Mathilde's house, they found her less agreeable son, Vova, in charge. Vova announced that doctors had forbidden his mother to take part in any meeting that might upset her. Anna was outraged to find that she was the one now knocking vainly at the door. She expressed no sympathy for Mathilde's condition: 'But I must see her. I must. Absolutely... Any more of this and I'm leaving.'

Two weeks later the French film crew filmed Mathilde reading out a statement in which she referred to her earlier meeting with Anna in 1928. After this meeting she and her husband had both declared themselves convinced that Anna was the Grand Duchess. But the statement she read out now was equivocal. 'The comparison I was able to make between her and the unknown woman could only be relative... My impressions must not be taken as an affirmation...' However the director left the recorder running afterwards; Mathilde now expressed an altogether different opinion: 'I am still certain it is she. When she looked at me, you understand, with those eyes... That was it, it was the Emperor... It was the exact same look. It was the Emperor's look. And anyone who saw the Emperor's eyes will never forget them... It is she, you know, I am certain it is she.'

***

When Anna returned to Unterlengenhardt, she may have felt her life had become rather empty. There was a hiatus in the court proceedings and, while she was forever railing against the iniquities of lawyers, she probably felt a cooling of interest.

Whatever the reason, it became clear to her supporters that she was increasingly preoccupied with Gleb's plan that she join him in Charlottesville. When several friends suggested she put down the more disabled of her pets, she simply replied: 'America'.

A garden party was held on the hundredth anniversary of the birth of the Tsar in May 1968; Anna watched disconsolately from her window. By the end of the month her lack of party spirit had developed into dark paranoia. For four full days she saw no one and, as far as her friends knew, ate nothing. Eventually one of her elderly carers ordered that the door be broken down; Anna was lying on the floor moaning: 'Mamma, Mamma where is Mamma? I'm dying.' Friends disagreed about whether this collapse was brought on by painful associations with the Tsar's birthday or by Prince Frederick's unpopular decision to remove her compost heap.

She was taken to hospital where she was annoyed to be told that her house was being cleaned. Her annoyance turned to horror when she was told that her 40 cats had been gassed and Baby (the dog) destroyed. She became convinced that the Baroness had injected her with an incapacitating dose of morphine while 'the criminal', Prince Frederick, carried out the killings. She pronounced herself more than ready to leave Europe.

Gleb, on his side, was now desperately casting about for ways of bringing his plan to fruition. He needed someone to bring Anna to Charlottesville, someone organised enough to make the travel arrangements and tactful enough to maintain harmonious relations with Anna for the duration of a long journey. His final choice was Alexis Miliukov.

In the five years since their initial meeting, Miliukov and Anna had established a rapport of sorts. Among recent shared interests had been, curiously, Castle Seeon. At some point they had heard that it was for sale and hit upon the unlikely idea of converting it into a hotel. They had soon convinced each other there would be no problem persuading Gleb's millionaire friend, Jack Manahan, to stump up the cash. Anna's obvious shortcomings as a housekeeper do not seem to have entered into the discussion.

When Miliukov arrived at Unterlengenhardt in July 1968 to escort Anna to America, the pair could barely contain their excitement. They decided they must leave for Charlottesville as soon as possible, in order to begin their negotiations with Jack Manahan. They might even stay in Washington for a few nights for a spot of sightseeing. Miliukov taped their discussion.

Anna: 'Yes, I pay to the President a visit... Yes I will speak with him.'

Miliukov: 'What would you like to speak with him?'

Anna: 'I... ask him, "How do you do, Mr President?" And he surely will tell, "Thank you".'

Miliukov: 'And what else?'

Anna: 'And then goodbye.'

How long Anna planned to stay in America is not known; she was probably unclear herself. She did know, however, that she had had enough of life in Unterlengenhardt; she had not forgiven the mayor for issuing orders to clean her property. And as Miliukov tried to organise her passport, the extent of her alienation from her friends became clear. Anna's anger with the Baroness was such that she had recently locked her out of her house while not letting her out of the compound. The Baroness, in her eighties, had been trapped in the garden, in the blazing sun, for several hours. Now, discussing her travel plans with Miliukov, Anna dismissed outright the idea of enlisting help from either the Baroness or the Prince.

Anna: 'I don't see the Baroness Miltitz, for life and death not...'

Miliukov: 'Well then I tell them that I...'

Anna: 'The Baroness Miltitz I don't see.'

Miliukov: 'Okay.'

Anna: 'You can do what on earth you want. Never! I never do that.'

Miliukov: 'Alright, okay.'

Anna: 'Under no any condition will I see this woman.'

Miliukov: 'How about Prinz Friedrich? You see him?'

Anna: 'Neither. Never.'

Miliukov: 'You don't like Prinz Friedrich?'

Anna: 'No!'

Miliukov: 'But... thirty years you like him very much!'

Anna: 'I didn't never like him. You forgot that I hardly saw him. Hardly, that is the truth.'

Having finally arranged a passport and American visa,

Miliukov left Unterlengenhardt with Anna on 13 July. The pair flew from Frankfurt to Dulles airport, in Washington. They had arrived in Charlottesville before any of her friends in Unterlengenhardt knew she had left. She said goodbye to no one.

The loyal Anastasians, who for so many years had dug deep into their own pockets to support her, endured a final insult when they entered the house and, amongst the debris, came upon piles of uncashed cheques.

CHAPTER SEVEN
The death of Gleb

Anna would have known little of Charlottesville beyond news gleaned from Gleb's letters. But she must have been intrigued by the idea of meeting Jack Manahan at last. She would doubtless have found the tales of his wealth appealing. After years of eking out a humble existence in Unterlengenhardt, she probably yearned for the grand hospitality of her castle-hopping days.

Would she, then, have been sufficiently impressed by Jack's house at University Circle? Though smart, it was hardly baronial. And who knows what she made of her new patron. Years later, Jack said that when he and Gleb had met Anna in Washington, she had been somewhat under the weather. 'Her mind was certainly cloudy at the time she got off the plane at

Dulles as to what her future would be and she was rather a pathetic individual at that time.'

Anna and Gleb, meanwhile, were being reunited for the first time in 30 years. Gleb must have been deeply moved to have Anna finally restored to him in America. He would have been in a particularly heightened state of emotion as he was still in mourning following the death of his wife, Nadine, just six months before. The Botkins had been together for 48 years.

There is no record of Anna's thoughts on being reunited with her *chevalier*. But it is perhaps a mark of her feelings for Gleb that, within hours of her arrival, she had referred to his bereavement. Anna was not known for her powers of empathy. Gleb would have been the first to appreciate that seventeen words of condolence amounted, from her, to an outpouring of sympathy. 'I felt terrible sorry for you. So long as wife about you, I know safe and support.'

Anna's views on Nadine's qualities as a wife had not always been so favourable. Years earlier, while staying with Miss Jennings, Anna would complain about Nadine, claiming that Gleb had told her 'she would never work'. Her other complaint was, obscurely, that Nadine, perhaps with ideas beyond her means, wished to 'be bought everything at the delicatessen shop'.

Gleb had pulled no punches when he presented his case for Charlottesville as the perfect location for his reunion with Anna. He insisted that the city reminded him of Tsarskoye Selo where he and the Grand Duchess Anastasia had grown up.

He had once described Tsarskoye Selo as 'a sort of terrestrial paradise' for monarchists. His description of Charlottesville was more muted: 'It is a beautiful city. Its climate is very pleasant.' But then the similarities lay not so much in any shared grandeur as in their cosy friendliness. Though he had only recently moved to Charlottesville from New Jersey, Gleb was already a well-known figure. He was fond of relating how he was walking down Main Street when a bus stopped beside him and the driver asked: 'Mr Botkin would you like a ride?'

We do not know what Anna's initial impressions were. But at first she seemed intent on not disappointing her adoring host. She presented Jack with a handkerchief bearing the Tsar's initials, at which he declared himself 'overpowered'. She then produced nine pieces of cutlery from the silver mines, she claimed, of the Reuss family. The pieces, to be divided evenly between Jack Gleb and Miliukov, gave Anna an opportunity to shine: 'The Princess Reuss was my kind friend.' Jack, in turn, treated himself to several minutes on names, titles and dates associated with the Reuss family.

Buoyed up by the spirit of accord, Anna made a dramatic gesture. Rummaging in her bag, she declared: 'Now I am safe. Now I do not need this.' On the breakfast table she placed a short, sharp dagger.

On Miliukov's tapes can be heard the mostly happy exchange with which Gleb and Anna marked their reunion. Jack is heard only intermittently as he makes game efforts, as always, to smooth over awkward moments. Gleb begins gallantly, offering an improbably favourable comparison of Anna's appearance with that of the *Anastasia* star, Ingrid Bergman.

Gleb: 'To have selected such an actress – a big Swedish horse.'

Anna: 'Is he not sweet?'

He continues with a simple anecdote about wild pigs threatening a baby on the estate of Anna's former lawyer, Leverkuehn. 'Someone put a sign up saying "Keep the Gate Closed". They had a woman who cleaned and she hadn't come for three days... They went down to the village and asked her what was wrong. She said she couldn't get in because the sign said "Keep the Gate Closed".'

The hoped-for laughter is not forthcoming. Jack can now be heard coming to the rescue.

Jack: '...There's a man up in court for stealing a rug. They said: "Why did you steal it?" He says the lady in the shop gave it to me and said "beat it"... It's slang for "run away".'

Anna remains unmoved; with her taste for high living, she has not managed to tear herself away from the Leverkuehns' estate: 'This was lovely place,' she muses: 'Trees, blueberries, lakes.'

Treachery proves a popular topic. Indeed Gleb and Anna become so overexcited recalling the perfidies of her unfortunate lawyer Vermehren – or 'Vermin' as they call him – that Jack feels he must step in.

Gleb: 'Vermehren was just a crook.'

Anna: 'Eighty thousand marks. Do you hear? He threatened

always, Vermehren always... This happened Mr Manahan.'

Jack: 'The raisins are good... And the ice cream.'

Gleb: 'It was a difficult situation.'

Anna: 'He bought house in Bavaria with movie money. Tried to blackmail the American movie picture company.'

Gleb: '...The company came to me and said if you want exclusive rights we need more money...'

Jack: 'Butter pecan?... Orange sherbet?'

Jack is not averse to exposing traitors, but he is in favour of a cooler, more systematic approach. At another point on the tapes, he can be heard going through a book index, marking off friends and enemies. The friends are awarded a star and the enemies a minus; a third symbol, zero, is for the 'don't knows'. Anna adds a fourth category which she renders almost indistinguishable from minus: 'mess'.

The stars are few and far between. Minuses multiply: Colonel Nicholas Kulikovsky, the husband of 'Aunt' Olga, comes in for particular criticism. According to Anna, he was literally a 'mess'. 'He was a pig, dirty, unwashed with dirt under his nails.' Baroness Sophie Buxhoeveden, the Tsarina's former lady-in-waiting, who once denounced Anna as 'too short for Tatiana', fares no better. A fond friend of the Tsarina who followed the Imperial Family to Siberia, travelling for part of the journey on a train carriage roof, she was still judged by Anna to have betrayed the Romanovs and is therefore awarded a large minus and the epithet 'my greatest enemy on this earth'.

In the course of the awards procedure, Anna comes out with some startling revelations. Her former American benefactor

Billy Leeds (star) has, she insists, had a sex change. Yakov Yurovsky (minus), the Bolshevik commandant in charge of the shooting of the Romanovs, was 'man and woman in one'.

***

Jack's plan was that Anna would stay at his larger property, Fair View Farms, in Scottsville, with an old friend of his mother called Alicia Flynn. He would pick her up every day and take her back to the house on University Circle. She and Jack would spend nights at different locations for the sake of propriety. Over the next few weeks, Jack embraced the unlikely role of conventional host, escorting his elderly protégée around local tourist attractions such as Monticello, the spectacular house designed and built by Thomas Jefferson.

The couple walked happily everywhere, but always in single file. According to Jack, Anna's passion for hierachy meant she had to walk either ahead or behind. Jack took her to an exclusive country club where she became known for dietary peculiarities, not least her refusal of sauces and runny gravy. Jack was ready with an explanation: 'She saw too much blood running in that cellar in Ekaterinburg.'

Over the first few weeks of Anna's visit, Jack did his best to help her maintain her relationship with Gleb. Every few days he and Anna would visit Gleb's modestly sized clapboard house on Stonefield Lane, 'The House of Love', as it was occasionally called.

Gleb and Nadine had been obliged to move from their 'hut'

in New Jersey after a forest fire. They had lived with their son in a small town in Maryland before moving to Charlottesville, in 1963, to join their daughter, Marina, and her husband, Richard Schweitzer. Gleb had chosen his location well. Both Schweitzers gave him unstinting support; neither doubted his recognition of his childhood friend. Richard Schweitzer now says: 'I observed that with both Gleb and Tatiana (Gleb's sister) it was not a question of "believing in" the identity of A. She was someone they both had known from a very young age. They "knew" her.' Over the years the Schweitzers also succeeded in maintaining a relationship with Anna, even appointing her godmother to one of their children.

When Nadine died, Gleb said he found the pain of bereavement alleviated by the comforts of his life in Charlottesville. He wrote to Miliukov in March 1968: 'I should wish nothing better than to stay here... The house I inhabit is comfortable and cosy and now dearer to me than ever, since it is here that Nadine has spent her last years with me... All our local friends and neighbours have always been touchingly fond of Nadine and continue to be as touchingly kind to me. The prospect of ending my terrestrial sojourn in their midst is thus a very pleasing one.'

Gleb's espousal of the Church of Aphrodite did, however, arouse controversy. There were those who maintained his consecrated robes were no more than converted curtains. He was also accused of succumbing to a sort of spiritual promiscuity, in which he was liable to experiment with necromancy and even satanism.

In fact Gleb ran the Church of Aphrodite along reassuringly disciplined and conventional lines. He held services at the house three times a week. Jack and Anna occasionally attended services, though it is not known to what extent they subscribed to the Aphrodisian ideology. In one room Gleb had created a gold-covered altar which he decorated with candles and vases of plastic flowers. On the altar he installed a five-foot plaster copy of the Venus de Medici.

At the core of Gleb's ideology was the force of love. As he once wrote: 'A good gardener pulls out the weeds, not because he hates them, but because he loves flowers. Were a gardener to start hating weeds, he would end by pulling out also all his flowers, lest some weeds should hide under them.' His fun-loving religion had a concept of heaven, but none of hell. There were no negative commandments. Aphrodite, he proclaimed, simply looked on evil and sinfulness with sorrow. 'In Christianity you have the dilemma of either following the straight and narrow path and going to heaven or having fun here and going to hell... Aphrodite believes you can lead a very happy life here and be assured a happy life in the beyond.'

Gleb's promotion of happiness did not preclude a serious dedication to worship; he held regular 45-minute services on Friday and Saturday evenings and a communion service on Sunday. He also held vespers on Tuesday evening and a liturgical reading on Wednesday mornings. The small, makeshift chapel seated only ten, so it was as well that attendance was generally a modest three to seven. As Gleb once pointed out: 'It is not the kind of religion that you go out and shout and yell about and crowds arrive. I don't believe in conversion in the sense that you can put ideas in their heads. It is a matter of clarifying ideas... There must be millions of people who are basically Aphrodisians.'

The Aphrodisian service featured a credo: 'I believe in Aphrodite, the flower-faced, sweetly smiling, laughter-loving goddess of love and beauty, the self-existing, eternal and only supreme deity, creator and mother of the cosmos...' The congregants would then sing the fulsome *Thanksgiving Hymn* from *The Ritual of The Church of Aphrodite* in which thanks were offered: 'For the light and warmth of our sun, for the radiance of our moon, for the brilliance of our stars, we thank Thee, O Aphrodite... Blessed Thou art, O Mother of the cosmos, and our gratitude to Thee is like the sky that has no bounds, like eternity that has no ending, like Thy (sic) Own beauty that no words could describe...'

Gleb's enthusiastic embrace of what might be termed 'free love' gave rise to comment in the *Richmond Times-Dispatch*. From the article, Gleb emerges less as the author of several books about the Russian Revolution than a sort of Slavic Timothy Leary. Before quoting Gleb, the reporter warned readers that the words would shock any Bible-reading Christian. 'Sexual expression is as fully divine as any other expression... Love is a bond that should completely unite us. If a sexual relationship, whether within marriage or out of marriage, is a fulfilment of complete love between two people, it is acceptable, and people should be able to express that love.'

Gleb had always been good-looking and attractive to the

opposite sex. He in turn was attracted to women: whether this made his liberal stance more or less difficult cannot be known. He wrote in November 1968 that he had given a talk on religion: 'I could not have wished for a more charming and intelligent audience.' His talk was addressed to the University Law Wives Club.

As a grizzled elderly man, Gleb's enjoyment of the company of Charlottesville wives might have seemed acceptable. Less acceptable, however, would have been his belief in open marriage. He could have defended himself by pointing out that his own wife, who was most concerned, never raised objections to his theories. But there is every indication that he never fully grasped how subversive his views were; he certainly made no effort to temper either them or the breezy manner in which he expressed them: 'A person comes to me and says he loves my music, my country, my children. Fine. But in our society, if he comes to me and says he loves my wife, I am supposed to take a butcher's knife and cut him up. This is illogical. If he loves my wife, he must be a brother of mine because he must have been attracted by the same things about her that attracted me. If his love for her is pleasing to her, I see nothing wrong with it.' There was nothing morally reprehensible in the husband who commits adultery. He was simply like the musician 'who loves to play Bach and suddenly he wants to play Beethoven'.

Anna and Jack did not allow the Aphrodisian embrace of love to deter them as they continued to mark off Anna's old acquaintances with disapproving 'minuses'. Her anger with her devoted friend and supporter Prince Frederick showed no sign of abating. Years of financial and moral support were brushed aside with accusations that he had stolen her possessions and poisoned her pets. He remained unforgiven, and labelled a 'murderer'.

Gleb's own love tenets were put to the test as he found himself increasingly irritated by Jack's maverick tendencies. The two men had previously agreed that Anna's visit to Charlottesville should be kept private. Indeed Jack stipulated, in one of the first 20-minute interviews in a local paper, that his name be kept out of the article. Anna added mysteriously that the address must also be kept secret, otherwise her enemies might try to silence her.

Now there seemed to be little possibility of either of them being silenced. Jack had evidently decided to break his agreement with Gleb and go public; journalists were turning up at University Circle on an almost daily basis. The ensuing publicity – '"Anastasia" finds Haven in Virginia – Mystery Woman to Stay' in the Charlottesville *Daily Progress;* 'Fight to Prove Identity Wearisome – She Doesn't Care Anymore' in the *Halifax Gazette;* '"Daughter" of Last Tsar Steals Show at City DAR Luncheon' in the *Evening Star* – put Gleb in an awkward position; he had assured the German consul that Anna's visit would be kept private.

He described his awkward situation in an angry letter to a friend. 'Manahan, who, having solemnly promised to me that he will keep all newspaper reporters away from Anasastia, did the very opposite and started inviting them to his house,' he wrote. 'In addition, he keeps arranging banquets and talking incredible nonsense about some imaginary "conspiracies" and writing crazy letters to everybody he can think of, not only in this country, but also in Europe.'

While Gleb seemed to recognise early signs of Jack's mental instability, the newspaper reporters were content to take him at face value as a proficient genealogist with a certain simple and benevolent wisdom. Jack's reply, when asked why he had taken Anna into his home was, indeed, sober and sympathetic: 'To get the history written straight and to see that she has a happy and a safe life and to help her win her case in court.'

In terms of eccentricity, Jack probably found Anna a wonderful foil. As journalists turned up at the appointed hour, he would be the one appearing at the door with personable greetings: Anna, meanwhile, would be nowhere in sight. When she failed to appear, Jack would be ready with a variety of jolly excuses: she hated having her photograph taken, her bedroom clock had broken or she was in the bath. If visitors began showing signs of impatience, it fell to Jack to coax her out of hiding: 'Anaaastasia... Come on out now.'

Anna never mastered the art of creating a good first impression. Her air of being involved in something covert was exacerbated by her continuing habit of holding a tissue over her mouth. Journalists were struck by what they saw as her want of a regal bearing; they remarked on her clothes: battered flowery hats, fluffy white slippers and dark red trousers, occasionally with the zip undone. One of them noted that she ate ice cream at close-range, with a spoon in her fist.

The longed-for memories of Imperial Russia proved elusive: 'That is so far back and so dead, all so past, Russia doesn't exist,' she would snap. 'Mess' and 'dead' were her favourite words; she referred to her quest for recognition and decades of litigation as a 'big mess'. During one interview she pointed at the long-suffering Gleb, who happened to be present: 'That's the only one alive of my friends. My old friends are all dead.'

With her depressing outlook, it is not surprising that Anna felt discussing the past would endanger her health: 'One becomes ill when one must again and again repeat.' Happily, Jack was generally able to step in, entertaining visitors with readings from books about Anna. At heart-rending moments she would appear to shake with sobs behind a fistful of tissues. One reporter from the *Washington Post* noted that the tissues she held to her face remained dry.

She was more inclined to discuss her recent German past and the perfidy of her German friends. The villain Prince Frederick had conspired with the Baroness Miltitz to destroy her cats. Even the German doctors were at fault; during one hospital stay, she was still insisting, she had been given morphine shots against her will. With these unpleasant memories, it was perhaps surprising that, for some weeks, Anna clung to the idea of returning to Germany and still toyed with the unlikely dream of setting herself up at Castle Seeon as a hotelier.

These hopeful speculations were shunted on to the back-burner by the unexpected arrival of Rasputin's daughter,

Maria. In 1929 Maria had told the *New York Times* she was convinced Anna was not who she claimed to be. She had known the Grand Duchess Anastasia intimately when they were children, she said, and the photograph she had seen bore no resemblance to the girl she remembered. She expressed surprise that her view on the claimant had not been sought before. She did not seem to take into account that there might have been difficulties locating her: she had been working as a dancer at a Berlin circus.

In August 1968 Maria arrived at Jack's farm in Scottsville, accompanied by a Californian publicist called Patte Barham. She claimed that the last time she had seen the Grand Duchess Anastasia was when the Imperial Family had travelled on a boat past the Rasputins' village in Siberia. She maintained she had snuck on board to say goodbye, dressed as a peasant.

Jack summoned Gleb as well as a reporter from the local paper to witness what should have been a historic reunion. Things seemed to be looking up when Anna apparently addressed Maria as 'Mara', a pet name known only to her most intimate friends. But Maria somehow missed the clue and failed to recognise her childhood friend. It was only after the pair had been closeted together in another room – ostensibly to examine several of Anna's birthmarks and scars – that Maria pronounced herself convinced.

Patte Barham had dramatic recollections of Maria being so upset that she was unable to sleep. She 'paced the floor instead of sleeping', saying '"Bless God it is (she), but it is such a decision, I am afraid almost to think about it... It gives me the chills".'

Maria said later that she had been impressed when Anna remembered her dressing up as a Red Cross nurse, an episode she herself had forgotten. The journalist, Rey Barry, who wrote for the Charlottesville *Daily Progress* as well as *Associated Press*, is convinced that Maria was telling the truth at the time: 'She said "This is Anastasia". There was no duplicity in her voice, manner or face when she said it,' he says. However he admits that he struggled with her subsequent claim that she was a lion-tamer with the Ringling Brothers Circus. 'She just didn't have that kind of confidence. She wasn't that kind of strong woman. She was very feminine.'

Gleb remained unimpressed; he was initially opposed to Maria simply because of who she was: 'A Rasputin gives the case a bad name,' he declared. Upon meeting her, he was filled with distaste: 'I found her to be just what one would expect – a very homely Siberian peasant with the small eyes of a sly pig and saccharin manners of very doubtful sincerity.' He was, however, characteristically unfazed, immediately confronting her, demanding to know why she had not come forward to support Anna before. 'My question embarrassed her visibly and she mumbled something to the effect that she had been very busy and had not heard about Anastasia until recently, which was, of course, a lie.'

In the same letter Gleb alluded to Maria's companion, Patte Barham, mentioning that she was writing a biography of

Rasputin. He scoffed at her proposed title, *The Rape of Rasputin*, declaring it 'as unappetising as it is baffling'.

Jack took a sunnier view of the developments. He lost no time in persuading Maria to accompany him to a downtown bank, now the Jefferson National Bank, where she dictated and signed a statement confirming her identification of the Grand Duchess Anastasia. Jack deemed the statement persuasive enough to be sent to lawyers in Germany.

Three months later, Maria and Patte Barham returned to Charlottesville for a second visit. Their plan was to persuade Anna to accompany them back to Patte Barham's home in Hollywood. They had already made plans for a lavish gala tea in her honour; the tea-party was to be held at Ms Barham's house and invitations had been printed and sent out. Gleb thoroughly disapproved: 'They tried to induce the Grand Duchess to go with them to California and allow herself to be exhibited at some kind of monster gathering for the purpose of helping them publicise their book about Rasputin and promote some kind of dubious charities.'

Anna first agreed to go, then abruptly changed her mind. Much put out, the two ladies consoled themselves with an evening at the Gaslight restaurant, in Charlottesville, with Rey Barry. At that point Maria was still adamant that Anna was who she said she was. As Barry wrote: 'Over hamburgers and too much to drink, Maria told me why she was convinced Anna Anderson was really Anastasia. She said that, during their meetings, she would start to recount some childhood experience no one but she and the Grand Duchess had shared, and Anastasia would finish the story... It didn't happen once or twice, it happened in a score of specific instances. Very matter-of-factly, Maria told me, it was certain beyond question that Anna Anderson was the real Anastasia.'

Less certain, once again, were the increasingly dramatic tales Maria told of her own life-story. She now said that, before becoming a lion-tamer, she had been mauled by a bear in Peru. She touched upon her childhood and alluded to her father, boasting that he had slept with the Tsarina while a 'religious adviser' at the Russian Court. Patte Barham chimed in, declaring that her biography of Maria's father promised to be what she called 'sexsational'. Barham was later to claim that Rasputin's penis was being kept in a velvet box in Paris by fanatical émigrés.

Barry recalls that the evening was further enriched when the Gaslight barman, John Tuck, revealed that the father of one of his boyhood chums had been with the group of assassins who murdered Rasputin. Maria challenged him: 'Why didn't he like my father?' Tuck probably wished he had stuck to serving the drinks.

The two ladies set off back to California from Charlottesville the following day. And then everything seemed to fall apart. At Dulles airport they made an official statement denying that they had ever recognised the Grand Duchess Anastasia. Maria claimed Anna's distinguishing birthmarks and scars had now disappeared, while Barham declared Anna to be 'the cleverest fraud we've ever seen'. Maria put it more picturesquely: 'I've been bluffed by her.'

After they had left, Gleb wrote in fury: 'Those horrible women from California, the Misses Barham and Rasputin turned out to be precisely the kind of dirty creatures I had been warning everyone from the start that they are... the two California bitches instantly turned from friends and admirers into AN's (Anna's) bitterest enemies, declared her an impostor and began to write horrible articles and give out equally horrible interviews.'

With characteristic lack of judgement, Jack read out the articles to Anna; she then formed the impression that he had either written them or paid for them to be written himself. She began ringing Gleb several times a day saying that she could no longer stay with Jack. 'I'm doing my best to calm her, but have no idea how all will end,' lamented Gleb.

He consoled himself with the thought that Anna complained almost continuously whatever her circumstances. He also recognised that Jack's lapses of judgement were aspects of an otherwise appealing naivety. In the same letter Gleb paid tribute to Jack's efforts: 'At least he is very kind to her and permits her to do anything she pleases.'

Within two months of Anna's arrival in Charlottesville, Gleb was in the town's Martha Jefferson Hospital with a prostate infection. Though Gleb had been complaining of poor health for some time, it's possible that the vicissitudes of his new life with Anna were taking an additional toll. Gleb's correspondence was temporarily taken over by a Hugh D. Cook. In his replies, on Gleb's richly annotated notepaper, Cook declared that he had been associated with the Church of

Aphrodite for about a year and was now studying for the priesthood. Beneath his name he typed 'Hieros' – Greek for holy. Gleb set store by officialdom; he was slightly put out when Ian Lilburn neglected to accord him his title of Archbishop.

Gleb emerged from hospital looking more ascetic than ever. Anna, usually absorbed in her own difficulties, confounded her new friends by first remarking on the change in his appearance and then announcing that she planned to stay in Charlottesville to look after him.

By now Anna was either losing interest in or, more likely, had completely forgotten her German hotel plans. Indeed her attitude to Europe had become decidedly negative; when asked whether she would like to return, she snapped: 'Never. I have too many enemies there.' Prince Frederick and Baroness von Miltitz stood accused of purloining documents worth ten million dollars.

Nonetheless, the pending expiry of her American visa in January seemed to cause Anna no worries. She was busily ensconced in a burgeoning social life. She and Jack received an unexpected invitation to Richard Nixon's inauguration; although they decided, for some reason, not to attend, Jack carefully preserved the invitation. On a more intimate level, Anna enjoyed chats over Danish cherry wine with her neighbour, Mildred Ewell. Mrs Ewell, an old friend of Jack's, quickly formed an attachment to Anna. She says she was immediately struck by the way Anna nodded her head and waved her hand 'exactly like the Royals'. Anna's embrace of the all-American life was completed with a sobering announcement that she planned to take driving lessons.

First, though, Jack and Gleb had to work out how to persuade the authorities to let Anna stay in Charlottesville. After several lengthy and probably confused discussions, they decided that the only way to prolong Anna's stay in the United States was for her to marry an American citizen. Though now a widower, Gleb immediately declared himself unsuitable. First he had very little money; he clearly did not set much store by contemporary news reports estimating Anna's potential fortune at 28 million dollars. Secondly he was suffering from a heart condition and was in no position to look after anyone else. His third, more gracious excuse probably harked back to the difficulties he had suffered in his relationship with Anna as a young man. Marrying Anna, as he put it, would be like 'marrying his sovereign'.

Jack gallantly stepped forward to offer himself in what the couple would term 'a marriage of protection'. But he also stood to gain from the marriage. His father had specified in his will that, if Jack did not marry, all the Manahan property would go to the University of Virginia.

***

Five months after their first meeting, Anna and Jack were married in the Charlottesville city hall by City Sergeant Raymond Pace. On the marriage certificate Anna listed her name as Anna Anderson née Romanov. Her father's name she gave as

Nicholas Romanov; for her mother's maiden name she wrote Alexandra Hesse-Darmstadt. Her education she gave as 'taught by governess'; the address she listed was Fair View Farms. Jack asked Gleb what the Tsar would have thought of his new son-in-law. Gleb's reply was characteristically delicate: 'I think he would have been grateful.'

A photograph still exists of the couple shortly after they were married. The journalist Rey Barry asked them to pose with something that they felt best represented their new spouse. Anna's smile is wide enough but she somehow seems to leer over their invitation to Nixon's inauguration. Jack, grinning and altogether easier in his manner, holds a picture of the Tsar.

On 28 January Gleb wrote very positively of the newly-weds: 'The Manahan marriage gives every indication of being a success. Last Sunday they attended liturgy in my chapel and both were in the best of moods.' He adopted a sanguine view of the opinion of Anna's European friends. 'I have not heard from either Prince Frederick or Baroness von Miltitz directly, but, judging by their letters to other persons, some of which I saw, I think that they are relieved, rather than horrified, by the Grand Duchess's marriage.' In fact, many of them *were* horrified, believing that Anna had married beneath her. The level-headed Baroness regarded Jack as a sort of clown.

Gleb's feelings about Jack, meanwhile, continued to vacillate. An ongoing annoyance was Jack's continued insistence upon giving interviews to the press. Reporters from local papers trailed the couple as they attended countless meetings of the historical societies to which Jack belonged. Gleb felt that these

277

repeated appearances in the press detracted from Anna's dignity.

Another threat to Anna's dignity was the vast collection of mechanical toys littering the house at University Circle. Gleb's irritation with the collection reached a peak one night when he was meant to be enjoying dinner with the couple. An argument broke out and Anna let out a high-pitched scream. The scream activated a five-foot high mechanical penguin which then marched into the room. Gleb told his daughter, Marina, that this was the last straw. 'From now on I am keeping completely out of it.'

Jack and Anna in their early days together

Of course Gleb's attachment to Anna was such that he could not stick to his resolve. Though he saw less of the couple, he was continually in touch with them until he became seriously ill in the winter of 1969. Relations between the two men remained sufficiently good for Jack to brave a snowstorm and deliver Christmas presents to Stonefield Lane. Within days of Jack's visit, Gleb died of a heart attack. He was 69 years old.

Anna was by this time, as she put it, 'ill, deranged and tired'. For this reason it is difficult to gauge her upset over Gleb's death. From a pragmatic point of view she had lost her most effective supporter; on an emotional level she had lost her fondest friend. With all her muddled perceptions, Anna must have been affected by the particularly charged relationship she shared with Gleb. Mildred Ewell says Anna believed she loved him. Anna managed a succinct quote to the *New York Times*: 'Everything is changed entirely with his death.' Her grief may have been sharpened by her conviction that he had been murdered. So many of her friends, she insisted, had met a strange end.

Jack, Anna and Gleb

CHAPTER EIGHT
Married life in Charlottesville

The timing of Gleb's death was particularly unfortunate: Anna's case was about to be argued before the Supreme Court in Karlsruhe. The Lawyer Stackelberg had written repeatedly asking Jack to persuade his new wife to make an appearance in court. Prince Frederick had also written, suggesting, slightly sourly, that she might return to Europe to thank her supporters for their help. With characteristic optimism, he maintained the judge would be impressed to see her as she really was 'natural and straightforward'.

Shortly before his death, Gleb had written an enthusiastic letter to the Prince in which he pledged support for the new legal project. He expressed, at length, his approval of the engagement of Stackelberg: 'My father was on very friendly terms with one of the Stackelbergs and thought highly of the whole Stackelberg family. If I am not mistaken, it was a niece of Countess Grabbe who married my cousin, Michael von Enden.' The feeling may not have been reciprocated; Steno von Stackelberg described Gleb as a 'charlatan'.

Anna

Gleb did, however, feel it would be unwise for Anna to travel to Germany: 'On occasion she can still be most gracious and charming and simply bewitch the persons she meets. But unhappily she is just as often – and perhaps even more often – in an angry and suspicious mood and can even become intolerably rude. Were she in an angry and suspicious mood at the time of her appearance at the Supreme Court of Karlsruhe, I am afraid the effect of her behaviour and the nonsensical statements she is likely to make could prove disastrous.'

The difficulties with regard to her temperament showed little sign of abating; two months after her arrival in Charlottesville, the Prince sent photographs for her to identify. These effectively disappeared. As Jack wrote: 'She seized the pictures out of my hand and refused to return them to me for transmission to you.'

Before closing his reply, Gleb took pains to reassure the Prince that Anna was still, in general, content in Charlottesville. 'Thus, except for her unfortunate state of mind and frequent oubursts of pathological anger – one night she was greatly angered by a new moon which was lying down instead of standing up – the tragic story of Grand Duchess Anastasia's life may be said to have been given a happy ending.'

As soon as Gleb died, however, the Prince felt free to take liberties with the wishes of his old adversary. He now wrote to Anna assuring her that Gleb had always wanted her to return to Germany. This cheeky move resulted in the Prince receiving a sharp letter from an Andrew Hartsook in Zanesville, Ohio. Declaring himself acting successor of Gleb Botkin as 'Archbishop of the Church of Aphrodite', Hartsook accused the Prince of misleading Anna: 'It is with disapproval that I note in your letter to Her Imperial Highness that you state that Gleb Botkin had written to you in his last letter that Grand Duchess Anastasia should return to Germany.' Incidentally Hartsook now says Gleb never had a true successor, adding that the Aphrodisian movement died with its founder.

In the end Anna refused to go to Germany, insisting that her so-called friends in Europe would imprison her and prevent her from returning to America. Instead Jack sent a portrait of his wife to the President of the Court, signed with the best wishes of 'Anastasia and John E. Manahan'.

The court ruling was seen as a sort of draw – *non liquet* – neither established nor refuted. The judge said: 'We have not decided that the plaintiff is not Grand Duchess Anastasia but only that the Hamburg court made its decision without legal mistakes and without procedural errors.' Neither Anna nor Jack were particularly interested. Anna issued several of her enigmatic comments: 'It was wrong to have it in the newspapers. It cannot be risked again and it won't be... We go on.'

It is hard to imagine the nature of any rapport between Jack and Anna in these early days. It is known that Jack washed and tinted Anna's hair throughout her life, indicating some sort of relaxed intimacy. The writer Michael Thornton, who had known Anna for some years and spent time at Unterlengenhardt, visited the couple in 1970. He travelled from England shortly after hearing that Anna was spreading word that he had died mysteriously in a car crash in New York: 'She got a terrible fright when I rang up,' he recalls.

He remembers little now about the state of house. However, he observed their relationship with interest. 'The Baroness had said: "How can Anastasia be happy?" But I felt she was clearly fond of him. It was just that he irritated her. That was not surprising. He WAS irritating. He was madder than she was. They retired to their own rooms for their own good.'

Still, no one could dispute Anna and Jack's shared inclination towards unconventional living. Neither felt any constraints where personal appearance was concerned: Jack was invariably dressed in plaid jacket and tam o'shanter, while Anna rejoiced in her brilliant red outfits.

They were both also indefatigable hoarders, with little regard for storage arrangements. In the living room, Jack's rows of books, seven deep, now competed with an assortment of Anna's mementoes, ranging from priceless Romanov icons to rotting pieces of bric-a-brac.

Meanwhile, the garden at University Circle was allowed to deteriorate. Amongst the towering weeds, Anna scattered branches, tree-stumps and sacks of coal. She claimed this was a regrettable but necessary step to keep visitors at bay; she was not deterred when she herself fell on a piece of jagged wood and narrowly missed losing an eye. On the doorstep was strewn banana peel. The peel was sadly apposite: one neighbour, describing Anna to a friend, remarked that she had one foot in the grave and the other on a banana skin.

At variance with this disorder was the couple's punishing schedule of visits to genealogical conferences and meetings. These were recorded at great length in what was, for Jack, the equivalent of a diary: the *Coppage Family Bulletin*. He evidently set great store by his maternal grandparents, Frederick and Myrtle Coppage Becker. Myrtle he described as a 'noted beauty' though also a 'victim of melancholia'. In the *Bulletin*, Jack wrote: 'At the recent National Assembly of the Huguenot Society of Manakin held in Dallas, Texas, at the Sheraton-Dallas, your editor was unanimously elected Honorary Nation President.

'Accompanied by his wife Anastasia, last Grand Duchess of

Russia still surviving, who took an emu Easter egg with her and made Dallas headlines, he made in the month of May a 3,027-mile trip by car, visiting twice Emily Virginia Mills in Pine Bluff, Arkansas, who introduced them to Mrs H.L. Knorr, National Honorary President General of the Order of the Crown, who has in her house the largest card index file of Virginia marriages in existence...'

In 1972, a woman in Tampa, Florida, contacted the Manahans offering them a portrait of the Tsar for 30,000 dollars. Jack replied that the price was too high – even when she hastily dropped it to 15,000 dollars. Despite this, the couple decided to drive all the way to Florida for a viewing. As they equivocated over the purchase, the owner pulled out all the stops. She said: 'You know Mrs Merriweather Post wanted this painting for 25,000 dollars. We were ready to crate it up and send it to her. On the night we were going to do it, I dreamt that the Tsar came in and there were tears weeping down his face. I said to my husband, we can never let Mrs Post have this painting.'

In such free time as remained, Jack maintained enlivening correspondences. In January 1970 he was prompt with his grand reply to a letter sent from the Philippines to Anna in Charlottesville, via Unterlengenhart. He sent a signed portrait of Anna on the back of which he wrote an enthusiastic message: 'Best wishes to all our friends in the Philippines including Lenor Doromal of Ilolio City, formerly of Radford College Virginia.'

Jack's first Christmas present to Anna was a genealogical

chart featuring 1000 of her ancestors. He felt the chart would help him understand her character. He professed himself delighted to find that she was, in fact, Spanish. 'The stars in the outer ring (of the chart) and there are 88 of them, if they are all on there... Each is a separate line of descent from Ferdinand and Isabella.'

It is not known whether Jack was ever able to make any kind of assessment of his wife's character but it is unlikely that he drew any accurate conclusions from his chart. He certainly either failed to recognise, or decided to disregard, her most-trumpeted characteristic: shyness. The couple would argue about social outings for an hour, then Jack would shout through the door: 'We're going out to the car now, and I'm going to honk four times when we're ready to leave.' He would pile the dogs into the station wagon then simply lean on the horn until she emerged.

Jack and Anna's turbulent foray into Charlottesville society had its successes. They established a small but solid following. Jack would have been gratified by evidence soon emerging of Anna's lesser-known taste for public life. For weeks she cherished a restaurant table card with the slogan 'If you drink a glass of this wine, you'll think you're Anastasia too'. The couple's acceptance into the community seemed assured as they were photographed entertaining bemused newcomers to Charlottesville at a 'Welcome Wagon Club' luncheon.

But Anna's most loyal supporters remained Mildred Ewell and her husband, Dr Nathaniel Ewell. Dr Ewell, a paediatric physician, had been a fraternity brother of Jack's at the

University of Virginia. Mrs Ewell never doubted Anna's claim. 'She was a little aloof, reticent and very reserved... Very prim and proper and very strait-laced.' She recalls watching the television news with Anna in August 1979 when it was announced that Lord Mountbatten had been killed by the IRA. 'She didn't jump up. She threw up her hands: *"Mein Gott"*. She was really shaken. At that moment it was clear that she was not a peasant from Austria. No way.'

Bill Sublette, an editor of the *University of Virginia Alumni News* magazine, was impressed by her apparent indifference to her cause. 'She was never interested in proving that she was Anastasia. She didn't care that much about getting into the debate – Jack did that – and I thought that said something.' Another supporter, Alexander Peaslee, witnessed what he deemed a poignant sight during the Queen's visit to Charlottesville in 1976: 'The last of the Romanovs standing there with a banner, a flag of the Romanovs and a picture of the Tsar'. Needless to say, the Queen did not acknowledge her.

But perhaps it says something about Charlottesville that the couple boasted so many loyal friends who nevertheless doubted Anna's claim. Johanna Shalloway first encountered Jack in the downtown mall. He heard her German accent and struck up conversation with her. As she recalls: 'He asked me if I'd heard of the Tsar's daughter. He told me she was going to come here and that I should come and meet her in his villa.'

Mrs Shalloway felt almost immediately that Anna's claim was false. She had problems reconciling Jack and Anna's bizarre life-style with Anna's supposed beginnings at the Russian

Court. The strange appearance of the couple and the deteriorating conditions in which they lived proved continual stumbling blocks to some would-be believers. 'I did feel you could tell there was something untruthful about her. If she was raised in the Tsar's Court she would have everything super clean. A person like this would not put up with this dirty business.' Her view was supported by a friend who was a Professor of Slavonic studies. 'Anastasia had only been here a week before he said she was phoney. He detected a Polish accent. He said: "Johanna don't believe her. She is nothing but a cheap Polish backyard maid".'

The lawyer, Rae Ely, echoes Mrs Shalloway's view. 'There was a feeling of rooting for the home team. We hoped she would turn out to be the real Grand Duchess. But the average person would ask themselves how a child of such royal bearing at the beginning could have turned into such a peculiar person.'

Rey Barry, the journalist who had witnessed the meeting between Anna and Maria Rasputin, became a good friend while doubting her claim. His doubts, however, had nothing to do with her pecularities. 'I was one of the few people she talked to easily. She usually kept her chin covered to hide a scar. If she appeared without her chin covered, that was a way you knew she'd accepted you... If you create a picture based upon what she would be like – taking into account the insanity-producing aspect of her life between the ages of six and 21 – she came out right where she should. She was self-willed and very egotistical. She was a little kooky.'

Another neighbour of the couple, Jack Davis, praises Jack's good-natured disposition, while refraining from commenting about the claim. 'Jack was a good man. He was a good neighbour who always did the right thing.' He was more reticent about Anna: 'I didn't see much of her. But I admit she was a person who you didn't look forward to talking to. She was a messy thing, if you'll excuse that impertinent statement.' He later added that he had once seen Anna sitting in the couple's station wagon while only 'about half dressed'. He hesitated to criticise the couple's management of the house, though he did finally concede that it 'could use some cleaning'.

While Anna was usually viewed as the odder of the couple, she was frequently matched, and occasionally outdone, by Jack. At one point an advertising director of the *Daily Progress* recalled Jack visiting her college during a history class. He announced that he was going to run a competition in which students had to guess his title; the correct answer, to the bemusement of the competitors, was 'Tsar'. On another occasion, a prominent University of Virginia professor stalked out of one of Jack's talks. Jack had overstepped the mark, producing a handkerchief and proclaiming: 'This belonged to my late father-in-law, the Tsar of Russia.'

During the rare periods when they were at home, the Manahans still received a stream of reporters. Jack evidently saw no contradiction between the traps laid in the front garden and his eagerness to welcome in the press. The reporters emerged reeling from the unsettling combination of

Anna's random comments and Jack's garrulousness. He would talk grandly about Anna's connection with the International Communist Conspiracy or about his prediction of a second George Washington emerging to preside over a true American independence. He was capable of talking for hours without drawing breath; she, meanwhile, would snap: 'Don't believe a word he says,' and finally '*Mach ein Ende.*'

In 1976 Anthony Summers and Tom Mangold published *The File on the Tsar* in which they put forward evidence that the Tsarina and the four Grand Duchesses had not been killed at Ekaterinburg. The new evidence suggested the Tsarina and her daughters had been sent by train to the nearby town of Perm. The Tsar and Tsarevich, meanwhile, had been executed the day after the shootings were meant to have taken place. The book contained an entire chapter on Anna's life and an account of evidence presented in her court cases; the writers put forward the idea that the Grand Duchess Anastasia had escaped to the West. Jack was sufficiently excited by the book to present signed copies to visitors. Anna, predictably, harboured objections; however, these apparently centred on an unflattering photograph.

Soon after its publication, a Prince Alexis Romanov came forward claiming that his grandfather, Prince Nicholas Romanov-Dolgoruky, had been told by an assistant of Trotsky's that one of the Imperial children had survived. Prince Alexis also claimed, even more improbably, that Yussoupov had made a deathbed confession that he knew the Grand Duchess Anastasia was alive.

Anna's own accounts of the aftermath of the killings were becoming increasingly confused. With claims that the whole family had survived, she breezily brushed aside her traumatic experiences in the cellar at Ekaterinburg, not to mention her dramatic escape through Roumania, the Tschaikovsky brothers and even her long-lost son. Her new suggestion was that the Tsar had died in obscurity in Denmark in 1928 and that he had remained unrecognised because he had shaved off his beard. Anna's sisters, meanwhile had, she claimed, sought refuge with the Grand Duke of Hesse. In the Summers and Mangold book she was quoted as saying: 'There was no massacre there, but I cannot tell the rest.' She later told the *Daily Progress* that the family had escaped on a blue train which, improbably, they operated themselves.

Jack now weighed in, insisting that Grand Duchess Marie had lived in Germany and Italy, that Grand Duchess Tatiana had died within the past two years and that Alexis was still alive. 'It's all very complex,' he admitted. In February 1978 a programme was aired, *In Search of... Anastasia*, in which she announced: 'I am the daughter of the Tsar.' The Manahans were invited to watch the programme in the offices of the *Daily Progress*. Anna watched a re-creation of the Ekaterinburg murders without registering any emotion. Asked to comment afterwards she said: 'It's a mess.'

One of her further claims, that the family had been replaced by 'doubles' bore fruit two years later when a retired dentist from Richmond, Virginia, insisted that his uncle had been the Tsar's double. Pledging support for Anna, Dr Charles

L. Meistroff said his Uncle Herschel and Aunt Leah (doubling for the Tsarina) had been executed in Ekaterinburg. Jack thanked him for his support but rejected the claim adding, slightly implausibly, that Anna had once told him the name of the Tsar's double but she would not reveal it publicly. Anna was, as always, more peremptory: 'Write no more. Enough has been said. It is all a nonsense. Throw it in the fire.'

In 1976, Jack's servant, James, died; he had been with the Manahan family for 29 years and had latterly presided unwillingly over the decline in standards of tidiness and hygiene. While Anna had apparently disliked James because he was black, she proved reluctant to replace him. The house duly deteriorated further, visiting reporters now being obliged to meet the Manahans in the nearby Farmington Club.

At one point Jack procured a tree-stump which he hoped would remind Anna of the Black Forest. The massive stump was installed in the living room for several years before being singled out as the piece of clutter ready for the dump. Jack and Anna were spotted driving away from University Circle one day with the stump on the roof. A friend recalls seeing Jack's station wagon inching along the road, the stump wobbling from side to side. His offers to secure the stump were, however, rejected with easy optimism by Jack: 'That will not be necessary.'

At the heart of the continuing deterioration was, as at Unterlengenhardt, a burgeoning band of cats. The five cats Anna had adopted soon after her arrival had multiplied to 30. Even she was disconcerted when, on one occasion, she found an opossum and a dead rabbit among the latest batch of kittens. 'Look what I have come to! I must live like a gypsy.' A new ungracious bitterness emerged during an interview in which she complained: 'I don't like this home. In America they don't have grand palaces like they do in Europe.'

Johanna Shalloway recalls Anna's attachment to her cats; she remembers Anna collecting leftover food during their meetings in restaurants. The doggy bags would be meticulously filled with each element of the meal, from pieces of meat to icecream sundae. But Johanna also recalls Anna neglecting her pets; she once saw one of the Manahans' cats with an open wound between its eye and ear. 'There were maggots crawling in and out, it must have been in horrible pain. I went with a friend of mine who also had animals; she tried to persuade the Manahans to give her the cat. But Anastasia simply wanted us to leave. She believed in reincarnation; she believed the cat was one of her relations.' When the cats did eventually die, Anna took to cremating them in the living room fireplace. Neighbours filed complaints about the smell with the local health authorities.

The Manahans' neighbour, Jack Davis, who had once run an automobile business, admits that the couple's station wagon had more than kept pace with the house in terms of deterioration: 'Jack brought the car in to have work done and the cops happened to be in there. They told me I didn't have to work on it because it was so dirty. It was...', he pauses, 'frankly filthy.'

By now the Manahans' property was surrounded by a low chicken wire. The front door was boarded over, the windows were barricaded and junk was piled in the yard. The path leading to the kitchen door at the side was festooned with rocks, tree-stumps and even knives. The postman refused to go to the side of the house, so boxes of huge canvas bags filled with mail now lay in the street.

An Englishman, Michael Wynne-Parker, visited Anna and Jack in the late 70s. He was due to give a talk in Charlottesville for the English Speaking Union. The evening before he left for America, he dined with Lord Mountbatten, who warned him against meeting Anna. 'Whatever you do,' he recalls Mountbatten saying, 'don't have anything to do with that woman.' Wynne-Parker's recollection is delivered with gusto: Mountbatten's warning probably served as more of an incentive than a deterrent.

In any case, Wynne-Parker seems to have had no compunction about allowing his host in Charlottesville to ring Jack and arrange an appointment to meet Anna. Before the meeting, both men soaked their handkerchiefs in aftershave lotion; his host explained that they would need to clasp these handkerchiefs to their noses as they entered the house.

Wynne-Parker recalls wading through shoulder-high undergrowth: 'There was barbed wire and nettles. But I did not feel it was just neglect; they were trying to hide. It was a veritable Fort Knox.' The two men finally reached a clearing in the garden, in the centre of which was a table covered with an assortment of documents, papers and photographs. Jack joined them and began to talk at length about his belief in Anna; they were lulled into a submissive daze. Both apparently awoke with Jack pressing a question on them: 'Do you believe in reincarnation?' While Wynne-Parker contemplated his answer, Jack interrupted him, pointing to the six labrador puppies under the table: 'Can I introduce you to the Imperial Family?'

Wynne-Parker and his friend exchanged glances and told Jack they were becoming concerned about the time. Jack had already told them that Anna had once kept Maria Rasputin waiting two or three hours. When Wynne-Parker pointed out that he needed to leave soon for the airport, Jack replied loftily: 'Her Royal Highness is a law unto herself. She is no respecter of planes.'

Suddenly the three men were disturbed by a sharp rattling of the window. 'This was the Royal Command. We went inside, stepping on piles of books. The smell hit one and out came the handkerchiefs,' recalls Wynne-Parker. 'A white-haired lady in a crumpled, old coat appeared at the top of a staircase. She said, "Would you be so kind as to take best greetings to my cousin the Queen?" We nodded and then there was an ear-piercing shriek from some cat biting another cat and she rushed off. Our audience lasted roughly three minutes.'

Ian Lilburn, who stayed with Jack and Anna for several weeks around this time, quickly formed the impression that Jack was deranged. 'He was a nutcase but he did save her.

What would have become of her otherwise?' He noticed that Jack was snappy with Anna and ordered her about, but he also noted that Anna remained unfazed, even oblivious, to Jack's rants. He felt that the proliferation of pets stemmed from a sort of competition between the couple. 'Anastasia would get cats and Jack countered with Dobermans.'

Anna in later years

Lilburn had gone to Charlottesville with Prince Frederick. The visit originally came about because Jack had been asked to give a talk in Williamsburg. Jack felt Prince Frederick would do the job better and had written asking the Prince to come to Charlottesville. Anna had evidently been persuaded, somehow, to forgive the Prince all his past misdemeanours.

When Prince Frederick replied that he had no money, Jack agreed to finance the trip. 'Jack asked the nearest businessman how much the Prince would need and he was told 2000 dollars. That's what he sent us.' Lilburn still grimaces as he recalls his visit; he and the Prince braved an apartment in the second of Jack's two houses on University Circle. 'There were cockroaches all over the floor. Jack simply jumped on them. He prepared breakfast for us which he brought in these nests made of tinfoil. There would be a fried egg or bacon which looked like it had been prepared by the cats. Without wishing to offend him, the truth is we threw the breakfasts down the loo.'

The rest of the meals, to Lilburn's relief, were taken out. 'Anastasia would drink coffee and after just one cup she'd start babbling. Jack would say: "If you want her to talk, get coffee".' On one occasion during Lilburn's stay, Anna was upset by a breach of etiquette which occurred while the party was at the Ewells' house. Mrs Ewell offered a plate of *hors-d'oeuvres* to Anna before the Prince. Anna quietly corrected her: the Prince apparently needed to be served before his cousin.

Much of the day was spent in the car, with Jack taking every opportunity to show off his smart European guests. 'Jack couldn't resist buying books; he would emerge from shops with armfuls of books. Anastasia would turn to us and say: "I've married a *lumpensammler* (a rag and bone man)". Whenever we spoke to people, Jack would make a play of introducing the Prince. The Prince hated this sort of fishing for publicity and I felt Jack introduced him simply to boost his own ego. We would be in the launderette and he would be saying: "May I introduce Prinz Friedrich of Saxony?"'

Lilburn felt greatly privileged to be granted what was regarded as a fond farewell from Anna. 'We drove to the airport and, as I got out, she made a special effort to turn round in her seat and offer me her hand. This was a great honour as she was terrified that people would shake her hand too violently. Prinz Friedrich said: "She has not given me her hand in 30 years". I was flattered', adds Lilburn, with feeling.

Anna was characteristically dismissive of new tests conducted in Germany in 1977 which seemed to prove, once again, that she was the Grand Duchess. The conclusions were based on comparisons of her ear with the ear of the young Grand Duchess Anastasia: they were identical in seventeen anatomical points and tissue formations. The expert added that, in West German courts, twelve points were normally regarded as sufficient to establish identity. Anna simply used the news to renew her attacks on the hapless Prince Frederick: 'If the Prince goes on misusing the power of attorney as he has, it will be taken away. He is the one behind this mess... He is after the money and nothing else.' On a more personal note, she added: 'I am ill of this dirt. I will not read this dirt. Is my ear so important?' During one of her television interviews she took her comment a stage further: 'I spit on it.'

The writer Michael Thornton, meanwhile, took a copy of the report on Anna's ear to show to Mountbatten; his feeling is that Mountbatten was shocked by it and feared he might have made a terrible mistake. The copies were in German and English. 'He read it first in German then in English. He said: "This just cannot be so". His face was a picture of doubt and confusion.'

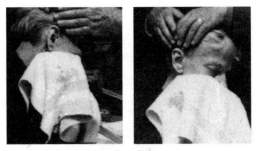

Anna's right ear

A photograph of Anastasia clearly
showing her right ear

Meanwhile the Manahans continued to cut what dash they could, accepting an invitation to Fort Worth, Texas, to see the *première* of a ballet about Rasputin. They flew on a private plane and were put up in the presidential suite of the Fort Worth Hilton Hotel. In a grand ceremony, Anna was presented with the key to the city. Before the couple's departure for Texas, Jack revealed that Anna had bought a new outfit for the ceremony. 'It will be a yellow dress with gold slippers. I wanted her to wear a small tiara but she wouldn't.'

A local amateur dramatic company, the 'Barboursville Players', staged a play about Anna. On the opening night Jack leapt, uninvited, on to the stage to give a talk about Anna's claim. He finally sat down after the producer promised he could give a ten-minute talk before every subsequent performance. He dutifully gave the talks, but could not be dissuaded from leaping up between scenes to add extra details. Anna made just one appearance, on the first night, before declaring that she preferred to remain outside, locked in the car.

In September 1978 the couple were taken to court on charges of 'failing to maintain clean and sanitary premises and allowing weeds and brush to grow in excess of eighteen inches.' Six residents on University Circle took out warrants against the couple. The formal complaint was that they were maintaining rat harbourages; Jack, in response, brought in a caribou antler which he said had been installed in the house for a long time but which had remained untouched by rats. It was a known fact, he explained, that rats liked to chew antlers. In a further defence, he added that vines were invading his property. He pointed out that the kudzu vine could grow a full 27 inches on a hot, wet July night.

After the judge alluded to the accumulation of trash, Jack commented that his wife's dogs ate 90 cans of food every week. 'I am hard put to it to keep the family going, to feed all the livestock (at the farm) and pick up all the cans.' He added that he had not used a vacuum for six years and now it was too late.

When Anna was called to testify, she refused to move. 'I think she doesn't feel she is subject to American law,' said Jack. The judge found Jack guilty and gave him three weeks to clean up the property. The cats and dogs would have to be transferred to the farm at Scottsville. 'Charlottesville has been known for its diverse people, and I don't want to punish you for your diversity. But I want spectacular improvements on those conditions.'

One morning in 1979, Jack arrived on the Ewells' doorstep in a panic because Anna had fallen ill. He was scheduled to give a talk in Richmond to the Huguenot Society and did not want to leave her on her own. Doctor Ewell immediately agreed to examine Anna; he established that she had a serious intestinal blockage and would be obliged to go to hospital. Mrs Ewell recalls the occasion vividly: 'She got real sick... Nat told Anastasia she had to go to hospital and she said, "No". So Nat said: "Do you want to live?" and she said, "Yes". He said: "Then you've got to go to hospital". Jack went to Richmond, leaving a note saying that Nat had responsiblity for Anna.'

Anna developed arthritis in her feet. It should not have been enough to confine her to a wheelchair but, after her stay in hospital, Anna was disinclined to walk. She began to treat the car increasingly as a sort of mobile home in which she stored, at her feet, cherry tarts and port wine.

***

While a random element attached itself to much of the Manahans' social life, Anna's birthday – the Grand Duchess Anastasia's birthday, 18 June – established itself as a fixed highpoint in the couple's diary. The *Daily Progress* would be invited to capture the celebrations. In curiously dismal photographs, the Manahans parade their ill-judged efforts at party dress. Their outfits are more than matched by that of their guest of honour, the elderly and lavishly bearded Col Elbert Radford, but the overall effect is more macabre than festive. Anna's face is the picture of a combination of detachment and confusion: she has forgotten it is her birthday but suspects something is up. Jack's wholehearted attempts to lift the occasion are doomed to failure, only so much can be achieved with a smile and jaunty tilt of the head.

Anna's 80th birthday celebration was attended by 75 guests including Gleb's daughter, Marina Schweitzer. Jack and Anna were photographed wearing, respectively, a tri-cornered Napoleonic hat and a pink, feathered straw boater. Anna was almost entirely silent while Jack, according to one generous report, regaled guests with detailed evidence of his wife's heritage: 'Her features, feet, hands, ears, eyes and stature – even her jaw and teeth are those of Anastasia of Russia.' Anna's only comment concerned her intestinal complaint. 'I came twelve days to the end. I was poisoned.'

She celebrated what would have been Anastasia's 82nd birthday, in 1983, with 25 guests, including mysteriously strait-laced young couples looking as though they had just walked off the set of *Bewitched*. She was presented with a poem by a Mary Faye Craft from Washington DC:

'Anastasia, my dear,/I wish you a happy birthday,/And pray that this year,/Will bring much joy your way.

I wish you good health,/And many birthdays to observe./I wish you great wealth./And the recognition you/ deserve.

I pray that you shall find peace,/As you enter this new year,/That your anxieties will/ cease,/That you will conquer every fear.

Anastasia, many love you,/And wish you happiness/today,/But from one, it is/particularly true,/Your friend, Mary Faye.'

Among the guests one year was Dr Richard C. Shrum, who had performed the operation on her intestine. Dr Shrum and Anna had struck up a friendship during her five-week stay in hospital. Following their frequent conversations, usually conducted in German, Dr Shrum had come to believe fervently in her claim. He later revealed himself sufficiently confident of the results to urge the speeding up of DNA tests. 'I think they ought to do it and get the thing settled.'

In 1981 Jack and Anna gave an interview to the *Shenandoah Valley* magazine, in which they were quoted at length. The writer noted that Anna took her belongings everywhere in plastic bags and, curiously, would eat only off metal plates. She recorded verbatim, with little comment or question, their curious conversation.

Jack: 'Now Vladimir is the oldest male, but Anastasia says he cannot be Tsar, since he was not born in Russia. Well, that's neither here nor there, if you need a Tsar, why you've got to get one from the family.'

Anna: 'I don't want to be Tsar of Russia. No. Never!'

Jack: '...They had at least six children and, of those six, only Vassily is still alive. He is President of the Romanov Family Association at the moment and he will never yield that Anastasia is any relation of his.'

Interviewer: 'Is it the money do you think?'

Anna: 'The money, the money, the money.'

The interviewer then said that it was now assumed by many that nothing happened in the cellar at Ekaterinburg. Recognising a familiar theme, Anna chimed in: 'Nothing happened. Nothing."

A year later Jack demonstrated his mixture of lucidity and madness with the issue of a sort of official complaint about what he clearly regarded as a persecution campaign. The complaint was entitled: 'Succinct Recital of Untoward Happenings to Property of John E. Manahan'. He listed stolen items including an electric organ, birdcages and commodes: Anna had occasionally been heard by visitors screaming at Jack to put her on the potty.

However the worst incidents concerned the dogs. 'Repeatedly about 4 o'clock in the morning our dogs were mangled in steel traps set in our front driveway. To date 41 of our dogs are missing without trace of a body; 20 more have been found dead, all under mysterious circumstances; one lived with two bullet tracks and one (had) six bullets removed by the vet at a cost of 78 dollars.'

The last time Rey Barry saw the couple was when several of their dogs ran riot after a basketball game. They had locked the dogs in the station wagon while they, improbably, enjoyed the game. When they opened the doors to leave, the dogs bowled out. 'I spent 45 minutes helping to catch them. They eventually came – after all they were pets,' he adds reassuringly.

The couple were increasingly incapable of looking after themselves. At one point Jack had to be admitted to hospital with an attack of Rocky Mountain spotted fever; Anna had to accompany him because no other means could be found of looking after her.

Jack would now be seen lying in the driveway or on the bonnet of the car. Anna, known obscurely as 'Apple Annie', would spend days and even nights outside in the car, screaming for Hans, her name for Jack. Her reluctance to leave the car became well known all over Virginia. Once, when the car broke down, a companion tried to explain to the state police that Anna would have to be towed inside the car. The policeman replied: 'Don't worry about it. We all know these two.'

Inside the house, the electricity was frequently turned off. Despite the lack of heating, the couple insisted all doors remain open at all times. Anna said she preferred the cold to the germs she believed lurked in heating systems. Jack dismissed any suggestion that the couple were not managing, insisting that they were healthier than the officials sent in every so often to help them: 'In fifteen years of married life we haven't had a sniffle until our contact with our "jailors" who've all been sick with colds.'

Their house deteriorated to such an extent that finally the couple moved into one of Jack's apartments, It then also deteriorated and they were obliged, according to one report, to move to a motel. But they were never friendless. Mrs Ewell would take Anna food; Jack's lawyer, Jim Hingeley, made several attempts to help Jack clear the house at University Circle, at least to a standard which put it within the law.

Public interest in Anna showed no sign of lessening; in September 1982 a new play based on her story, *I Am Who I Am*, opened in New York. One of the last interviews Jack and Anna gave was to *The Virginian-Pilot and the Ledger-Star*, during which the journalist dined, after a fashion, with the couple. The trio drove to a Ken Johnson's Cafeteria, where Jack ordered a baked potato, carrots, noodles, onions and a cup of coffee with six packets of sugar. He delivered the heavily sweetened coffee to Anna in the car; he then enjoyed his lunch with the reporter inside. Jack declared matter-of-factly that Anna would change her birthright if she could. Meanwhile, he explained, he was helping her through her travails by singing her the Singing Nun's song, *Dominique*.

In the summer of 1983 the Charlottesville circuit court put Anna in the temporary care of William Preston, a well-known city attorney. Jack was told he could not resume his role as carer until he had undergone a psychiatric evaluation. The result of the evaluation was that Jack could look after himself but not Anna.

A few months later, in October, Preston was appointed a permanent guardian to Anna. Jack resented Preston's interference. He had been suspicious of the lawyer from the beginning: this new appointment only served to increase his paranoia. 'Jack said I was an interloper, interfering with his marriage. It was a terrible job but, as a lawyer, I couldn't refuse to take it,' recalls Preston. His exasperation with the couple drove him to desperate measures; at one point he found himself almost exchanging blows with Jack. The story is the more harrowing for being told in the level tones of a clearly genial and temperate man: 'I made it clear that Jack was not allowed to take her anywhere. Then I got a call to say they'd gone. I drove down and found him in the house. When I said: "Where is she?" he refused to answer and just ran off. I tackled him, grabbed his leg and we rolled down the hill. I finally found Anastasia; she turned out to be locked in the car 20 yards down the road.'

Preston's subsequent decision to have Anna committed to the Blue Ridge Hospital proved controversial. Some of the Manahans' friends felt the committal was premature. Mrs Ewell, who saw Anna two days before she went into hospital, insists her friend seemed fine. 'She looked spry and was talking up a storm. Her clothes looked nice. She rolled down the truck window and just chatted away. I told her she looked well and she said, "I'm going to walk by Christmas".'

***

It is hard to know how buoyant Anna could have been feeling at this time of her life. As the Grand Duchess Anastasia, Anna would have been 82; her actual age was 87. She must have been aware, if only dimly, of her increasing frailty, even of her approaching death. If she had been given the choice, at this point, between an institution and remaining at home with Jack, which would she have chosen? While an institution would offer routine and security, Anna might have opted for Jack's haphazard but more familiar care programme. Was she still capable of making a proper choice?

For Jack there was no choice: his wife should be with him. He found Anna's incarceration deeply discomfiting. Over sixteen years Anna had become his life's work: he now found himself at a loose end. How far he analysed his feelings or his motivations cannot be known. What is clear is that he became convinced that he must, at all costs, get his wife out of hospital. He later claimed he reached this drastic decision after hearing she was scheduled for a CAT scan. As he put it: 'I thought about it overnight and decided that absolutely I was going to prevent that from being done. I was afraid, like an ignorant person would be, of anything on the brain.'

On the morning of the scan, Jack drove to the hospital with the intention of kidnapping his wife. He had stocked up enough money and supplies to last the couple six days.

Jack knew Anna would have to be transferred to a different building for the scan. His plan was to grab her from the entrance hall. Having parked as close to the entrance as possible, he proceeded up to the ward where he pronounced himself ready to accompany his wife. The nurse in charge clearly never thought to view the couple with suspicion: Jack, though eccentric in appearance, seemed every bit the thoughtful husband to his elderly, wheelchair-bound wife. Having successfully installed them in the front hall, the nurse left them alone while she telephoned for an ambulance to take them to the main building. But the minute her back was turned, Jack seized Anna, bundled her into the car and sped out of the car park. By 10.15am a felony abduction warrant had been issued for Jack, along with a thirteen-state police bulletin.

During their three days on the run, Jack and Anna enjoyed a relaxed time, seeing a few friends, having the car greased and buying some Russian fur hats. They spent one night in the Amherst motel, checking in under their own names. The next two nights they spent in an abandoned house, found for them by a friend. They were finally caught thanks to a tip-off from a restaurant owner who had recognised Jack after spotting him in the local shopping centre.

When the police found the house, they came upon Anna alone, sitting in the front seat of the station wagon. The car had broken down and Jack had gone to find someone to carry out repairs. Upon his return, fifteen minutes later, he was curiously jaunty, congratulating the police for having found them. Lieutenant Jimmy Higgins later said he formed the impression the couple had not left the station wagon for three days, even for the bathroom. Driving them into town, he added, he was obliged to keep the window open. Anna received the police with dramatic hostility, crying: 'I won't be taken alive.' When they asked her name, she replied, 'Jones'.

Jack emerged well from the media coverage of the abduction, as a misguided hero. But Preston disputes the view that Jack acted out of concern for his wife. As he sees it, Jack was actually guilty, once again, of jeopardising Anna's fragile health: this time by exposing her to the freezing November weather. 'Jack always acted in his own interests. He was brutal to his wife.'

The kidnapping led to speculation that plans were afoot to transport Anna to Russia. The Soviet leader, Yuri Andropov, had not been seen for months and some conspiracy theorists believed there was about to be a monarchist coup. The *National Examiner* quoted what it referred to as a top intelligence source: 'We can only speculate that the Soviets are poised to replace their Communist leader with their long-lost queen.' The cutting was one of Jack's favourites; he put it under a librarian's office door for storage at the University of Virginia library and later arranged it prominently among cuttings on the altar at Anna's funeral.

In an unexpected development, Anna was now declared sane; she could therefore no longer be kept in a mental institution. Preston was obliged to move her to a small nursing home. Here, she refused to eat anything except Lipton's Cup-a-Soup mixes and boiled eggs – and these only if they were peeled in front of her.

A little over a week before Anna died the German *Sonntag Aktuell* newspaper ran an article recording the fond memories of Thérèse Kustner, a room maid at Castle Seeon. She spoke of the Duke of Leuchtenberg's devotion to Anna. The Grand Duchess Anastasia, she reported, had eaten mostly alone and had particularly enjoyed roast pork. Thérèse was convinced the lady was Anastasia: she had a distinctive face and her attractions were '*kaiserlich*'.

Anna may well have suffered a stroke in January 1984; she

was not fully sentient when taken to Martha Jefferson Hospital. She died there on 12 February 1984. Jack left the hospital carrying Anna's belongings in a 25-pound dog food bag. She was cremated the day she died. Mrs Ewell commented: 'She always said that you would be reincarnated if you were cremated.' Anna's death certificate records her father as 'Czar Nikolai' and her mother as 'Alix of Hesse-Darmstadt'. Her birthplace is listed as 'Peterhof, Russia'. Under 'Usual or Last Occupation' is typed 'Royalty'.

CHAPTER NINE
The remains of Anna

A 'Memorial Service For Anastasia Nikolaevna Romanov Tschaikowsky Anderson Manahan' was held on Tuesday 14 February 1984 at the University Chapel. Mrs Ewell took over the organisation: 'I thought I had to take charge of it. Poor Jack didn't know which way to turn.' Among the 200 mourners was Gleb's daughter, Marina Schweitzer. A short piece of prose by Gleb, entitled *Obit*, was printed on the programme : 'Under the radiant smile death itself becomes the unfathomable joy of awakening from the dream of this earth to the true life of Thy Heaven.'

In the back of the chapel, Jack placed assorted memorabilia and stacks of newspaper articles supporting his wife's claim. On the altar was a candelabra decorated with the Russian double-headed eagle and a pair of playing cards. In his

30-minute oration he said that Anna had seen the Tsar in 1921. According to one report, he also said Queen Elizabeth II was 'the black queen' and referred to her as 'a drug dealer' – a reference not repeated in the local press.

After the ceremony he made further controversial claims: 'The end of Anastasia was infinitely pathetic... Had she not been committed to the hospital, she would have lived another nine or ten years.' On Leap Day 1984, he wrote a heartfelt reply to a letter of condolence from a Professor B. O'Neal. 'Your prompt and comforting note showed a wonderful grasp of my psychology and the puzzling situation posed by the deliberate murder of my wife by attorneys who subjected her to a minimum of 40 new attendants per week for 25 weeks – 1000 in all'.

While Charlottesville laid its claim to the Anastasia legacy, her European supporters weighed in with elaborate plans to bury her ashes at Castle Seeon. Jack had no objections; he gamely flew to Germany for the burial. The ceremony, during which her ashes were interred in an urn by the lake, took place on the Grand Duchess Anastasia's birthday. A simple gravestone bore the inscription: 'Our heart is unquiet until it rests with you, Lord'. Above the inscription were carved a Russian cross and the name 'Anastasia' in Cyrillic letters. Among the smarter attenders were Prince Frederick, Olga, Countess of Pourtales (one of the Kleists), and an aristocrat loosely described as a relation of the Kaiser's, Prinzessin Schoneich-Carolath.

A reporter for the German magazine, *Bild + Funk,*

described the burial as a moving event in which his hand was clutched fervently by two mourners. For the actual ceremony, the reporter found himself placed next to Jack, referred to optimistically in a rival newspaper as an '*unkomplizierte Amerikaner*'. Jack's uncomplicated air was enhanced by his light blue suit and the way he clutched a heart-shaped medallion containing locks of Anna's hair. At one point he produced a handkerchief and, wiping away his tears, sobbed: 'Is it not terrible that she could not be who she was? I know she spoke the truth.'

Prince Frederick apparently sputtered names and dates connected with the Anastasians' abortive attempts at establishing recognition. He kept asking the same question: 'Why could people not recognise her?' Ian Lilburn, who attended the burial, says that he remained curiously unaffected. 'I didn't find it actually moving – nor did Prinz Friedrich. There was no priest officiating. Jack was prancing around making mad allegations. He started repeating his claims that Anastasia had been murdered.'

Jack managed to give a talk outside the Munchner Hauptbarnhof. Despite the heat he wore a Russian fur cap. He announced that he had resolved not to cry, but his voice frequently broke. Confusingly, he gave the impression he had initially travelled to Germany to fetch Anna and take her to the United States. Then he digressed to his favourite topic: heraldry.

***

The completion of the last ceremony marking Anna's death could have left Jack at something of a loss. On the surface, his prospects did not appear promising. Now aged 65, his chances of finding a new wife would seem slim. He had little interest in art, music, sport, or any area of high living; the *Coppage Family Bulletin* would surely not fill the gap.

But as Jack returned to Charlottesville, he may have had mixed feelings. Competing with his sorrow would have been altogether happier thoughts about a curious new woman in his life, one Althea Hurt, who had accosted him after Anna's funeral in February. She had offered to step in as his business partner, an offer which had been favourably received, not least because she was vivacious, blonde and 25.

Within months of his return to Charlottesville, Jack was infatuated with Althea, crowning her with ever grander genealogical links and finally declaring her: 'The True Czarina Of All The Russias'. He drew up a hereditary chart listing her as 'The Centre Of The Universe', related to Napoleon, Thomas Jefferson and Conan the Barbarian.

While Althea was not prepared to marry her new admirer, she was happy to adopt a wifely role where his property was concerned. She had trees cut down at the farm and autho-rised the clearance of old newspapers. Later it was claimed that she took Romanov artefacts to the Charlottesville dump. Anna's collection had apparently included an oil portrait of the Dowager Empress Marie when she was Princess Dagmar, a 500-year-old icon, one of the Tsar's monogrammed handkerchiefs, a signed photograph of the Tsarina, an illuminated and embossed invitation to the Tsar's coronation and a hand-lettered menu from the wedding banquet of the Tsar and Tsarina.

In January 1987 Jack made a will leaving his property, the 660-acre farm in Scottsville and his second house in Charlottesville, to Althea. He died three years later, in 1990, after developing diabetes and suffering a series of strokes.

Four years after Jack's death, three of his cousins tried to have his will invalidated. The cousins' argument was that Jack's most recent will was invalid because he had made it while of unsound mind. A neuropsychiatrist, Gregory O'Shanick, of Richmond, testified that Manahan had suffered a history of psychotic delusions. Dr Gregory Saathof, a psychiatrist at the University of Virginia and a friend of the Manahans, added that he had seen Jack after his car had been stolen; Jack had seemed less concerned about the car than some maple syrup he had left on the back seat. Another friend said Jack had become excited when he had found a lost 'kitty'. On closer inspection, the kitten turned out to be dead and covered with flies.

But in the end, one crucial piece of evidence seemed to give the final word to Althea. She produced a 35-minute tape in which Jack professed full support for her. The tape had been recorded during the actual signing process: '(She) is a remarkably efficient person and everything she puts her hand to, she improves... The idea that Althea is putting some pressure on me is not true.' While a jury ruled in the cousins' favour, the verdict was overruled a month later by the judge.

Anna never quite went away. In 1986, a TV mini-series, *Anastasia: The Mystery of Anna,* was broadcast; this particularly unlikely version of the story portrayed poor Gleb as a publicity-crazed journalist who abandons his old friend in a New York hotel room. Anna herself is depicted naked in bed with a character obviously based on Prince Frederick. It is not known whether the principal actresses were aware of the liberties taken with the truth, but both said there were moments when they believed Anna's claim. Olivia de Havilland, who played the Dowager Empress, said at the time: 'Many times I thought yes and then began to doubt again, but that's the magic of the movie.' The actress playing Anna, Amy Irving, was less equivocal: 'I do admire Anna Anderson. She was a real quirky character, but if you went through seeing your family murdered and survived, you'd be quirky too.'

***

Nine years after the death of Anna Anderson, several tests were conducted in which DNA from the Romanov bones was compared with DNA from Prince Philip. There was a positive match. As they assembled the bones, scientists also established that two bodies remained missing: those of Anastasia and Alexis. The news of the missing bodies was received with enthusiasm by Anna's supporters in Charlottesville.

Among several impressive pillars of the establishment now coming forward was the University of Virginia Rector, Hovey S. Dabney. 'Her background, her demeanour, her knowledge of the Imperial Family. I felt like she knew entirely too much about the family not to be the Princess.'

Paul Saunier, a retired University of Virginia administrator and Congressional aide, added his voice: 'There were just more pluses than minuses to her claim, especially the recognition from Botkin (Gleb) and others who knew the Russian Royal family well.' The Charlottesville police chief, John deK. Bowen, confessed that he could not wait for tests to be conducted on Anna's DNA. 'I wish they'd run that DNA thing and cut through all of it. I would not be surprised if she was who she said she was.'

The testing of Anna's DNA became a real possibility in 1992, when locks of her hair were found in an envelope in a Chapel Hill, North Carolina, bookstore. Jack had originally wanted to leave his books to the Mormon Church but in the end Althea sold them off to various bookdealers.

As one dealer went through the leaves of one of the books, an envelope fluttered out with 'Anastasia's Hair' written in pencil on the outside. The dealer, evidently uninterested in his find, readily sold the envelope and its contents to a woman called Susan Burkhart for 20 dollars. Burkhart later offered a description of the hair, which had been taken from a brush: 'It is kind of salt and pepper grey with sort of streaks of auburn in it... It has roots and bits of scalp attached to it.'

Under the auspices of the historian Peter Kurth, six strands of the hair underwent DNA tests at Penn State. Kurth also took samples to a British lab. The scientists concluded that the owner of the hair could not be related to the Tsarina. Jack would have received the result with particular dismay; he had always been proud to call his wife's hair 'Romanov brown'.

At roughly the same time, a more full-proof source of Anna's DNA came to the fore in the form of a tissue sample stored at the Martha Jefferson Hospital. The tissue had been stored as part of routine procedure following the operation she underwent on her intestine. Several parties now made legal bids for rights over the tissue: in the ensuing year-long battle, the piece of intestine took on an unlikely central role, acquiring a sort of celebrity status of its own.

Penny Jenkins, the acting director of medical records, defended the hospital's insistence upon protecting the tissue. 'We all had an agenda. I saw the film (about Anna) in the 50s and since then I had believed. It was an enchantment from my childhood. I guess I wanted to see her come out to be the Princess because of the romance of it all. Some were sure she was, while others certainly didn't think so. It was a feel-good story. That made us all very much want to make this work. But we also have a responsibility to our patients and to our whole community. We had to stick absolutely by the letter of the law.'

The principal adversaries in the dispute were Marina and Richard Schweitzer, who wanted tests conducted in England and the Russian Nobility Association, who insisted they be conducted at Berkeley in California. Rights were also claimed by the daughter of Anna's former patron Princess Xenia, Nancy Wynkoop, and, more bizarrely, a woman from Idaho claiming to be Anna's long-lost daughter. This new 'Anastasia Romanov', otherwise known as Ellen Kailing, was one of more than 30 women who, at one point or another, came forward claiming to be Anna's daughter.

Mrs Kailing said she learned she was the daughter of Anna in 1990 after a conversation with a woman she would only identify as Mother Alexandra, abbess of an Orthodox monastery in Ellwood City, Pennsylvania. She claimed, in a further twist, that Jack Manahan was her father. She brought a tape to court in which Jack says: 'I have a new child. My wife and I are very happy. Something in here... I have a child now.' Jack was actually reading a letter from a former student.

This second-generation 'Anastasia' claimed to have suffered a tempestuous life, featuring a separation from her mother after an accident during the Second World War. She insisted that sinister attempts had been made to kill her; at one point her dental crowns were laced with arsenic. In corroboration of her claim, she revealed that her sixteen-year-old son bore an uncanny resemblance to Tsar Nicholas II. She boasted a thick German accent: 'I saw the picture of Jack Manahan and Anna Mananan and I knew it was my story.' Matthew B. Murray, the lawyer for the Martha Jefferson Hospital, took a dim view of the proceedings: 'We're not in novel territory, we're in outer space.'

In the end, on 16 March 1994, Schweitzer skilfully overrode all other claims by appointing a friend and fellow lawyer, Ed Deets, as administrator of Anna's estate in Virginia. There was no official opposition to the appointment and Deets was now able to make a request for the tissue to be sent to the eminent British scientist Dr Peter Gill, who had carried out the tests on the Romanov bones. Marina Schweitzer had sent a blood sample to Gill's Aldermaston laboratory to help him identify the bones of her grandfather, Dr Botkin. Her sample consisted simply of the paper tissue she had used to stem the blood from a finger prick.

In June 1994, Dr Peter Gill came to collect the precious DNA samples in person. Several photographs exist of him at the Martha Jefferson Hospital; in one he looks particularly stiff and British, contrasting sharply with the beaming, relaxed, Virginian doctor in the background. Dr Gill could not have failed to be aware of the watchful gaze of the Schweitzers, who had come to witness the procedure. He gave a cautious statement to the press: 'I can't be sure at the moment how likely it is we'll get DNA from the samples. One problem is that they have been subject to harsh chemical treatment which destroys DNA. We also have to bear in mind the age of the samples.'

Upon his return to England, Gill compared the DNA in the fingernail-sized portion of Anna's intestinal tissue with DNA from Prince Philip. He also compared the tissue with a blood sample taken from Karel Maucher, a relative of Franziska Schanzkowska. The results came through in October 1994. Dr Peter Gill announced, in effect, that Anna Anderson was not the Grand Duchess Anastasia. 'If you accept that these samples came from Anna Anderson, then Anna Anderson could not be related to Tsar Nicholas or Empress Alexandra.' The comparison of Franziska's sample to Karel Maucher's was equally conclusive, with Gill pronouncing it 'a 100 per cent match, an absolute identity'.

The Schweitzers were bitterly disappointed. Richard Schweitzer said: 'It's going to be hard, but I'm looking for a mistake... There's so many things that other people wanted to cover up in that period of history... I still feel it's not over. For those of us who knew her, she could not possibly be a Polish peasant.' He felt, in short, that the 'rational experience' of those who knew Anna outweighed the scientific evidence. 'It's like saying she was a man,' he added. Gleb had expressed the same view in his conclusion to his savage critique of Gilliard's book on Anna Anderson: 'Anastasia could no more be mistaken for a peasant – Polish or otherwise – than Emperor William could be mistaken for Queen Victoria.'

Marina Schweitzer added thoughts of her own: 'I know this will sound insane. But I think Russians had something to do with it, and I think it's connected to Queen Elizabeth's visit to Russia... My father knew the Grand Duchess as a child and went through Siberia with the family. When she reappeared he didn't want to believe the story, but the moment he met her, he knew it was she and he never faltered in his conviction. I'm disappointed in the results, but they don't change my opinion.'

Andrew Hartsook, the man who had been close to Gleb and had, at one point, been associated with the Church of Aphrodite, was in no doubt that the tests were invalid. He insisted, mysteriously, that the tissue had been discovered by an avowed (and unnamed) enemy. In a letter to the *Washington Post* from his home in Zanesville he wrote: 'It is this same individual who located Franziska's descendants. The tissue sample was kept in an ordinary room with an ordinary lock and potentially was accessible to unauthorised people. There is no question that the DNA testing was honest, but the question remains: Whose tissue was it really?'

In England, Ian Lilburn, too, finds the result hard to believe. He subscribes to the notion that DNA is a science still in its developing stage. 'They conducted an experiment in which 200 people had their DNA tested. It was tested again a month later and one in five of the results were different. There's evidence that DNA can migrate from one dead body to another if they are lying next to each other.'

Back in Charlottesville, many of Anna's supporters questioned the results. The editor of the *Charlottesville Weekly*, Hawes Spencer, says there were supporters who felt that the Martha Jefferson Hospital was not secure enough; they shared Hartsook's view that the tissue could have been tampered with. Mrs Ewell still voices her concerns: 'There has got to be more than this to convince me... There has to still be a great mystery here.' She refers to what appeared to be Anna's intimate knowledge of life at the Russian Court: 'How could a Polish peasant know it?' Rey Barry maintains that many people in Charlottesville were disappointed by the tests: 'I myself think the DNA was probably fraudulent,' he adds. 'It was handled by many people, it was not like court evidence, kept under seal. It would have been possible to switch it.'

But nothing has ever persuaded him to accept Anna's claim. 'I'm still not convinced. She could have been a Polish peasant.' He now throws in a new possibility: 'She could have known Anastasia as a young girl.'

Paul Saunier, the retired University of Virginia administrator, expressed his disappointment. 'I was on her side, I thought she was who she said she was.' He said Gleb had convinced him that Anna's claim was real: 'He said that she told him things about the household that no one else could have known. I just thought it was logical. I'm sort of sorry that it turned out that way.'

Police officer Cornilia Johnson was walking her beat in the downtown mall when she heard the news. 'I was hoping she was. I really like that royalty stuff. I was praying she was, but what a shame.' John Conover, a print shop owner and former city councillor, also expressed his regrets: 'I enjoyed her being Anastasia.' Pam Kelly, who worked in a bank on the University Corner, often served Jack and, over the years, had become convinced of Anna's claim. 'I was sure she was. I guess because you assume a person knows her own family history and would have evidence to back that up.'

To further muddy the waters, a Sandra Romanov came foward claiming that her husband, Heino Tammet, had been Alexis. Heino claimed to have been rescued after the shootings at Ekaterinburg by a Russian farmer. Sandra sent her husband's teeth to DNA scientists in Florida, England and Russia. The teeth sent to Florida and England seemed to go astray; Dr Pavel Ivanov admitted to being in possession of one tooth, but claimed he had no money to carry out tests. The stalwart Mrs Romanov immediately declared herself victim of a conspiracy. She probably relished the opposition; for years before going public she had gamely shrugged off the discrepancies between Alexis and her husband: unlike the weakly Tsarevich, Heino had been a keen swimmer and ballroom dancer.

***

By 1995 the American wing of the Russian Orthodox Church had canonised the Romanovs and their servants. Five years later, the Russian Orthodox Church canonised all seven members of the Imperial Family. A dispute began over where to bury the nine sets of bones. Though St Petersburg was the first place to be considered, there were proposals for a burial in Moscow and, at one point, Ekaterinburg. The House of Special Purpose had been destroyed in September 1977 by a reluctant Boris Yeltsin. 'What am I to tell the people?' he had asked the authorities in Moscow. 'Whatever you like, only get rid of the building,' came the reply. Previously the house had been seen as something of a feather in Ekaterinburg's hat, with dignitaries using the fateful cellar wall as a backdrop for photographs.

The least popular proposal, as far as the Schweitzers were concerned, was for Dr Botkin and the three other retainers to be buried separately in Ekaterinburg. There had been some opposition to the idea of burying the servants with the Imperial Family, with one commentator even suggesting it marked a triumph of Communism. But Marina Schweitzer felt the bodies should remain together; if they were to be separated, she would prefer her grandfather to be buried in the family plot in St Petersburg. As Richard Schweitzer said of the Ekaterinburg proposal: 'If they (the nine bodies) are to be buried together that's fine. They died together. (But) There was nothing that tied my wife's grandfather to that place except misery and death.' Prince Nicholas Romanov, seen by the majority of the Romanovs as the head of the family, was adamant that all nine bodies be buried together.

But as Prince Nicholas voiced his views, a further argument developed over who should be the chief mourner. The daughter of the former head of the family, the late Grand Duke Vladimir, Grand Duchess Maria, declared herself the obvious choice. In a heated retort, Prince Nicholas ridiculed the notion of any kind of hierachy and, though adamantly opposed to Anna Anderson, he paid a warm tribute to Marina Schweitzer as grand-daughter of the loyal Doctor Botkin. 'It is not a question of whether I stand in front of Maria or whether Maria stands in front of me. But Mrs Schweitzer, she should stand beside us. No. She should stand in front of us.'

The sentiment was echoed by the grandson of Anna's opponent, Grand Duchess Xenia, Prince Rostislav Romanov, the same Rostislav who had unmasked the hapless Mrs Smith in Chicago all those years ago. The Prince was then living in Sussex and working in London. At the time of the DNA testings he sent his own contribution: a clump of hair. He expressed his fondness and admiration for the Schweitzers: 'I hope they will be at the funeral'.

Rostislav had been the only member of the Romanov family to attend Dr Gill's London press conference regarding the DNA results. He wanted to attend because he felt that a member of the Romanov family should be there. In 1998 he shook his head in wonder as he recalled his thoughts at the hearing: 'If the DNA had matched, what would we have done?' At the time of the tests, he was quoted more succinctly: 'It's over.'

Sources

Prologue
Reunion, Charlottesville, 1968

15: 'I was living this dirt!': Extracts from CDs and tapes belonging to Julian Nott and Greg Rittenhouse.

16: Jack's ancestry from *The Manahan Family and Allied Families*, 2nd Edition, May 1952.

Chapter One
The Murders: Ekaterinburg, 1918.

19: 'half fainting with fear... ': *I, Anastasia: An Autobiography with Notes* by Roland Krug von Nidda (New York: Harcourt, Brace and Co, 1958), p. 60.

20: 'smiled naturally at us... ': *The Fate of the Romanovs* by Greg King and Penny Wilson (New Jersey: John Wiley & Sons Inc, 2003), p. 304.

21: eight kilograms of jewels: *The Lost Fortune of the Tsars* by William Clarke (London: Orion, 2000), p. 94.

23: He himself returned upstairs... : *The Fate of the Romanovs* by Greg King and Penny Wilson, p. 313.

23: 'she cried out and covered her face... ': *The Fate of the Romanovs* by Greg King and Penny Wilson, p. 313.

23: According to Gleb Botkin, two men... : *The Woman Who Rose Again* by Gleb Botkin (New York: Fleming H Revell Company, 1937), p. 100.

23: Henry Ford, who had acquired... : *The Woman Who Rose Again* by Gleb Botkin, p. 100.

24: Strekotin later confessed.... : *The Fate of The Romanovs* by Greg King and Penny Wilson, p. 313.

24: 'It had become clear to me... ': *The Fate of The Romanovs* by Greg King and Penny Wilson, p. 314.

25: Ermokov mumbled that perhaps... : *The Fate of The Romanovs* by Greg King and Penny Wilson, p. 317.

27: Michael Leteman: *The Fate of The Romanovs* by Greg King and Penny Wilson, p. 516.

28: Ermakov was unable to... : *The Quest for Anastasia* by John Klier and Helen Mingay (London: Smith Gryphon, 1995), p. 166.

Chapter Two
The Botkins and the Romanovs

31: a bear of a man who... : *The Russian Revolution 1899-1919* by Richard Pipes (London: Collins Harvill, 1990), p. 57.

31: 'not look upon as a gentleman': *Nicholas and Alexandra* by Robert K Massie (New York: Atheneum, 1967), p. 9.

32: 'girlie': *The Fate of the Romanovs* by Greg King and Penny Wilson, p. 31.

32: pelting him with... : *The Russian Revolution 1899-1919* by Richard Pipes, p. 58.

33: 'sawbones': Richard Schweitzer e-mail. 14.3.03.

34: 'How strange. Am I already dead?': *The Real Romanovs* by Gleb Botkin (New York: Fleming H Revell, 1931), p. 55.

34: Tsar Alexander's first offer... : *The Real Romanovs* by Gleb Botkin, p. 55.

35: 'He was never like other children... ': *The Fate of The Romanovs* by Greg King and Penny Wilson, p. 61.

35: 'The Commission does not have any evidence... ': *The Fate of the Romanovs* by Greg King and Penny Wilson, p. 498.

36: 'Tsarskoye Selo was a world apart... ': *The Real Romanovs* by Gleb Botkin, p. 18.

37: Receiving implausibly supportive... : *The Real Romanovs* by Gleb Botkin, p. 124.

37: At one point she decided... : *Nicholas and Alexandra* by Robert K Massie, p. 367.

38: 'Your brother is a true friend... ': Letter from Tsar to Peter Botkin from *The Fate of the Romanovs* by Greg King and Penny Wilson, p. 62.

40: 'Of course the Heir was angry... ': *The Real Romanovs* by Gleb Botkin, p. 32.

41: 'Isn't this a dull... ': *The Real Romanovs* by Gleb Botkin, p. 64.

41: 'poor young woman': *The Fate of the Romanovs* by Greg King and Penny Wilson, p. 62.

41: 'Your failure to do so... ': *The Real Romanovs* by Gleb Botkin, p. 34.

42: But the example he offered... : *The Real Romanovs* by Gleb Botkin, p. 22.

42: 'His composure is... ': *Nicholas and Alexandra* by Robert K Massie, p. 90.

43: after the Revolution she insisted... : *Nicholas and Alexandra* by Robert K Massie, p. 152

43: 'healthy as a bull': *The Real Romanovs* by Gleb Botkin, p. 59.

44: 'The devil neither smokes... ': *The Real Romanovs* by Gleb Botkin, p. 81.

45: 'How strange... ': *The Real Romanovs* by Gleb Botkin, p. 65.

45: 'What better symbol...': *The Woman Who Rose Again* by Gleb Botkin, p. 17.

45: They used to play a game... : *The Real Romanovs* by Gleb Botkin, p. 30.

47: In 1912 an American magazine... : *The Fate of the Romanovs* by Greg King and Penny Wilson, p. 51.

47: 'Even when the two eldest... ': *The Fate of the Romanovs* by Greg King and Penny Wilson, p. 51.

47: 'poor Goliath': memoirs of Margaret Eager quoted in *From Cradle to Crown* by Charlotte Zeepvat (Stroud, UK: Sutton Publishing, 2006), p. 92.

50: Other times she would climb... : *The Romanovs, The Final Chapter* by Robert K Massie (London: Jonathan Cape, Random House, 1995), p. 166.

50: 'frightfully temperamental': *The Romanovs, The Final Chapter* by Robert K Massie, p. 167.

50: One of her English nannies… : *From Cradle to Crown* by Charlotte Zeepvat, p. 81.

50: 'the Fat One': *The Fate of the Romanovs* by Greg King and Penny Wilson, p. 53.

51: 'While I fully shared the general devotion... ': *The Woman Who Rose Again* by Gleb Botkin, p. 22.

52: 'I can't send that paper… ': *The Real Romanovs* by Gleb Botkin, p. 76.

53: 'while all those agonising... ': *The Real Romanovs* by Gleb Botkin, p. 72.

53: 'The Grand Duchesses and the Tsarevich... ': *The Woman Who Rose Again* by Gleb Botkin, p. 21.

54: 'For Anastasia was less beautiful... ': *The Woman Who Rose Again* by Gleb Botkin, p. 22.

55: 'I have never met a person... ': *The Woman Who Rose Again* by Gleb Botkin, p. 22.

55: 'She was always most... ': *The Real Romanovs* by Gleb Botkin, p. 23.

56: He won a second victory... : *The Woman Who Rose Again* by Gleb Botkin, p. 26.

57: 'She graciously allowed... ': *The Woman Who Rose Again* by Gleb Botkin, p. 26.

57: In 1913, the Grand Duchess Tatiana... : *The Real Romanovs* by Gleb Botkin, p. 90.

58: 'If Gleb can do it... ': *The Woman Who Rose Again* by Gleb Botkin, p. 28.

58: 'Fie what a lovely... ': *The Woman Who Rose Again* by Gleb Botkin, p. 18.

60: more worryingly, he had depicted... : *The Real Romanovs* by Gleb Botkin, p. 78.

60: 'These picture books must... ': *The Real Romanovs* by Gleb Botkin, p. 75.

61: 'astonishing calm': *The Real Romanovs* by Gleb Botkin, p. 87.

61: 'Believe me, one must not... ': *The Russian Revolution 1899-1919* by Richard Pipes, p. 191.

62: 'an elderly man with a... ': *Nicholas and Alexandra* by Robert K Massie, p. 205.

62: 'He may be old but he is wise... ': *The Real Romanovs* by Gleb Botkin, p. 109.

63: 'I declare hereby that Germany... ': *The Real Romanovs* by Gleb Botkin, p. 108.

64: While the crowd at the... : *Nicholas and Alexandra* by Robert K Massie, p. 264.

64: With characteristic quirkiness... : *The Real Romanovs* by Gleb Botkin, p. 119.

65: 'Tsar of the land of Russia... ': *The Fate of the Romanovs* by Greg King and Penny Wilson, p. 10.

65: 'Rasputin dead will be... ': *The Real Romanovs* by Gleb Botkin, p. 127.

68: The warning was carried... : *The Quest for Anastasia* by John Klier and Helen Mingay, p. 16.

68: He heard of the families... : *The Real Romanovs* by Gleb Botkin, p. 140.

69: 'Why not doom oneself?... ': *The God Who Didn't Laugh* by Gleb Botkin, 187.

69: 'Don't be alarmed... ': *The Real Romanovs* by Gleb Botkin, p. 140.

71: Vyrubova's father... : *The Real Romanovs* by Gleb Botkin, p. 132.

71: 'I beheld a small, clean-shaven... ': *Nicholas and Alexandra* by Robert K Massie, p. 429.

72: Children were forced... : *Natasha's Dance* by Orlando Figes (London: Allen Lane, The Penguin Press, 2002), p. 56.

73: 'The moment I found myself... ': *The Real Romanovs* by Gleb Botkin, p. 151.

74: 'All I did was to kill... ': *The Real Romanovs* by Gleb Botkin, p. 158.

75: 'Do not waste your time bemoaning... ': *The Real Romanovs* by Gleb Botkin, p. 162.

76: 'I consider that the grief of a second... ': *The Real Romanovs* by Gleb Botkin, p. 164.

77: 'Papa is sad today... ': *The Real Romanovs* by Gleb Botkin, p. 179.

77: 'her sturdy legs and bottom... ': *Tutor to the Tsarevich* by JC Trewin (London: Macmillan, 1975), p. 82.

77: 'deliberately losing at the most dramatic... ': *The Real Romanovs* by Gleb Botkin, p. 180.

79: Gleb offers characteristically lurid... : *The Real Romanovs* by Gleb Botkin, p. 202.

80: 'I felt I was transferred... ': *The Real Romanovs* by Gleb Botkin, p. 203.

82: 'Why should such a handsome girl... ': *The Real Romanovs* by Gleb Botkin, p. 207.

82: He was rewarded with the sight of... : *The Woman Who Rose Again* by Gleb Botkin, p. 35.

82: 'Nobody is permitted... ': *The Real Romanovs* by Gleb Botkin, p. 208.

83: As the Bolshevik grip on the area... : *The Real Romanovs* by Gleb Botkin, p. 210.

84: Neither of them wanted to accept... : *The Real Romanovs* by Gleb Botkin, p. 220.

86: At the slightest hint of trouble... : *The Real Romanovs* by Gleb Botkin, p. 229.

87: Rasputin's son-in-law... : *The Real Romanovs* by Gleb Botkin, p. 233.

87: A fourth Tatiana was reported in 1920... : *The Lost Fortune of the Tsars* by William Clarke, p. 148.

88: Anna claimed to have been rescued... : *The Woman Who Rose Again* by Gleb Botkin, p. 37.

89: According to Anna... : *The Romanovs, The Final Chapter* by Robert K Massie, p. 164.

89: Unfortunately she also apparently... : *The Romanovs, The Final Chapter* by Robert K Massie, p. 164.

90: She related how she then decided... : *The Real Romanovs* by Gleb Botkin, p. 252.

91: He told Victor he was desperate to leave... : *The Real Romanovs* by Gleb Botkin, p. 237.

92: 'She was kind of never invited': *The Quest for Anastasia* by John Klier and Helen Mingay, p. 108.

93: 'Now they come in crowds... ': *The Real Romanovs* by Gleb Botkin, p. 247.

94: The sight of a woman's naked body... ': *The God Who Didn't Laugh* by Gleb Botkin (London: Victor Gollancz Ltd, 1929), p. 156.

95: 'An abyss that suddenly opened under their feet... ': *The God Who Didn't Laugh* by Gleb Botkin, p. 74.

Chapter Three
Anna in Germany 1920-1927

97: She had no identification... : *The Romanovs, The Final Chapter* by Robert K Massie, p. 163.

99: Her older half-brother... : *The Quest for Anastasia* by John Klier and Helen Mingay, p. 223.

99: 'My Auntie Franziska was the cleverest... ': *Washington Post*, October 6, 1994.

99: 'There cannot be the question of any... ': Fallows Collection, Houghton Library.

100: Franziska meanwhile began working... : *The Romanovs, The Final Chapter* by Robert K Massie, p. 249.

102: 'I know who you are... ': *Anastasia: The Survivor of Ekaterinburg* by Harriet von Rathlef (New York: Payson and Clarke, 1929), p. 34.

104: Another early champion... : *The Woman Who Rose Again* by Gleb Botkin, p. 39.

104: 'She's too short... ': *The Romanovs, The Final Chapter* by Robert K Massie, p. 163.

108: Anna began to feel comfortable... : *Anastasia, The Lost Princess* by James Blair Lovell (Washington: Regnery Gateway, 1991), p. 85.

108: 'It was at Grunberg's house... ': *The Woman Who Rose Again* by Gleb Botkin, p. 40.

108: 'I saw immediately that she could not... ': *The Romanovs, The Final Chapter* by Robert K Massie, p. 167.

110: 'She had a habit, when annoyed... ': 'Analysis of the False Anastasia' by Gleb Botkin, printed April 25, 1929, pp. 56-57. Fallows Collection, Houghton Library.

110: At one point, a young man... : *The Woman Who Rose Again* by Gleb Botkin, p. 106.

111: Schwabe eventually got his own back... : *The Quest for Anastasia* by John Klier and Helen Mingay, p. 151.

111: 'Half a year I bother... ': Quote from Harriet von Rathlef, June 20,

1925. Fallows Collection, Houghton Library.

112: 'Impression: primitive, noisy, official... ': Fallows Collection, Houghton Library.

114: Dr Rudnev later became an important witness... : *Anastasia: The Survivor of Ekaterinburg* by Harriet von Rathlef, p. 236.

116: A visit of this kind... : *The Romanovs, The Final Chapter* by Robert K Massie, p. 178.

116: If Grand Duke Ernest was intent... : *The Woman Who Rose Again* by Gleb Botkin, p. 41.

118: 'The feet look like... ': *The Romanovs, The Final Chapter* by Robert K Massie, p. 172.

118: Her first comment... : *New York Times* article, dated March 28, 1926. Greg Rittenhouse collection.

119: They believe Olga decided, then and there... : *The Real Romanovs* by Gleb Botkin, p. 293.

120: 'At least we shan't have to beg... ': *The Romanovs, The Final Chapter* by Robert K Massie, p. 184.

120: When he died, in 1937, his estate... : *The Quest for Anastasia* by John Klier and Helen Mingay, p. 123.

120: At one point, before the Revolution... : *The Lost Fortune of the Tsars* by William Clarke, p. 256.

121: It is known that, while... : *The Quest for Anastasia* by John Klier and Helen Mingay, p. 170.

122: She now denounced the scar... : *Tihon: The Tsar's Nephew* by Hans Neerbek, (Sweden Royal Books, 2005), p. 33.

122: "For nearly four years, they stuffed... ': *Boston Evening Telegraph*, April 1929.

123: Olga's sister, the Grand Duchess Xenia... ': *The Lost Fortune of the Tsars* by William Clarke, p. 139.

123: 'Do not acknowledge... ': *The Real Romanovs* by Gleb Botkin, p. 266.

123: In fact, as late as 1958... : 'Olga Romanov Exile and a Woman Named Miss Unknown' confessions to James Rattray's niece Marjorie Wooten. Greg Rittenhouse collection.

124: 'Though I have not found anything... ': Letter from Shura to Harriet von Rathlef, dated January 6, 1926. Fallows Collection, Houghton Library.

124: 'As a matter of fact... ': 'Analysis of the False Anastasia' by Gleb Botkin, dated April 25, 1929, p. 99.

125: 'Well, Madame Tchaikovsky is either... ': *The Quest for Anastasia* by John Klier and Helen Mingay, p. 145.

126: 'Her whole nature... ': *The Woman Who Rose Again* by Gleb Botkin, p. 111.

127: schoolmarmish: Author interview with Ian Lilburn, January 13, 2004.

127: 'When Anastasia Nikolaievna laughed... ': *The Romanovs, The Final Chapter* by Robert K Massie, p. 166.

129: 'I think my poor dear Roger... ': *The Man Who Lost Himself* by Robyn Annear (London: Robinson, 2002), p. 84.

129: 'I am perfectly satisfied that... ': *The Man Who Lost Himself* by Robyn Annear, p. 104.

132: She said Franziska... : *The Romanovs, The Final Chapter* by Robert K Massie, p. 179.

133: But Anna's supporters were quick to point out... : *The Romanovs, The Final Chapter* by Robert K Massie, p. 179.

133: At one point, she even declared... : *The Quest for Anastasia* by John Klier and Helen Mingay, p. 106.

133: 'One would hardly treat... ': Faith Lavington diary, Ian Lilburn collection.

Chapter Four
Anna and Gleb in America, 1928-1931

136: 'funny animals': *The Woman Who Rose Again* by Gleb Botkin, p. 52.

136: Felix mysteriously changed... : *The Real Romanovs* by Gleb Botkin, p. 284.

137: 'She isn't my sister': Affidavit, dated May 9, 1927. Ian Lilburn collection.

137: 'I saw the Grand Duchess on the day... ': 'Analysis of the False Anastasia' by Gleb Botkin, dated April 25, 1929, p. 183.

138: 'It was all so awful': *The Woman Who Rose Again* by Gleb Botkin, p. 75.

138: 'The gold of her hair... ': *The Woman Who Rose Again* by Gleb Botkin, p. 61.

139: 'located in the worst slums... ': *The Woman Who Rose Again* by Gleb Botkin p. 85.

140: 'Who does she think she is?': *The Romanovs, The Final Chapter* by Robert K Massie, p. 181.

140: 'I am the daughter of your Emperor': *The Woman Who Rose Again* by Gleb Botkin, p. 48.

140: 'A case of pull devil... ': Faith Lavington diary, Ian Lilburn collection.

141: He spoke to her in French...: *Anastasia, The Life of Anna Anderson* by Peter Kurth (London: Jonathan Cape, 1983), p. 186.

141: 'According to one account, the conversation... ': *Anastasia, The Lost Princess* by James Blair Lovell, p. 131.

141: 'I killed Rasputin and I will... ': *The Murder of Rasputin* by Greg King (London: Century, 1996), p. 237.

141: 'If you had seen her... ': *The Murder of Rasputin* by Greg King, p. 238.

142: 'I don't know who she is... ': Faith Lavington diary, Ian Lilburn collection.

144: 'butterfly mouth': *The Woman Who Rose Again* by Gleb Botkin, p. 131.

144: 'I mused to have... ': *The Woman Who Rose Again* by Gleb Botkin, p. 140.

145: 'Has Gleb really not got... ': Letter from Andrew to Serge, dated December 25, 1927. Ian Lilburn collection.

145: 'Two days I have spent with her... ': Letter, dated February 4, 1928. Ian Lilburn collection.

146: 'He was friendly... ': Interview given May 8, 1929. Fallows Collection, Houghton Library.

147: 'A strange sensation it was... ': *The Woman Who Rose Again* by Gleb Botkin, p. 152.

148: 'I hardly dared to believe my eyes... ': *The Woman Who Rose Again* by Gleb Botkin, p. 159.

149: This certainly is letting the cat...': *The Woman Who Rose Again* by Gleb Botkin, p. 169.

149: 'She knows so much about the intimate... ': *Anastasia, The Life of Anna Anderson* by Peter Kurth, p. 212.

150: There are a lot of things which are lacking... ': *The Woman Who Rose Again* by Gleb Botkin, p. 175.

151: 'I am very pleased with the book... ': Fallows Collection, Houghton Library.

154: 'As long as you know him... ': Author interview with Ian Lilburn, February 2, 2004.

156: 'Alexandra threw her arms around... ': *The Baron's Fancy* by Gleb Botkin (New York: Doubleday, Doran & Company, Inc, 1930), p. 142.

157: 'He could not permit... ': *The Baron's Fancy* by Gleb Botkin, p. 152.

157: 'You can rest assured... ': *The Woman Who Rose Again* by Gleb Botkin, p. 193.

158: Gleb did receive a visit... : *The Quest for Anastasia* by John Klier and Helen Mingay, p. 112.

158: 'The fight you have put up for DA... ': *The Baron's Fancy* by Gleb Botkin, p. 168.

159: 'You lied to me... ': Testimony from Xenia Leeds in Hamburg, dated March 17, 1959. Ian Lilburn collection.

161: 'When it comes to such technical... ': *The Woman Who Rose Again* by Gleb Botkin, p. 209.

162: In about a month's time... : *Anastasia, The Lost Princess* by James Blair Lovell, p. 149.

163: 'I received your letter... ': Letter from Xenia to Gleb, dated July 18, 1928. Ian Lilburn collection.

165: 'You'll make Alexandra... ': *The Baron's Fancy* by Gleb Botkin, p. 117.

166: 'How generous!... ': *The Woman Who Rose Again* by Gleb Botkin, p. 245.

170: 'valuable hunting lodge': Letter from Fallows to lawyer, dated April 20, 1928. Fallows Collection, Houghton Library.

170: 'Speaking now not as a lawyer... ': New York paper, undated, University of Virginia library collection.

170: At the signing of the agreement... : Statement August 15, 1928. Ian Lilburn collection.

171: Grandanor: *The Romanovs, The Final Chapter* by Robert K Massie, p. 184.

171: Miss Jennings was among several rich people... : *Anastasia, The Lost Princess* by James Blair Lovell, p. 171.

171: 'she registered as Gleb's sister... ': *The Woman Who Rose Again* by Gleb Botkin, p. 275.

172: 'It makes a gruesome impression... ': Letter from Gleb to Grand Duchess Xenia, dated October 20, 1928.

173: Rachmaninov was one of the few... : *Anastasia, The Lost Princess* by James Blair Lovell, p. 157.

173: 'I told Xenia that... ': *The Woman Who Rose Again* by Gleb Botkin, p. 287.

174: 'Anastasia, who was one of the... ': *The Woman Who Rose Again* by Gleb Botkin, p. 289.

178: 'It was however a form of cruelty... ': *The Woman Who Rose Again* by Gleb Botkin, p. 312.

179: Gleb was so worn out after the ensuing... : *The Real Romanovs* by Gleb Botkin, p. 311.

180: 'I hope my illness hasn't... ': *The Baron's Fancy* by Gleb Botkin, p. 285.

181: 'This she tried to achieve... ': Letter from Gleb to Fallows, dated March 13, 1930. Ian Lilburn collection.

182: 'Her personality hasn't changed... ': *North American Review*, University of Virginia collection.

184: She refused to accept that he was... : *Anastasia, The Lost Princess* by James Blair Lovell, p. 174.

184: 'Is the person to whom... ': Fifteen pages of questions and answers, undated. Fallows Collection, Houghton Library.

185: She failed to appreciate... : Letter from Lloyd Smith to Fallows, dated August 22, 1930. Fallows Collection, Houghton Library.

186: The only information Lloyd Smith... : Letter from Lloyd Smith to Fallows, dated August 22, 1930. Fallows Collection, Houghton Library.

187: 'I have made other arrangements... ': Letter to Fallows from Anna Anderson, dated May 30, 1930. Ian Lilburn collection.

188: 'Dear Mr Lloyd-Smith, Miss Jill... ': Letter from *Times* correspondent to Lloyd-Smith, dated June 19, 1930. Fallows Collection, Houghton Library.

189: At one point she set about... : *Anastasia, The Lost Princess* by James Blair Lovell, p. 176.

189: The crisis came one evening... : *Anastasia, The Lost Princess* by James Blair Lovell, p. 176.

190: 'I know of your attitude... ': Letter from Miss Jennings to Anna Anderson, dated July 17, 1930. Ian Lilburn collection.

190: 'Miss Anderson, without any near relatives... ': State of New York Department of Mental Hygiene, Form 472. Ian Lilburn collection.

191: On 24 July 1930, a nurse and two orderlies... : *Anastasia, The Life of Anna Anderson* by Peter Kurth, p. 252.

Chapter Five
Anna returns to Germany

192: 'The whole thing has been... ': Letter from Gleb to Adeline Moffatt, dated September 19, 1931. Ian Lilburn collection.

193: Actually they had agreed... : *The Romanovs, The Final Chapter*, Robert K Massie, p. 186.

194: 'Newspaper reports absurd... ': Telegram from Lloyd-Smith to Fallows, dated August 18, 1930. Fallows Collection, Houghton Library.

195: By the second day... : *Anastasia, The Life of Anna Anderson* by Peter Kurth, p. 259.

196: The newspaper claimed that... : *News of the World*, Fallows Collection, Houghton Library.

196: The case lapsed... : *The Quest for Anastasia* by John Klier and Helen Mingay, p. 127.

196: 'Tuesday April 25, 1939... ': Fallows Collection, Houghton Library.

197: The article, which Fallows carefully... : *Sunday Express*, dated January 29, 1939. Fallows Collection, Houghton Library.

198: 'Who is the Princess of Reuss?': Author interview with Michael Thornton, October 2003.

198: 'Look for the smile': Author interview with Ian Lilburn, February 2, 2004.

200: 'One of those people... ': Letter from Mountbatten to Steno von Stackelberg, dated January 10, 1968. Hartley Library.

200: In early 1932, Anna left... : *Anastasia, The Life of Anna Anderson* by Peter Kurth, p. 274.

200: 'Frau Lange' and... : *Anastasia, The Lost Princess* by James Blair Lovell, p. 187.

200: In 1933, Anna had a meeting... : *Anastasia, The Life of Anna Anderson* by Peter Kurth p. 277.

201: Michael's widow, Natasha Brassov, had become... : *Michael and Natasha, The Life and Loves of The Last Tsar of Russia* by Rosemary and Donald Crawford (London: Weidenfeld and Nicolson, 1997), p. 395.

201: Fallows himself shook off... : Fallows diary, July 6, 1938. Fallows Collection, Houghton Library.

202: Gertrude Madsack, meanwhile... : *Anastasia, The Life of Anna Anderson* by Peter Kurth, p. 281.

204: 'Dear E.H.... ': Letter from Gleb to Fallows, dated July 23, 1937. Fallows Collection, Houghton Library.

205: Lord Louis Mountbatten, presuming... : *Anastasia, The Lost Princess*, James Blair Lovell, p. 196.

205: 'I can assure you that... ': *Mountbatten* by Philip Ziegler, p. 679.

205: 'They held lunch... ': Fallows diary, dated April 14, 1938. Fallows Collection, Houghton Library.

206: On one visit to her apartment... : Letter to Leverkuehn, dated October 5, 1938. Fallows Collection, Houghton Library.

206: 'Never in my life... ': Letter from Fallows to Dr Albert F Coyle, dated March 25, 1938. Fallows Collection, Houghton Library.

207: 'I also am requesting... ': Letter from Fallows to Miss Jennings, dated May 20, 1938. Fallows Collection, Houghton Library.

208: 'We all hoped here that... ': Letter from Fallows to JJ Edwards, dated June 17, 1938. Fallows Collection, Houghton Library.

209: The Schanzkowski siblings gained... : Author interview with Michael Thornton, May 24, 2005.

210: 'You *are* my sister... ': *The Romanovs, The Final Chapter* by Robert K Massie, p. 180; *Anastasia, The Life of Anna Anderson* by Peter Kurth, p. 283; *Anastasia, The Lost Princess* by James Blair Lovell, p. 187.

211: 'natural dignity in her stance... ': Author interview with Ian Lilburn, January 13, 2004.

212: Anna claimed to have been paid special... : *Anastasia, The Lost Princess* by James Blair Lovell, p. 198.

214: His daughter Marina and her husband... : *The Quest for Anastasia* by John Klier and Helen Mingay, p. 207.

215: 'longing very very much... ': Letter from Prince Frederick to Gleb, dated March 10, 1947. Fallows Collection, Houghton Library.

215: That same year, Prince Frederick... : *Anastasia, The Life of Anna Anderson* by Peter Kurth, p. 287.

216: 'Mrs Anderson': Letter from Gleb to Anna Anderson, dated December 14, 1949. Greg Rittenhouse collection.

216: 'Your prolonged silence worries me... ': Letter from Gleb to Anna Anderson, dated May 28, 1950. Greg Rittenhouse collection.

218: Prince Sigismund, whose questions... : *Anastasia, The Lost Princess* by James Blair Lovell, p. 225.

219: 'In memory of Olga Nikolaievna... ': *Charlottesville Daily Progress*, November 20, 1983.

219: In 1954 she had a triumphant... : *Anastasia, The Life of Anna Anderson* by Peter Kurth, p. 287; *Anastasia, The Lost Princess* by James Blair Lovell, p. 215.

220: 'If that woman is Anastasia, I'm a Chinaman': *The Romanovs, The Final Chapter* by Robert K Massie, p. 187.

220: 'A monk came... strange-looking... ': Cassette from Julian Nott, recorded 1968.

220: 'He had defects... ': 'Analysis of the False Anastasia' by Gleb Botkin, p. 137.

221: Otherwise they restricted themselves to... : Author interview with Michael Thornton, May 24, 2005.

222: 'Her face lit up... ': Author interview with Michael Thornton, October 2003.

223: 'People want me to die... ': *Life* magazine, February 14, 1955. Greg Rittenhouse collection.

223: 'Suddenly, accompanied by... ': *Le Figaro*, August 1960, Dominique Aucleres.

224: The growth of Anna's popularity... : *Anastasia, The Life of Anna Anderson* by Peter Kurth, p. 268; *Anastasia, The Lost Princess* by James Blair Lovell, p. 216.

Chapter Six
Anna goes to court, 1933-1968

228: She certainly preferred Leverkuehn... : Author interview with Ian Lilburn, February 2, 2004.

229: Anna's lawyers were now persuaded... : *Anastasia, The Life of Anna Anderson* by Peter Kurth, p. 289; *Anastasia, The Lost Princess* by James Blair Lovell, p. 230.

230: 'Mrs Tchaikovsky's eyes are long... ': 'Analysis of the False Anastasia' by Gleb Botkin, p. 177.

232: Anna vowed never... : *Anastasia, The Lost Princess* by James Blair Lovell, p. 236.

233: Finally a neighbour... : Anastasia archive, U von Gienath, January 1990. Greg Rittenhouse collection.

234: At one point he flourished... : Author interview with Ian Lilburn, February 2, 2004.

234: He added that he had been sent... : Author interview with Michael Thornton, May 24, 2005.

235: Following the publication... : *The Lost Fortune of the Tsars* by William Clarke, p. 150.

236: Among several new details... : *Life* magazine, October 18, 1963.

236: In an interview he gave... : Author interview with Prince Rostislav Romanov, 1998.

239: In a detailed letter... : Letter from Gleb to Miliukov, dated May 2, 1960. Greg Rittenhouse collection.

240: Gleb did eventually get a phone... : Letter to Greg Rittenhouse from Tatiana Botkin, dated April 15, 1970. Greg Rittenhouse collection.

240: 'She had those Yardley things... ': Letter from Gleb to Miliukov, dated June 3, 1960. Greg Rittenhouse collection.

241: At one point she insisted that the Tsarevich... : *Anastasia, The Lost Princess* by James Blair Lovell, p. 274.

242: slept in by Queen Victoria... : *Anastasia, The Lost Princess* by James Blair Lovell, p. 215.

243: One of Anna's last encounters... : Author interview with Ian Lilburn, February 2, 2004.

243: 'She was a lady even when... ': Author interview with Ian Lilburn, February 12, 2004.

245: The third of her original four dogs... : *The Romanovs, The Final Chapter* by Robert K Massie, p. 191.

245: 'fed good hamburger meat... ': Anastasia archive, U von Gienath, 1990. Greg Rittenhouse collection.

245: 'But the Baroness was like a second mother... ': Author interview with Ian Lilburn, February 12, 2004.

246: 'He wanted to be the hero... ': Author interview with Ian Lilburn, 2003.

246: 'Are you married to... ': Author interview with Ian Lilburn, 2003.

247: The judge bowed to the romance... : *Anastasia, The Life of Anna Anderson* by Peter Kurth, p. 341.

247: 'Our circles knew about it... ': *The Romanovs, The Final Chapter* by Robert K Massie, p. 178.

248: 'Based on a completely misconceived... ': Letter from Steno von Stackelberg to Mountbatten, dated December 26, 1967. Hartley Library.

249: However, her friends were delighted when... : *Anastasia, The Life of Anna Anderson* by Peter Kurth, p. 366.

250: Indeed Lilburn says it was... : Author interview with Ian Lilburn, 2003.

251: But when Anna and her supporters arrived... : Author interview with Ian Lilburn, 2003.

252: 'I am still certain it is she... ': *The Romanovs, The Final Chapter* by Robert K Massie, p. 175.

255: The Baroness, in her eighties... : Author interview with Michael Thornton, May 24, 2005.

256: The loyal Anastasians, who for... : Author interview with Ian Lilburn, 2003.

Chapter Seven
The death of Gleb
258: 'be bought everything at... ': Letters, University of Virginia library.

258: He insisted that the city... : *Anastasia, The Lost Princess* by James Blair Lovell, p. 259.

259: 'It is a beautiful city... ': Letter from Gleb to Miliukov, dated March 8, 1968. Greg Rittenhouse collection.

259: 'Mr Botkin would you like... ': Author interview with Greg Rittenhouse, March 1, 2004.

259: 'Now I am safe... ': *Anastasia, The Lost Princess* by James Blair Lovell, p. 309.

262: The couple walked happily everywhere... : *Daily Progress*, April 7, 1972.

262: 'She saw too much blood... ': *Daily Progress*, April 7, 1972.

262: 'The House of Love': Author interview with Deborah Wyatt, 2003.

263: 'I observed that with both... ': Author e-mail from Richard Schweitzer, dated March 14, 2003.

264: 'A good gardener pulls out... ': *In Search of Reality* by Gleb Botkin, p. 7. University of Virginia library collection.

265: 'I believe in Aphrodite... ': *In Search of Reality* by Gleb Botkin, p. 34. University of Virginia library collection.

265: 'Sexual expression is as fully divine... ': *Emphasis Magazine*, July 1968. Greg Rittenhouse collection.

266: 'A person comes to me... ': *Emphasis Magazine*, July 1968. Greg Rittenhouse collection.

267: 'Manahan, who, having solemnly... ': Letter from Gleb to Greg Rittenhouse, dated August 30, 1968.

268: 'To get the history written straight... ': *Star*, August 12, 1968.

270: She maintained she had snuck on board... : Cutting from the Mountbatten collection, Hartley library.

271: 'She said: "This is Anastasia"... ': Author interview with Rey Barry, March 1, 2004.

271: 'A Rasputin gives the case a bad name... ': *Washington Post*, August 24, 1968.

271: 'I found her to be just what... ': Letter from Gleb to Greg Rittenhouse, dated August 30, 1968. Greg Rittenhouse collection.

272: He lost no time... : *Anastasia, The Lost Princess* by James Blair Lovell, p. 318.

273: Barham was later to claim that Rasputin's penis... : *The Murder of Rasputin* by Greg King (London: Century, 1996), p. 172.

274: Gleb's correspondence was temporarily... : Letter from Hugh Cooke, dated September 10, 1968. Greg Rittenhouse collection.

276: His father had specified... : Author interview with Evelyn Meese, April 2004.

277: 'I think he would have been grateful': *The Romanovs, The Final Chapter* by Robert K Massie, p. 192.

277: 'The Manahan marriage gives every indication... ': Letter from Gleb to Greg Rittenhouse, dated January 28, 1969. Greg Rittenhouse collection.

278: The scream activated a five-foot high... : *Anastasia, The Lost Princess* by James Blair Lovell, p. 326.

279: Mildred Ewell says Anna believed... : Author interview with Mildred Ewell, November 2003.

279: 'Everything is changed... ': *Richmond Times Dispatch*, December 12, 1969.

Chapter Eight
Married life in Charlottesville

280: 'My father was on very friendly terms... ': Letter from Gleb to Prince Frederick, dated October 23, 1969. Ian Lilburn collection.

281: 'charlatan': Letter from Steno von Stackelberg, dated August 8, 1968. Mountbatten collection, Hartley library.

282: 'She seized the pictures out of my hand... ': Letter from Jack Manahan to Prince Frederick, dated September 6, 1968. Ian Lilburn collection.

282: 'Thus, except for her unfortunate... ': Letter from Gleb to Prince Frederick, dated October 23, 1969. Ian Lilburn collection.

282: 'It is with disapproval... ': Letter from Andrew Hartsook to Prince Frederick, dated January 11, 1970. Ian Lilburn collection.

282: Incidentally Hartsook now says Gleb... : Author e-mail from Andrew Hartsook, dated November 28, 2003.

283: It is known that Jack washed and tinted... : *The Quest for Anastasia* by John Klier and Helen Mingay, p. 221.

283: 'She got a terrible fright... ': Author interview with Michael Thornton, May 24, 2005.

284: a 'noted beauty': *Coppage Coppedge Chronicle 1542-1975* by John E Manahan and Arthur Max Coppage.

285: In 1972, a woman in Tampa, Florida... : *Anastasia, The Lost Princess* by James Blair Lovell, p. 329.

285: 'Best wishes to all our friends... ': *Woman's Home Companion*, March 15, 1973.

286: 'If you drink a glass of this wine... ': *Commonwealth Magazine of Virginia*, February 1984.

287: 'She didn't jump up... ': Author interview with Mildred Ewell, November 2003.

287: 'She was never interested in proving... ': *Daily Progress*, September 5, 1993.

287: 'The last of the Romanovs... ': *Daily Progress*, September 5, 1993.

287: 'He asked me if I'd heard... ': Author interview with Johanna Shalloway, January 22, 2004.

288: 'There was a feeling... ': Author interview with Rae Ely, April 2004.

288: 'I was one of the few people she... ': Author interview with Rey Barry, March 1, 2004.

289: 'Jack was a good man... ': Author interview with Jack Davis, January 22, 2004.

289: 'This belonged to my late father-in-law... ': *Daily Progress*, September 5, 1993.

290: Soon after its publication... : *Daily Telegraph*, August 14, 1976.

291: Her new suggestion was that... : *Palm Beach Post-Times*, July 16, 1978.

291: She later told the *Daily Progress*... : *Daily Progress*, June 28, 1981.

291: 'It's a mess': *Daily Progress*, February 11, 1978.

291: One of her further claims... : *Daily Progress*, August 7, 1979.

293: 'In America they don't have grand palaces... ': *Daily Progress*, undated.

293: Johanna Shalloway recalls... : Author interview with Johanna Shalloway, January 22, 2004.

293: collecting leftover food... : *Daily Progress*, October 31, 1976.

293: 'She believed in reincarnation... ': *Sunday Sun Baltimore*, December 19, 1976. Michael Wynne-Parker collection.

293: 'Jack brought the car in... ': Author interview with Jack Davis, January 22, 2004.

294: An Englishman, Michael Wynne-Parker... : Author interview with Michael Wynne-Parker, April 12, 2003.

296: 'Jack asked the nearest businessman... ': Author interview with Ian Lilburn, January 13, 2004.

297: Anna was upset by a breach of etiquette... : *Daily Progress*, article following DNA testing in 1994.

297: 'Jack couldn't resist... ': Author interview with Ian Lilburn, January 13, 2004.

298: 'If the Prince goes on misusing... ': *Daily Progress*, February 28, 1977.

298: 'He read it first in German... ': Author interview with Michael Thornton, January 5, 2004.

299: Meanwhile the Manahans continued to cut... : *Daily Progress*, April 26, 1978.

299: A local amateur dramatic company... : Letter from Sasha Bernath to Hugo Vickers.

300: Jack, in response, brought in a caribou antler... : *Daily Progress*, August 30, 1978.

300: he had not used a vacuum... : *Daily Progress*, August 30, 1978.

301: 'She got real sick... ': Author interview with Mildred Ewell, 2003.

302: 'I came twelve days to the end... ': *Daily Progress*, June 19, 1981.

303: 'I think they ought to do it... ': *Daily Progress*, August 17, 1993.

304: 'Succinct Recital of Untoward... ': Deborah Wyatt collection.

304: Anna had occasionally been heard... : Letter from Sasha Bernath to Hugo Vickers, undated.

305: 'Apple Annie': *Daily Progress*, December 5, 1986.

305: Anna said she preferred the cold... : *Daily Progress*, December 1, 1983.

305: 'In fifteen years of married life... ': *Daily Progress*, January 13, 1984.

306: Jack's lawyer, Jim Hingeley... : Author interview with Jim Hingeley, March 3, 2004.

306: The trio drove to a Ken Johnson's... : *The Virginian Pilot and the Ledger-Star*, October 16, 1983.

307: 'I made it clear that Jack was not... ': Author interview with William Preston, April 2004.

307: 'She looked spry and was talking up a storm... ': *Anastasia* by Peter Kurth, Afterword. Albemarle Historic Society.

308: 'I thought about it overnight... ': *Daily Progress*, January 13, 1984.

308: Jack knew Anna would have to be transferred... : *Daily Progress*, November 30, 1983.

309: When police found the house... : *Washington Post*, December 3, 1983.

309: Driving them into town... : *Daily Progress*, June 8, 1994.

309: 'Jones': *Anastasia* by Peter Kurth, Afterword.

310: The Soviet leader, Yuri Andropov... : *National Examiner*, December 27, 1984. Michael Wynne-Parker collection.

310: Preston was obliged to move her... : *Daily Progress*, December 21, 1983.

310: A little over a week before Anna died... : *Stuttgarter Zeitung*, February 5, 1984.

311: 'She always said that you would be reincarnated... ': *Charlottesville Weekly*, October 4-10, 1994.

Chapter Nine
The remains of Anna

312: 'I thought I had to take charge... ': Author interview with Mildred Ewell, 2003.

347

312: 'Under the radiant smile death itself... ': University of Virginia library collection.

312: Jack placed assorted memorabilia... : *Daily Progress*, February 15, 1984.

313: 'the black queen': *Anastasia, The Lost Princess* by James Blair Lovell, p. 373.

313: 'The end of Anastasia... ': *Cavalier Daily*, February 15, 1984.

313: 'Your prompt and comforting note... ': University of Virginia library collection.

313: 'Our heart is unquiet... ': *Washington Post*, October 6, 1994.

314: '*unkomplizierte Amerikaner*': *Munchner Merkur*, June 20/21, 1984.

314: 'I didn't find it actually... ': Author interview with Ian Lilburn, February 2, 2004.

315: 'The True Czarina Of All The Russias': Author Interview with Rae Ely, April 2004.

315: Conan The Barbarian: *Anastasia, The Lost Princess* by James Blair Lovell, p. 378.

315: Later it was claimed that she took... : *Anastasia, The Lost Princess* by James Blair Lovell, p. 377.

316: A neuropsychiatrist, Gregory O'Shanick... : *Daily Progress*, June 15, 1994.

316: Dr Gregory Saathof... : Papers from lawyers Wyatt and Armstrong in Charlottesville. Trial began June 7, 1994.

316: '(She) is a remarkably efficient... ': *Daily Progress*, June 16, 1994.

317: 'Many times I thought yes... ': *TV Guide* by Andrea Lee, produced by NBC, December 6, 1986.

317: 'Her background, her demeanour... ': *Daily Progress*, September 5, 1993.

318: Jack had originally... : Author interview with Deborah Wyatt, April 2004.

318: 'It is kind of salt and pepper grey... ': *Daily Progress*, July 30, 1993.

318: Kurth also took samples... : *Daily Progress*, July 30, 1993.

319: 'We all had an agenda... ': *The Quest for Anastasia* by John Klier and Helen Mingay, p. 208.

319: a woman from Idaho... : *Daily Progress*, September 20, 1993.

320: 'I have a new child... ': *Daily Progress*, June 22, 1997.

320: 'We're not in novel territory... ': *Daily Progress*, March 18, 1994.

320: Schweitzer skillfully overrode... : *The Romanovs, The Final Chapter* by Robert K Massie, p. 221.

320: Marina Schweitzer had sent... : *The Quest for Anastasia* by John Klier and Helen Mingay, p. 203.

321: Dr Peter Gill came to collect... : 'Health News', Martha Jefferson Hospital, Summer 1994.

321: 'a 100 per cent match... ': *The Romanovs, The Final Chapter*, p. 239.

322: 'I know this will sound insane... ': *Daily Progress*, October 1, 1994.

322: In a letter to the *Washington Post*... : *Washington Post*, September 27, 1995.

323: 'They conducted an experiment... ': Author interview with Ian Lilburn, December 2003.

323: 'There has still to be... ': Author interview with Mildred Ewell, November 24, 2003.

323: 'How could a Polish peasant know it?': *Daily Progress*, October 6, 1994.

324: Police officer Cornilia Johnson... : *Daily Progress*, October 6, 1994.

324: a Sandra Romanov came forward... : *Daily Progress*, July 17, 1994.

324: The teeth sent to Florida... : *The Lost Fortune of the Tsars* by William Clarke, p. 151.

325: Though St Petersburg was the first... : *Daily Progress*, January 31, 1998.

325: Previously the house had been seen... : *The Quest for Anastasia* by John Klier and Helen Mingay, p. 165.

325: she would prefer her grandfather to be... : *Daily Progress*, November 12, 1995.

326: 'It is not a question of whether... ': *Daily Progress*, December 10, 1995.

327: 'If the DNA had matched... ': Author interview with Prince Rostislav Romanov, 1998.

327: 'It's over': *Daily Progress*, October 6, 1994.

Select Bibliography

Annear, Robyn *The Man Who Lost Himself: The Unbelievable Story of the Tichborne Claimant* (London: Robinson 2002)

Botkin, Gleb *The God Who Didn't Laugh* (London: Victor Gollancz Ltd, 1929).

Botkin, Gleb *The Real Romanovs* (New York: Fleming H Revell, 1931).

Botkin, Gleb *The Woman Who Rose Again* (New York: Fleming H Revell, 1937).

Botkin, Gleb *The Firebird* (London and Edinburgh: Fleming H Revell Company)

Botkin, Gleb *The Baron's Fancy* (New York: Doubleday, Doran & Company, Inc, 1930)

Buxhoeveden, Baroness Sophie *Left Behind: Fourteen Months in Siberia during the Revolution* (New York and London: Longmans, Green, 1928)

Dehn, Lili *The Real Tsaritsa* (London: Thornton Butterworth, 1922)

King, Greg and Wilson, Penny *The Fate of the Romanovs* (New Jersey: John Wiley & Sons Inc 2003)

Klier, John and Mingay, Helen *The Quest For Anastasia* (London: Smith Gryphon, 1995)

Krug von Nidda, Roland (editor) *I, Anastasia – An Autobiography* (New York: Harcourt, Brace and co 1958)

Kurth, Peter *Anastasia, The Life of Anna Anderson* (London: Jonathan Cape, 1983)

Lovell, James Blair *Anastasia, The Lost Princess* (Washington:

Regnery Gateway, 1991)

Massie, Robert K *Nicholas and Alexandra* (New York: Atheneum, 1967)

Massie, Robert K *The Romanovs: The Final Chapter* (London: Jonathan Cape, Random House, 1995)

Montgomery-Massingberd, Hugh (editor) *Burke's Royal Families of the World, Volume 1: Europe and Latin America* (Burkes' Peerage Ltd, 1977).

Neerbek, Hans Tikhon *The Tsar's Nephew* (Sweden Royal Books 2005).

Rathlef-Keilmann, Harriet von *Anastasia, The Survivor of Ekaterinburg* (New York: Payson and Clarke, 1929)

Trewin J.C. *Tutor to the Tsarevich: An Intimate Portrait of the Last Days of the Russian Imperial Family compiled from the papers of Charles Sydney Gibbes* (London: Macmillan, 1975)

Additional Material: Author interviews for the *Sunday Telegraph* with Prince Rostislav Romanov (1998), Grand Duke Vladimir of Russia(1991) and Grand Duchess Maria of Russia (1998); Letters by Gleb and Tatiana Botkin, Grand Duke Andrew of Russia, Edward Fallows, Princess Xenia of Russia, Annie B Jennings, Jack Manahan and Admiral of the Fleet, Earl Mountbatten of Burma; Gleb Botkin's pamphlets: *In Search of Reality, The Religion of Aphrodite* and *This Is Anastasia* in *The North American Review*; Jack Manahan's pamphlets: *Coppage, Coppedge Chronicle* and *Anastasia's Money & The Czar's Wealth*; extract from *The Story of Hetty Richard: A*

Journey Worth The Taking, privately printed New York 1964; Faith Lavington's diary; affadavit of Felix Schanzkowski; testimony from the trial brought by the Manahan relatives. Newspapers and periodicals: *The Times, Daily Telegraph, Boston Evening Telegraph*, the *Washington Post*, the *Washington Star, New York Times, New York Herald Tribune, New York Evening Post, Life* magazine, *Royalty* magazine, *Baltimore Sun, The National Examiner*, the *Palm Beach Post-Times*, the *Richmond News*, the *Richmond Times-Dispatch*, the *Daily Progress*, Charlottesville, the *Charlottesville Weekly*, the *Virginian Pilot and The Ledger-Star*, the *Virginia Weekly, Albemarle* magazine, the *Wilmington Morning Star, Cavalier Daily, Sonntag Aktuell, Bild + Funk*, the *Munchner Merkur, Frau Im Spiegel, Martha Jefferson Hospital Health News, Emphasis Magazine, Woman's Home Companion.*

Acknowledgments

There are many people I would like to thank. Hugh Massingberd gallantly proof-read the book, and offered many useful suggestions: no-one could have been more helpful or encouraging. Aurea Carpenter and Emily Fox were unfailingly good hearted and efficient editors.

The historian and genealogist Ian Lilburn, a long-term friend and supporter of Anna Anderson, shared particularly poignant memories. Lilburn photocopied hundreds of documents for me, as well as lending me innumerable photographs, mostly of Anna Anderson and all five Romanov children.

Greg Rittenhouse, a former friend of Gleb Botkin, referred to as an Anastasia scholar, sent parcels of documents from his home in California, as well as providing phone numbers for important witnesses.

Brian Horan helped me contact Gleb Botkin's son-in-law, Richard Schweitzer. Schweitzer himself kindly sent several e-mails containing information about the Botkins. Andrew Hartsook, another close friend of Gleb, also sent interesting e-mails. Tatiana Yellachich offered telling memories of her mother's cousin and Gleb's sister, Tatiana Botkin.

Michael Thornton, who knew Anna well, readily shared colourful memories. Michael Wynne-Parker offered me a rich account of his visit to Charlottesville in the late 1970s as well as some papers given to him by Jack Manahan. Hugo Vickers sent useful documents. Julian Nott, who made a film about the DNA testing, helped me contact several crucial witnesses. The staff at the Houghton Library, in Harvard, where the Fallows papers are stored, were friendly and cooperatice. Staff at the Hartley Library, at the University of Southampton, where the Mountbatten papers are stored, were also helpful.

There are several people in Charlottesville I also wish to thank, including some who, while they spoke to me, would not have wished to be quoted directly.

Deborah Wyatt faxed me details of the Manahan family's court case and helped me track down people who had known Anna Anderson. William Preston, Anna's court-appointed guardian, gave me insights into the Manahans' last months together. Jim Hingeley offered testimony as Jack's friend and lawyer.

Mildred Ewell, one of their near neighbours, spared time to recall her close friendship with Jack and Anna. Jack Davis, an actual neighbour, gave his account of day-to-day life next door to the Manahans. Another friend, Johanna Shalloway, offered incisive details about the couple's way of life. Rey Barry gave me detailed descriptions of what he deemed almost historic encounters with the Manahans. Another of Jack's lawyers, Rae Ely, and Pat Francis, who interviewed Jack during his last years, both gave me useful information. Evelyn Meese volunteered information about Scottsville.

The librarian at the Albemarle Historical Society, Margaret O'Bryant, located and photocopied hundreds of documents relating to the Manahans. The staff at the University of Virginia library were also extremely helpful.

Finally, many thanks to Tara and Chris Chappel for having me to stay in their lovely house in Charlottesville. rewarding pastimes around.